Aoh

Jennifer Renson

This is a work of fiction. Names, characters, places, and incidents either are the product of the author's imagination or are used fictitiously. Any resemblance to actual persons living or dead, events, or locales is entirely coincidental.

Published and printed in the United States Of America

Cover design by Damonza (damonza@damonza.com)

Section separator design by gerges haleem (vecteezy.com)

PO Box 9013
Trenton, NJ 08650

Facebook: https://facebook.com/booksandpoetrybyJenniferRenson
Twitter: https://twitter.com/JennyRenson

This Book is dedicated to my husband, daughters, family, friends and to you dear reader.

Prologue

I could listen to that song every day for the rest of my life and never tire of it. Right over there, the young man playing the same song on the same flute every morning. His hands cracked and dirty from working with rocks and sand all day, and sometimes all night.

As cracked as they were, he still managed to play such a soothing melody every morning.

The sun would peak in the same spot, and just beyond it I could see miles of desert sand laid out like this sea of yellow and brown leading to the mountains in the distance. Every morning I'd look into that distance, staring at the open space of nothingness and look at the mountains. Sometimes I would catch a glimpse of a kite soaring in the sky who, unbeknownst to me, would one day become my eternal friend. For, no matter where my destiny takes me, he will always be there.

1

"Aoh! Aoh, are you awake?! Come down here!"

Every morning my mother would call for me from the rooftop to come down. Ever since I could walk, I could climb. I don't know what it was about overlooking the world I lived in, but I did it as often as I could. Even if it meant staying up all night.

My mother was very strict with our household. She had five children to care for while my father worked. All day he carved the stories of our history into the walls, columns, furniture, and statues of the city, and sometimes the palace. Carving and chipping away at the stone, painting the images with such precision through the heat of the day while the sun watched over him. Sometimes, he would work in the cold of the night with the moon lighting his creation.

If I could be honest...I didn't really know my father that well. I hardly saw him and when I did, it was through the doorway or from a distance. According to my mother, he worked continuously for eight days, only able to come home on the ninth and tenth days. All I knew was that he was a very hard working man, and that the work he did was praised.

The smell of the meal cooking over a burning fire filled the morning air. The children, full of energy, screamed with delight as they chased each other. They ran in between the homes, trying to find other children, passing farmers preparing for a new day. The sun was warm and bright floating in the morning sky.

"Aoh!" her mother called again from the bottom of the ladder, waving her hands into the air.

Silently, Aoh climbed down through the large opening in the ceiling. She found her mother trying to separate bread and cooked papyrus reeds roughly from the doorway.

Egypt was recovering from a famine. Due to the short supply in food, we were eating papyrus reeds with the scraps we had. It wasn't as horrible as it sounded. My siblings would say otherwise.

Aoh entered the room. feeling the heat from the fire, inhaling the scent. Approaching the food, she scooped some up and placed it on a thick, mud-hardened plate. Her mother opened the nearest window and greeted the passing young man carrying a lamb over his shoulders. The voices outside immediately increased in volume as more families began to fill the dirt streets of the town.

Sitting at the small table, Aoh began to munch on the cooked papyrus reeds, ripping them with her small teeth and swallowing with water. She took several pieces of flattened bread and cereal grains between bites of the papyrus. Thrashing several cloths outside the window, her mother turned and watched her daughter slowly eating. She pulled the bread, listening to the rattles from the bells around the sheep's necks and the patter of little boys feet. They followed their teacher while they carried their items in satchels over their small shoulders.

"Hurry up and eat. We need to bring those with us. Come on," her mother ordered, quickly folding and then putting the cloths down onto a small chair. She picked up a woven basket of sheep wool and thread. The basket resided next to the family Senet board and the serpent, dog, and jackal pieces.

Aoh ate quickly, barely able to swallow each piece before shoving more in. Before she could finish, her mother took her hand and they left. Barely out the door, Aoh's brothers and sisters ran past her, shrieking loudly, with children they played with every day. Aoh's mother ordered them to stop running and to be careful as they ran around large oxen pulling carts and men preparing to go to work. Tugging Aoh roughly, they continued onto the gravely dirt street, kicking up small pieces of sand unintentionally with each step. The bottom of their sandals crunched against the rough ground.

Aoh watched several women with their children as they passed each other. Oxen, cows, and donkeys were led by their owners, pulling heavy carts. The heavy odors of the animals and meals cooking was a daily scent that lingered until dark.

Turning a corner, Aoh saw nothing but white as priests walked single file exiting a small temple. Their hands were clasped closed near their faces, praying loudly. The temple was completely white, standing out from the rest of the homes and structures. Nothing but darkness with faint hints of a statue resided in the temple entrance.

Aoh strained her eyes to take another look at the priests. She watched as two of the priests gathered papyrus written with spells, before she heard her mother's impatient call. Passing in between homes and near watering holes, they arrived at a comforting home where more women were getting settled inside, preparing the threads with their daughters. Taking their seat on the thin mats, Aoh and her mother pulled out the items from the basket, hearing the other conversations already starting.

Together they continued working on a blanket made from shaved sheep's wool. They bartered for the wool with beads. As her mother used the tips of her fingers to patiently weave, Aoh sat next to her and watched intently. Around them, the mothers sat with their daughters, teaching them the same skill. Slowly the blankets were getting longer. They rolled several times towards the center of the group where women were telling stories with smiles and red cheeks.

Sitting together in a circle, all the women worked, listening to the sounds of the children playing outside. Conversations between multiple women filled the room as they worked together in a pattern-like motion. The windows were opened so wide, the smell of the Nile River embraced them. For hours they worked, delicately weaving and pricking their fingers, feeling the skin roughen.

Aoh's attention shifted from her mother's working hands to the younger women's conversations that seemed to revolve around attractive young men they've been admiring for some years. They giggled and laughed while sewing straight lines with precision and fluffing out the wool with the tips of their thin fingers. The sounds of beads across the room sliding into each other clicked with the tapping of a older woman's foot. She strung each bead silently, devoted to her work, tuning out the rest of the conversations circulating around her.

"Don't stare, Aoh."

Aoh obeyed her mother, turning back around. She shifted slightly, leaning over to observe how much progress her mother made in the short amount of time. The shifting of thread through the fluff became therapeutic.

Every so often my mother would flip the wool to show me the stitching she made with devotion. I tried to pay attention, but found it hard to when the several stories being told seemed more interesting.

The door slammed open, startling the room. The young woman responsible, panting near out of breath, spewed, "The pharaoh is calling for the people to his gates. The traitor has been caught! Quickly!"

The women rose to their knees, taking their pieces with the needles and thread and rolling them quickly. Outside the sounds of the peasants and workers taking to the roads intensified. Placing everything back into the basket, Aoh's mother took her hand tightly, following the women out the door. She called out to her younger children in the crowd. Together in their innocence, the children ran in between the legs of other peasants, laughing, before returning to her. Babies were wrapped in the arms of their mothers, and smaller children rode on the shoulders of their fathers.

Aoh held her mother's hand as she, and the rest of the town, followed each other upward towards the capital city. Upon arriving to the city, Aoh beheld several sights and sounds, children distracting her at every turn. Men and women walked together, dressed in clean, bright linens and animal skins, towards the white palace.

The capital city was full of people: artisans, merchants, farmers, alike. It was bright and glorious! Women donned in perfume walked together, dressing almost identically, like reflections in mirrors. Young men quickly called for each other as one by one shops were beginning to close. Spices covered, wooden pieces stored, jewelry quickly pocketed and large jars sealed. I lost sight of the city around me, as the crowds of people began to close in around my family. My younger siblings remained behind us, clasped side by side with their tiny hands, oblivious to the event we were about to witness.

Aoh glanced upward, squinting her small eyes as the bright sun hovered over the city. Taking some water from her mother, Aoh lifted her head gently, placing her lips over the rounded opening. She heard the shrieking of a kite in the sky several feet away from the tallest statue of the pharaoh worshiping the gods. Aoh swallowed, watching her friend glide through the air, searching for something to eat, screeching loudly. Feeling the small hands of her siblings pulling on the back of her dress, Aoh handed them the water as they quickly shared the remnants.

Approaching the palace, Aoh strained her neck, trying to see ahead of her beyond the backs of the citizens. When she tried to jump, her mother scolded her harshly and ordered her children to walk in front where she could see them.

I've never seen the palace up close. Only at a distance.

"My people!" a voice boomed.

I trembled at the sound of the voice. It was the voice of only one man.

The crowd of people rushed forward as loud groaning sounds of large doors opening swept over the city.

A dark shadow swallowed me as the tops of the palace towered over the city glowing in the sunlight.

"My people! MY PEOPLE!"

Aoh peered in between the small open spaces left between people all standing at attention with concerned expressions. She could hear the pharaoh's booming voice, sounding like a powerful thunderstorm, proclaiming itself over the sky, striking the clouds with bright lightning. She couldn't see him but heard him clearly as her hand never left the tightened grasp of her mother's. She glanced above her, noticing every face was turned to the attention of their king. Everyone was silent, listening, beholding the sight of the king like soldiers. Aoh slightly bounced, trying to see but was not able to jump high enough.

"Aoh," her mother scolded quickly for a second time.

Looking through the small spaces in between the rows of legs, Aoh could just see ahead of her the pure color of white.

She could see two feet, scuffed and dirty, standing in front of something hidden. She then saw another pair of feet, lighter than her in skin tone, covered in sandals made of pure gold, snugly strapped against the entire foot. The feet paced to and fro with slight hesitation, revealing signs of a limp in front of the dirty pair of feet covered in sand. The pharaoh's voice boomed loudly over the crowd as they roared in response. The more he spoke, the louder the voices became. Fists were raised into the air. The volume rising.

Like a flash of light, everything fell eerily silent. I released a heavyweight breath…

Startled by the sharp sound and loud gurgle, Aoh jumped slightly, watching as a young man fell onto the white stone floor. Red blood flowed from the horrid wound across his chest and stomach. She watched as his head and limbs curled and shook violently before ceasing. The gurgling stopped, but the blood continued to flow. The beautiful white color became overpowered by red.

Turning away, Aoh clasped her eyes closed, feeling a strike of fear run up and down her small body. But even when she closed her eyes, she could still see the dead body, laying on the white floor. She could see the wound, so deep that she noticed the mangled layers of flesh the blade cut through without struggle. Her eyes tightened, hearing the sounds of him dying in her ears.

She jumped when the loud sounds of the crowd roaring with praise erupted. They raised their arms into the air! They called out their pharaoh's name over and over, chanting! They cheered for him. They loved him.

I couldn't chase away the image of that young man from my mind. He haunted me for days unending, to the point I thought I was seeing him everywhere I went. I couldn't help but look at the men I passed almost daily, and feared that they would be killed, too, before a large crowd. I felt sick to my stomach. Perhaps the only reason I was able to free myself from such a haunting face was because of-

2

"Aoh!"

Frowning slightly, she glanced over the side of the rooftop, finding no one below her. Hearing her name repeated, she crawled over to the hole in the roof and looked down. Below, her brother stood in her room in the small space of cooling shade hiding just away from the sunlight. Her hair swayed as she leaned over, seeing him with a heavy linen satchel over his shoulders.

"Come down from there."

"I was just-"

"Now."

My brother was the oldest, learning the trade of my father that was passed down for several generations. When my younger brothers get older, they will begin learning the same craft. He painted and carved several monuments almost every day, working in the hot sun at astonishing heights. He felt honored to have such a task. He knew that all the work he did would last thousands of years, like the ones made before we existed. The pyramids withstood the forces of nature and war for hundreds of years. Statues, monuments, temples, all surviving that which we cannot control.

Though my brother's name would never be carved into his work, it didn't matter. He knew the work he did would be admired and loved. He was very brave, my brother.

Aoh followed him outside as they walked past a shepherd and his flock, and then three older women carrying covered baskets. Three dogs rushed around them, nearly colliding into another group of women carrying baskets of clothes needing to be cleaned. Passing several open windows, Aoh could hear men and women singing songs slowly in whispers.

Coming to a small nook, Aoh's brother took his walking stick, slightly hidden behind several mud brick pots containing a variety of holding tools. He struck the walking stick into the ground firmly, listening to it click against the hardened surface with every step. He groaned slightly, rolling his shoulder several times as though trying to loosen a tight muscle.

The sunlight warmed the town as it did countless days before, hiding behind thin clouds in the blue sky sometimes occupied by several birds of prey. Routinely, the sounds of workers singing the same song would lift from their mouths as young boys playing with wooden toy swords clanked into each other.

They walked past several rows of empty carts soon to be filled with jugs of the newly grown wheat and hay for storage. Aoh trailed her fingers across the uneven and rough outer mud brick walls of the homes they passed, moving away from the town and towards the open spaces at the river.

The soft sounds of the water flowing over thick rocks and against small boats tickled the insides of Aoh's ears as she tucked her hair behind them. In the distance, Aoh watched the royal boats moving slowly through the waters, carrying baskets full of food and newly-made furniture coming all the way from another city. Women gathered water, watching their steps as they walked through the reeds.

The echoes of children laughing followed her, combining with the voices of men casting nets to catch fish and the gentle groaning of the wooden boats rocking in the still water. She followed her older brother through the reeds, stepping through the broken branches. She heard the thick crunching under her rough feet as they came to the Nile.

He paused momentarily, looking at the water, poking the walking stick into several areas as though trying to find something. He stepped as the water rested above his scarred ankles. Aoh followed him across small but higher muddy land where the Nile water rose just underneath her knees. Her teeth clamored lightly, feeling a cold chill rush up her legs from the water.

Waves swept around them from the small boats, rocking each time fish were hurled aboard. Keeping steady steps, she continued forward, beginning to wonder where her brother was taking her. After crossing safely, they touched the ground again, passing through more rows of healthy reeds and then sand.

I couldn't resist another glance at the royal boats, almost still in the water. The way the objects they carried glistened in the sunlight…like a poem in motion.

Catching her looking at the boats again, he mumbled, "Aoh, try to pay attention, please."

"Haven't you wondered what kind of things those boats carry everyday? Have you wondered where they came from?" she asked.

"I'm afraid we won't know. I'm sure those items are worth more than our lives."

Aoh listened, tucking her hair behind her ears again, watching her feeble steps as the sight of the boats faded behind the reeds.

"We're almost there," he reminded, continuing forward.

Slowing his steps, he shifted the walking stick, rolling it side to side as his eyes remained planted on the ground. Suddenly he stopped, poking the walking stick into the sandy ground. He lowered himself, balancing all of his weight on his feet and rubbed his hand across the sand. He looked at the sand grains in between his thick fingers, holding it upward for Aoh to see.

"Aoh, come," he called firmly.

Aoh got onto her knees and rubbed the sand, feeling the texture.

"Feel that?" he asked.

"Feels damp," Aoh replied.

"Exactly. Where the surface of the ground is damp like this, it means there is water underneath. If you dig deep enough, you will find it."

He turned around, looking at the Nile River and pointed the walking stick in the direction it was flowing.

"The river is quite generous, spreading its wealth all around here," he continued. "Why else do you think the reeds are so bountiful?"

Aoh nodded, rubbing the cool ground with the palm of her hands.

"Water can also be found in depressions or holes in rocks. Sometimes when it rains in the desert, the rain will reside inside and sit. The collected rain water isn't enough to fill a cup, but enough to keep you alive."

Aoh nodded again, listening intently.

"Come, I want to show you," he ordered, standing back up.

Aoh got onto her feet, swiping her hands against the bottom of her dress and followed him, turning around briefly to notice how far they were from home.

I never wandered far from home. I suppose you could say I was like the kite I befriended. We stay where we are comfortable.

From the growing distance, Aoh could see the homes shrinking behind the people working just over the tops of the reeds. The sandy ground slowly hardened like rock, as Aoh followed his steps. They moved in and out of the sunlight, pushing palm tree limbs away from their faces. Just ahead of them, the ground began to slope as though suddenly dropping just before the dried land.

Her brother stopped just near the beginning of the slope and looked out at the desert with his narrow eyes.

"Look, Aoh. A desert of promise," he said, pointing with his walking stick.

Aoh stumbled slightly, standing next to him, looking out and seeing nothing but emptiness.

"Why are we out here?" she asked.

"Because I want to teach you something. Sit," he requested.

Aoh sat down next to him, feeling the hard ground on her bottom and the sand stick to her dry skin.

"That desert is the only thing that keeps us and the rest of the world separated. Many battles have been fought out there. We haven't won them all, but Egypt remains strong."

"Is there a war coming?" she asked, calmly.

"It has been quiet, however, war doesn't sleep for long. Aoh, I want you to try to understand that this world is only as tame as the gods allow it to be. We are their servants. We will always serve them."

He took a deep breath and faked a smile, noticing how intensely Aoh was looking at him.

"That is why I brought you out here," he continued. "You are growing and quickly you will be seeing the world from a different perspective than the rooftop. If Egypt were to awaken a more formidable enemy, they would attack us from that direction."

He pointed the walking stick in the direction firmly, so Aoh's eyes could follow.

"They would then come up there on their horses and by foot," he explained. "Shields at their chests. Swords in their belts. They would first shoot arrows at a distance. And they would not stop until everything was in flames. When that happens, you have to follow the path we took to this spot here."

He moved the stick from behind him forward and then pointed to the edge of the ground just ahead of them.

"This is the path you need to take," he repeated. "You cannot go anywhere else or they will kill you. Man, woman, child. It's all the same to them. You will go into the desert and not come back. The desert will care for you. You will survive."

Putting down the stick, he raised his knees to his chest to rest his heavy arms, tired from carrying large stones and tools for several days.

"I've been out there several times and have come close to death but never died," he reminisced. "I found water. I found food. Just enough, every time. You need not be afraid of the world, Aoh."

"How do you know all of this?"

"When you've painted and carved as long as I have, you learn."

From behind them, they heard the loud cries of excitement from several children near the bank of the river. Intrigued as to what the children were yelling about, they followed the sounds to a group standing over two men digging several feet deep into the ground. At the bottom, they were beginning to hit water for a new well. The water rose well over their feet and near their knees.

More children rushed over, hearing the excitement, and joined into the fray, pointing down at the rising water. With a quick wave of their hands and shouts, the children were chased away as the two men climbed their way out of the hole to obtain more help. The men worked together digging out the walls, using every tool on hand as the children waited to see the fresh water. They worked diligently until nightfall, almost completing their task. With any luck, the new well would provide water for more cattle and farms. A smile from the gods themselves with a promise to end the famine.

3

The next morning, Aoh's mother repeatedly called for her, as she sat on her bed trying to sew the long tear down the side of Aoh's dress from the other day. Running to her mother's call, she saw her holding a basket with one hand and pointed in the direction of the city with the other.

My mother's face was slightly red, ordering me to bring my brother the food he had forgotten to take with him earlier that morning. It was unlike him to forget anything. No matter how tired or weak he was. This only further proved my intuitions that something was wrong, and he had some awareness of it and refused to tell anyone.

Sending her on her way, Aoh wandered the streets up the usual path of traffic heading towards the capital city. She carried with her the animal skin basket containing food and water. Her steps firmly pressed against the rough ground as she looked around at the beautiful city, bustling and full of life from another world often not heard from.

She watched women sitting patiently as tweezers plucked away tiny hairs from their faces, fixing their eyebrows while, simultaneously, others tended to their fingernails. Through the next tent, Aoh watched as thick, potent powders and creams were made in several bowls, churned and spun with multiple utensils and then applied onto irritated skin and thin scars. Men and women waited, standing in a straight line for the relief while constantly rubbing their ragged skin.

Shopkeepers bargained as firmly as a woman standing in the doorway of a bar, waiting for her husband. Men sat in the shade, betting and trading as the merchants arrived with items never seen before. Most items came on carts, covered with linens until revealed before the shopkeepers.

Aoh hesitated, craning her neck to see what the items were. They were uncovered so delicately. held in the large hands away from the heat of the sunlight. Feeling eyes on her, Aoh glanced to her side and saw two women looking at her from the doorway across the street, leaning in the cool shade. She caught a whiff of the heavy perfume they wore, watching everyone who passed. Their skin was clear of any blemish or freckle, nearly hidden in the thick black wigs and lightly worn jewelry.

Feeling intimidated by their looks, Aoh tugged the basket tightly in her grip and continued towards the palace where two men were loudly arguing amid a mess of broken carts and loose oxen. Egyptian guards had already arrived, listening to the argument while several others tried to remove the damaged property. Passing the situation, Aoh walked in between large pillars, glancing in the direction of the towering doors she walked through days ago. Those doors closed off the city from the palace grounds, creating a barrier between the gods and mortals. Immediately, Aoh caught sight of a plethora of fresh flowers, carried in large vases. One after another, the bounty of colors and scents carried by florists and servants followed each other towards the palace, passing guards standing at attention.

Moving away, Aoh arrived at the construction area, greeted by the loud sounds of men working with heavy equipment and materials. They chiseled and carved delicately and precisely, some working on the same project from different angles and sections while following the detailed instructions on papyrus. Architects stood out dressed in white and red linens, gesturing with their arms and hands the desired sizes of the statues and where to place them. Smoke and dust filled the air as the tiny remnants covered the floor. The sand stuck to the sweated bodies whenever a breeze swept through the area. Looking around, Aoh saw images of the pharaoh all around her. He was carved with his family, sitting on his throne, and riding his chariot to certain victory.

Statues of the gods were erected, painted, and measured with tools, all under the instructions of several older men from the pharaoh's court. Mostly bald and donning clean robes with animal skins and colored sashes, they watched and guided. Every man varied in age and yet none were her brother. Looking upward, she covered her eyes for a moment, finding him up high working near the top of a magnificent column, chipping away the stone, constantly wiping his face.

Aoh clasped her hands over her mouth and called out his name. She watched him pause for a moment looking around. Calling his name, a second time, he looked and found her.

"Aoh? What are you doing out here?!" he called.

Aoh raised the basket in response.

Taking a quick drink of water, he called, "I'll be right down!"

Putting down his tools, he quickly climbed down several sets of wooden ladders, crossing wooden planks until finally reaching the ground.

Taking the basket, he laughed, "Thank you. Mother must have been pretty mad I left without it."

Aoh nodded slightly when suddenly a man called out to her brother loudly. Wiping his brow of his sweat, he called back, shaking his head in response.

"You haven't forgotten anything before," Aoh whispered, looking at the ground.

"You really shouldn't be here. Go on home before you get hurt. These pillars are bound to go up any day now."

"I didn't know you were upgraded to work in the palace?"

"I'm not. I'm still working on the obelisks and statues that will go up at the entrance of the city when complete. Trust me, if I was asked to become an elite craftsman, I would have told you."

Aoh kept her eyes on the ground and asked, "Where's father?"

"In there," he replied. nodding to the palace.

"The palace?"

Still nodding he explained, "Father has been in there every so often for the past month, speaking with the royal chief architects. He may be celebrated tonight, to be welcomed as a new elite craftsman."

Aoh's smile widened when another man called for her brother with a hint of impatience. He called back waving roughly.

"I have to get back. I'll see you at home."

Aoh however hesitated from leaving.

"Go on, go on."

As the sun began to set that evening, Aoh rested in her quiet room. Even in the solitude of her room she could not ignore her intuition that something was wrong. She tried to ignore those feelings but failed. In the distance she heard a flute playing. Aoh sat up in her bed, trying to listen. She climbed the ladder from her room to the rooftop as the darkness of the night already shadowed Egypt. Sitting on the rooftop, she stared out into the desert as the melody carried from a few homes away. Wrapping her arms over her knees, Aoh listened to the music, sitting peacefully away from her family. The flute drowned out her siblings still playing with each other while her mother relentlessly tried to teach them. The smells of her neighbors cooking still lingered. Below the shepherds slowly made their way back from the fields leading their flocks.

Aoh's attention was distracted by the sudden sounds of rejoicing coming from the palace. She could see from the rooftop the palace aglow, hearing the dim sounds of exotic music. Hearing the melodies, she sighed heavily, recognizing the sounds of her brother's feeble steps up the wooden ladder. Finding her at the rooftop, he struggled to sit down next to her. Stretching his arms, he exhaled heavily.

"Father is still working, isn't he?" Aoh asked lowly from between her hands.

"Yes, he is. And that celebration isn't for him," he replied.

Aoh blinked heavily. "I discovered that when I realized we weren't invited to the palace."

"That was when you realized? Honestly, I noticed when mother didn't mention anything about moving into the city."

"Where I could experience the process of smooth, cleaned nails on both my hands and feet."

"More than that in the city. Those women might as well be princesses in their own homes."

Releasing a sigh, he added, "Maybe father will become an elite next year. There is always next year."

Aoh's eyes rolled in disbelief, looking in the direction of the desert.

"See something?" he asked.

"You don't hear that?" she asked quickly.

"Hear what?"

"Voices from the desert."

He paused, tilting his head and listened cautiously.

Curling his lips, he replied, "No. Do you?"

"Now and again."

"Probably echoes from wanderers and thieves. Maybe wild animals feeding."

He noticed how tense Aoh's body was becoming. Her shoulders curling forward, as she leaned, staring out into the desert as if looking for someone.

"I'm sure it's nothing to worry about. You should get to bed. It's late."

"I'm not tired."

"If mother catches you up this late, she's not going to be happy," he warned walking towards the ladder.

"I want to wait for father to come home."

"Aoh, go to bed. You can see father tomorrow. Are you going to listen to me?" he asked, firmly.

"I will," Aoh replied, slowly turning around.

"Alright. Good night."

Climbing down the ladder, Aoh listened to his footsteps fade, lightly walking over the floor and pulling the door behind him to a solid close. Glancing over the side of the roof, Aoh carefully climbed down the corner, using her feet to balance her body against heavy cracks and indentations made from the hardened mud brick. Her feet gently touched the top of large sealed pottery, using it for balance as she straightened her legs and turned her body. Delicately climbing off the large pottery, she touched the ground feeling a slight chill in the air.

4

Aoh wandered the town, noticing several people out late, hardly visible in the heavy darkness. She heard the sounds of small fires crackling, creating a dim light in the windows. Shadows swept under the closed doors and across the roads. Aoh's nose picked up the scent of a tea brewing nearby. Someone wasn't sleeping and turned to the pleasures of an expensive tea to calm them. Sometimes when the breeze came through at the right moment, the sounds of the celebration at the palace traveled down the paths in between the houses.

Turning a corner, she encountered random men talking outside their homes, keeping their hands tucked under their arms. The faint odor of animals still lingered on their bodies. Their heavy eyes were wide open, even with the surrounding dark circles. Aoh stopped, watching them converse with deep hostility when they noticed her not far from them. They stopped talking and glared at her, questioning why she was there, when suddenly the sharp and quick sound of horses running caught their attention. They looked in the direction they heard the horses, remaining still and listening again. The sound grew louder before fading away.

A sharp thud startled them as an arrow struck a door post next to the two men. A second later, another arrow fell from the sky striking one of the two in the chest. He grunted, falling over dead, horrifying Aoh. She screamed at the top of her lungs when the sharp sound of a loud whistle soared across the sky. Following the sound, Aoh looked up and could see hundreds of arrows falling.

Diving quickly, she hid underneath several pieces of wood standing up against the wall, held up by sealed pottery. Her scream alarmed many from their deep slumber as the screeching of horses filled the air. Covering her ears, Aoh felt the wood throbbing and rocking as the arrows struck it, piercing through and barely missing her. Citizens were killed trying to flee their homes, as the rain of arrows continued again, sounding like hail against every object.

The sounds of a barbaric cry shook the ground as Aoh trembled, unable to move from the tight space, facing the sharp tips of arrows and splintered wood. The cries grew as horses ran past her, kicking up the sand. The sounds of swords freed from leather straps and the burning of wood rang in her ears as she cupped her hands over her face.

Locking the door, Aoh's older brother bared it with whatever furniture he could find as his mother and siblings descended down a small wooden ladder to a hideaway under the home. The children wept loudly as the crashing and screaming continued at an alarming pace. He wrapped a thick fabric through the hole in the door and around furniture viciously several times.

"Stop! It's good enough! Come down with us!" his mother shouted, harshly.

"Mother, go down there and don't come out!" he shouted in response.

"I'm not going-"

"You have to go down there to protect them! They need you! Stay down there and don't come out!"

He quickly looked at his siblings and frowned heavily.

"Where's Aoh?"

"I don't know," his mother replied, worriedly.

"What do you-"

"She wasn't in her bed."

"I'm going to find her and bring her back here. Stay down there with them and don't come out!" he ordered as she wept wildly.

As her feeble steps reached the bottom surrounded with her children, he closed the door, tugged it roughly, and tossed a ragged mat over it. Rushing to his small room, he tossed the layers of mats he slept on and revealed a small sword wrapped in a blanket. Tucking the sword into the belt at his waist, he climbed out the nearest window.

Aoh remained under the pieces of splintered wood, wishing the sounds of screaming would stop. After another round of arrows were fired, she stumbled onto her feet trying to find somewhere to hide, as her heart raced, hurting her chest. She covered her head from the heavy flames and increasingly thick smoke, as the citizens tried to escape their burning homes, suffocating on the thick air. Men collapsed, covered in arrows, pinned to the hard ground. Aoh screamed, terrified by every horrible sight, hearing the horses and men growing closer.

She clasped her sweaty hands over her mouth, breathing through her nose, feeling the heavy smoke burning her eyes as she tried to maneuver her way back home. Slipping her left hand from her mouth, she leaned against the homes, trying to stay balanced, feeling the trails of smoke slipping between her fingers. Her throat tingled, causing her to cough, while she tried to escape the smoke.

Seeing in the smoke a clearing, she darted forward. feeling the cold night air enter her body. She was shoved from both sides by panicked men, women, and children trying to free themselves from the fire. Water was splashed from the well, tossed onto the vicious fires as one by one families grabbed each other, trying to escape their town which had become a maze of death. Lifting her head to look at the sky of stars, Aoh winced…

Above me, thousands of arrows soared like diving birds, glowing red from the reflection of the flames, so thick I couldn't see the sky.

"Get down!"

Aoh was shoved forcefully under a cart as her brother followed behind her. The sound of the arrows striking the cart rang in their ears, slashing through the wood. She clutched her hands over her ears, hearing hundreds of people scream their last, picturing the families she had seen every day brutally killed. She screamed loudly, struggling to fight back from crying.

"Aoh? Aoh?"

Her brother shook her violently until she removed her hands from her ears, seeing him screaming at her. Her body jiggled with each violent shake as her woeful eyes were swallowed by his dark, intense ones.

"Listen to me. You have to listen to me. You can't stay here. If you do, you will die. Remember what I told you? Think, Aoh."

Aoh nodded roughly up and down, feeling stray tears run down her cheeks.

"Don't stop running," he continued, "no matter what you hear and no matter what you see. Keep going in that direction and don't come back! Don't come back! Understand?!"

Aoh bit her lips together and sputtered, "I…can't…leave-"

"You have to! If you want to live, you have to run! The second I tell you to you run, you run and do not turn back! Understand?"

The wisp of the release of thousands of arrows whistled into the air, crashing down onto the cart and all around them a second time. Aoh screamed, hearing the wood splinter and crack as her brother wrapped his arms around her tightly, tucking her head into his chest.

The second the last arrow was heard striking the ground he shouted, "Go and don't come back! Go!"

With a forceful shove, Aoh was thrown outside the small covering, beholding a sight of the ends of arrows sticking up from the ground, covering the backs of men, women, and children. Stunned, Aoh barely got onto her feet, grasping onto the side of the wall for support. She turned and saw for a brief moment her brother killing a man violently with a sword. She watched as the man screamed, his blood splattering all over himself and across her brother's face. Everything went black for half a second…

As she reopened her eyes, feeling the lower half of her body become numb, she watched her brother remove his sword from the dead man. She blinked heavily, as the pains in her chest increased with each heartbeat.

"Aoh! Go, now! NOW!"

Aoh felt him shove her again as he killed another man rushing at them like a wild beast.

Struggling to run without being able to feel my legs was unlike anything I have had to overcome to this point. My eyes were constantly shifting from left to right, as I moved away from the town as fast as I could, turning at every corner trying to avoid broken items scattered across the ground. Every second I saw someone killed, someone beg, someone hide, someone cry. I saw them…briefly, like shadows striking out of the darkness, slipping between homes and windows.

I saw blood in the air and on the ground. I saw it on the walls and doors. I felt the blood on my hands when I placed them on my pounding head. I saw fire burning. So much fire! The rooftops of homes completely collapsed with a monstrous groan shaking the ground. I stumbled several times, almost falling, trying to hold onto anything I could to keep my balance. For if I fell...I feared I would not rise ever again.

In between heavy breaths, Aoh's eyes opened and closed as scenes of death and devastation flashed in and out of the heavy darkness and smoke. As the feeling of numbness in her legs turned to severe pain.

"Where am I? Where am I?" Aoh repeated to herself aloud, constantly looking about, confused and disoriented from the violent distractions.

Tripping over a dead man who collapsed right in front of her, she felt the force of the ground hit her body. With a grunt, she looked upward, seeing nothing at first. Then she realized there was less blood and fire around her. The colors of the burning fire rose upward like columns, glowing in the growing distance like beacons. Struggling to turn her head, she turned around and found that she had progressively moved further from all of the destruction unfolding like pages from a book written by angry gods.

My legs went numb again, my body felt as though it had this invisible pressure on top of it that made it near impossible to move. I cried aloud for a moment, to release myself from all of the confusing emotions that battled each other to be heard. I shouted my brother's name more than once, but only received howling and shrieking in response. Crawling over the body and across the sand, feeling the rough grains scratch my skin, I saw the rows of reeds before the Nile River. Getting onto my feet and stumbling a second time, I ran towards the river as fast as I could, running through the endless, thick reeds, and falling several times over my feet.

Aoh rolled down the slight drop, feeling the dirt, papyrus reeds, and sand cover her, rattling her just slightly until she stopped at the bank of the river.

I forced myself up, feeling the wrath of death as the fires kept burning and the screaming echoes suffocated the air. I saw nothing but darkness around me, yet ahead of me lied water. Dark…water…I could not see through. Crawling, grasping for something solid in the soft sand, I grasped the papyrus reeds, pulling myself upward, pulling through the remnants of reeds until I felt the water against my knees. The cold touch sent shivers up and down my body as my feet fumbled against the floor, sliding me forward.

My breathing hadn't calmed, but heightened intensely. I slid into the water, pushing myself to walk across the path, when I slipped. Falling into the hidden depths, I quickly swam upward, trying to keep my head above the surface, watching as my vision constantly changed from seeing the other side of the river to the water covering me in small waves.

I pulled and kicked, gasping for air each time I came up, feeling my body painfully cramp each second I struggled. I cried aloud and shouted, fighting against my own body, trying to get onto the other side, dreading creatures who dwelled in these waters would find me. Spitting up the water, between clamoring teeth and my hair, uncontrollably swallowing some, I gasped as I finally reaching the other side... I dragged myself onto the sand, feeling my body collapse onto the papyrus reeds.

My body soaked, my hair covering half of my face...my skin was covered in goose bumps as I stared at the night sky so far from my reach. I exhaled slowly, seeing trails of my breath escape from my mouth... shivering uncontrollably on the ground until the glisten of flames reflecting off the river caught my attention.

Straining my back, I sat up and gazed towards the source of the fire. In between the flames and reeds, I saw more men crossing the river, trying to get to the other side to join the never ending massacre. They didn't speak, silent shadows of death, carrying weapons glowing against their bodies. Turning around, I lowered myself, hearing my knees crack. I dragged my body across the cold ground in between the rows of reeds. I was unwilling to give up, as painful as every movement became.

Finally freeing myself from the reeds, I stumbled, continuing into the sand, running away from the endless moving torches in the dark hands of the monsters. I don't know how far I ran or how long it took me... The outlines of large rocks and boulders came into view... I grasped onto them until I collapsed onto my knees, sliding downward across hard rock and sand, towards nothing but emptiness. Leaning against the rocks, I turned back and saw the black smoke filling the changing dark to blue sky, consuming it in poisonous colors. I couldn't hear the screaming anymore, but I could see the pain. I fell into the shade of the rocks as consciousness left me...

5

When I awoke, I saw nothing but grey skies…

Pulling herself upward, Aoh coughed heavily, feeling sand and dirt sticking to her lips. Sand decorated the tips of her long hair, painted across her skin. Small cuts covered the palms of her hands and tops of her toes. Rubbing her body, she felt the tiny shards of rough textures fall onto the ground. Aoh coughed aloud several more times, trying to build liquid into her mouth to spit. The air was clean, empty of any smoke and smelt like the river. Rising onto her feet, leaning her body against the side of a large boulder, she looked around her seeing nothing but desert in every direction.

I heard nothing… I saw nothing… Until suddenly I heard my friend calling out to me.

Aoh looked up at the sky and found the kite circling over her, casting itself across the grey colors. The shadow from its wings swooped over her like a swift spirit. Aoh raised her trembling left arm gently upward, waiting for her friend to perch. With another loud call, the kite swooped downward, hovering in the air with its wings spread outward like a tent before landing on her arm. Its long claws wrapped carefully over her skin without scratching. She smiled faintly, seeing that within the closed beak of the kite was a rich green branch with healthy leafy ends. Raising her other hand to the beak, the kite dropped the piece.

"Thank you," Aoh smiled, taking the branch and quickly eating it.

It was sweet, fresh, new. The taste was so cool down my throat. It awoke me.

The kite stared at Aoh, constantly twitching. Its small white head, speckled with grey, turned every second towards a different direction while it's sharp eyes remained frozen in place. Aoh tenderly stroked the soft chest with her fingers, feeling her insides growl and rumble with a hunger the branch couldn't fill. Tears swelled in her eyes as uncontrollable thoughts of her family haunted her with such a ferocity their screams rang all around her.

Like a vicious echo of a dying heart, their voices called out to me, over and over again. I could hear them in the air flying all around me. They were in the sky, in the mountains, in the ground beneath my feet. I wept. I tried to stop but every time, my tears would flow faster than a flooded river into open fields.

Rubbing her dirty hand across her mouth and nose, the kite watched, beginning to shriek. Aoh turned, looking at the kite who shifted radically, lifting itself gently from her arm. She watched it lift into the air, not far above her, and beginning to fly towards the direction of the large desert. Once it circled her several times, it shrieked loudly.

Aoh rubbed her face, taking small but strong steps forward, feeling her legs wobble slightly. She followed the kite, as the sun emerged from the grey sky. With the sun now revealed, the heat began to rise, burning the ground and turning the brittle sand to solid rock spread across the open space. Aoh remained as close as she could to the shade, often walking into the sunlight as she came across several crumbled pieces of larger stones.

Exasperated, she rushed to the large rocks. Her hands scanned each rock, over every edge and indent desperately. She picked up the smaller rocks, turning them in her hands. Small amounts of water slipped from the holes and into her mouth. Anxious and flustered, Aoh grabbed another and repeated the process, feeling small droplets soothe her mouth. The small amounts of water collected inside were hardly enough to refresh her, but just enough…just enough.

For hours, Aoh followed the kite, moving in between shade and sunlight, slurping up any water she could find in the rocks. Every so often, she'd lose sight of the beautiful bird only to catch him carrying some kind of plant for her to eat. Biting into thick green leaves, she sucked heavily trying to slurp more liquid, munching on the remnants.

As the sun began to fade and the wisp of cold air swooped in like a vicious vulture, Aoh found shelter in the small indent in a large rock foundation. Drawing her legs up to her chest, wrapping her arms across her body, she sat in the tight space, staring out at nothing but more desert and a pitch black sky. Constantly rubbing her arms up and down to create heat, her eyes fluttered open after falling asleep for an hour or two.

Trying to hum aloud songs she had heard all her life, Aoh constantly battled herself, trying to find some peace, fighting back the urge to cry thinking of her family.

The second I would think of them I would fall into this deep sadness that I felt as though I was crawling to get out of. Every time the depth would deepen and it would take me longer to escape. I repeated the same songs until I passed out.

Aoh entered the heat of another day, walking through the desert, kicking the sand with each step, feeling particles cling to the tight spaces between her toes. She constantly pulled her hair in between her hands, rubbing the sweat off her face and listening to the silence of the desert.

I lost all concept of time…

I had spent the majority of the day laying in the same shade of two large palm trees I discovered nearly lost, misplaced in the vast desert. In between the sandy bottom of the two trees, I laid on the small patches of grass, washing myself completely in the cool water. It was a very small oasis, left in the desert to hide away from the rest of the harsh world.

I stared at those tall, thin trees and the blue sky where, every so often, I'd see the kite circle for hours on end, so high he was near invisible. His shrieks traveled far, looking for something to feast upon while I feasted on whatever grew under the trees. My body, now clean, revealed tiny cuts and bruises. I slept well for the first time since that horrific night.

6

For days, Aoh nibbled on the leaves of the palm trees she plucked from the ground that fell some time ago. Sucking and biting into the green leaves, she tried to digest the tiny pieces into her roaring stomach.

Upon the fifth screech of the kite, Aoh could feel a low rumble under her feet. Tiny pieces of broken stone and hardened sand jumped and bounced on the ground. Remaining still, Aoh gently peered around the corner of the rocky wall and heard the sounds of horses growing louder. Within a second, she could just see the tops of heads coming up from the drop in the terrain calling out to their horses. She quickly dashed away from the wall and towards the large rocks to hide as the storm of running horses came by her, creating clouds of dust.

Lowering herself against the rock, Aoh sighed in relief when suddenly the sounds of the horses changed direction. They turned back, coming towards her as she stumbled to hide behind another large rock, keeping low and silent. The roar of the horses running came to an abrupt halt. She remained still, pressing herself against the rock until…

"You there! Behind the rocks!"

She winced, remaining silent.

"We know you're there! Come out!" the voice ordered, loudly.

Aoh didn't answer. Closing her eyes, she silently prayed they would leave.

"If you do not come out, we will come over there!"

The smoke cleared, revealing brutal horses grunting and gasping for breath.

With the rage of a violent storm, he bellowed, "This is your final warning! COME OUT, NOW!"

"Zurvan!"

Aoh opened her eyes, taken aback by the sound of a woman's voice.

"It's alright. Please come out," the female voice reassured.

Rubbing her hands across the rock, Aoh rose to her feet, staring at the small company of seven men on horseback. All seven men were garbed in several layers of long cloaks in black, dark blue, and white hues. The thick and strange looking garbs made of wool were wrapped over their heads. Each of their hands appeared painted with black markings. Their fingers were rough, some covered in rings, grasped tightly around the reigns of their large horses. Each of them had dark eyes, piercing through their firm faces so tight that, if they were to smile, surely their skin would crack like the ground on a hot day. Their horses looked equally firm, with large hooves and thick bushy manes and tails. Their eyes remained forward at all times, still like statues.

Aoh looked at all of them, feeling her throat swell. From the back of the row of horses one came forward, trotting gracefully. As it passed each man, they tugged their horse back in rhythm. The horse stopped at the front of the line, just before the large rocks Aoh was hiding behind.

Her eyes pierced through the long drape that covered her mouth, hanging from the wrapped cloths over her head. The tiny jewels and threads stitched upon it, glistened with the slightest turn of her head. They were curved as though painted onto her face with swift strokes of a brush. Lifting her hand to the drape that covered her mouth, she untied the small bow. With the release of the thread, a rather distinguished nose and two thin lips were revealed.

She was beautiful. As beautiful as I imagined a Queen of a faraway kingdom would be.

The woman's eyes looked upon Aoh, a child dirty and tired. Dried sand covered her cheeks and neck, dazzling her hair. Her skin looked rough and her feet barely covered by worn sandals. Seeing the beautiful woman, Aoh slowly moved to the side of the rock, keeping both hands positioned firmly to stay balanced.

I looked like nothing compared to the grandeur of this woman, who undoubtedly was from a palace of some kind. A multitude of colors surrounded her. I could see tinier jewels scattered across her, matching the jewels on three of her fingers. Long sleeves painted in such vibrant purples, blues, and greens with gold stitching, trailing the course of the front. Tiny sapphires continued down the middle from the high collar covering the neck, to the bottom of the dress. The dress hid her feet, rubbing against the leather saddle on a well fed grey and white horse. The grey color looked as though it was blended with the white skin, covered the nose, trailing up the legs and across the back.

"What is your name, child?" she asked.

Her voice nearly brought me to tears, sounding warm like my mother's.

"My name is Aoh…"

"Aoh…what a lovely name for a child."

"My queen, neglect this forsaken child and continue. This could be a trap," the tall man to her right said quickly with a deep frown.

"Our enemies are cruel, but never as cruel as to lure us into a false sense of security with a child," she reassured with a playful grin.

"Look at her…"

"I am looking at her, and you know what I see? I see a child who hasn't eaten a decent meal nor drank something cool in days, if not weeks."

"She's not alone."

"Of course she is. Aren't you?" she asked boldly.

"I am…" Aoh replied.

"Are you truly alone?" the man asked coldly.

Aoh nodded, remaining at the rock, trying to keep her feet straight on the slight slope.

"Come," she ordered.

Aoh didn't move, watching as the woman turned to her side, to reach for something she couldn't see under her long garb. Noticing Aoh wasn't moving, she turned to look at her again.

"Come child. It's alright."

"She ordered you to come forward! NOW!"

"Don't…don't yell at her, Zurvan. She's afraid."

I slowly moved, trying not to fall over my own weak feet. As I approached her, I could see nearly every stitch in her dress. Same could be said of what the men were wearing. They all wore matching uniforms of some sort of wool, something soft with an odd pleat to them I've never seen before. They carried with them flags made of silk, riding mighty mustangs that looked even more monstrous up close. I tried to avoid making eye contact with them, afraid they may turn hostile at the sight of my face.

"Here. Drink this."

She retrieved a soft bag full of water from the satchel attached to the back of the saddle. Gently, she lowered it for Aoh to reach. Once the bag reached Aoh's hands, she wildly began to drink. Her mouth sucked on the opening repeatedly, over and over as the liquid flowed down her throat and into her body.

I felt alive again. I knew it was only water, but there was something about it that made me feel as though I were floating. As though I was somehow in the sky or in the stars or with the gods. I felt so alive…

The kind woman watched Aoh as her painted lips curved into a warm smile.

Zurvan noted this immediately, and as though he were reading her mind warned, "Please do not take this child. We know nothing of her."

"But you see, Zurvan, I do know her," she replied kindly.

Aoh choked slightly as she finished the bag of water. She wiped her mouth, feeling the liquid gently wash away the sand from her chin and the palms of her hands.

Taking the bag, the woman gently shook it and smiled, "Oh, yes, you haven't eaten well or drank in ages. You must come back with me."

Upon hearing those words, Aoh's eyes slightly widened as Zurvan sighed heavily, loudly rubbing his fingers over his thick eyebrows and forehead.

"Come, child. I'm going to take you to my home in my palace."

"Queen Huriye-"

"You will have a bright future ahead of you, my child. Come, Aoh."

Queen Huriye stretched out her arm and opened her hand.

Her palm alone looked as smooth as silk.

Aoh grasped her arm and, with a heavy pull, she was lifted and sat in front of the queen, suddenly seeing her world from a slightly higher view. Zurvan glared at Aoh intently, as he looked behind him to make sure the rest of his company was prepared to ride again.

"There you go. Safe with me," Queen Huriye comforted.

Aoh turned and looked up at the queen, taken away by her very aura of benevolence she never knew could exist in anyone else but her own mother.

"You'll be safe, Aoh. You won't be alone anymore. Zurvan."

"RIDE!" Zurvan screamed.

The wind brushed against my face, swiping away the dirt and sand, freeing my hair. The sunlight burned my eyes each time I tried to look ahead of me. With each step of the grand horse, my body shifted from left to right against the queen's soft chest. With one arm containing her royal horse, she used the other to keep me safe in front of her lap.

For reasons I couldn't understand, I saw the desert differently that day. Before I saw it as nothing more than this empty land. But now...I saw it as this land of promise that my brother spoke of.

I watched as we passed boulders placed in several positions, large trees and small wells of fresh water. We raced past the wells and groups of shepherds, as it seemed the closer we were getting to our destination the more alive the desert appeared to be. I heard the chatter of wild dogs guiding the sheep and the whistles of the shepherds calling out to them. I noticed the terrain become less constricted.

The sounds of fire burning, women screaming, and men fighting rang in Aoh's ears like a violent storm. She kept hearing her brother's voice telling her to run with eyes full of a fear she had never seen before.

"Remember what I told you?" he had said.

"This world is only as tame as the gods allow it to be. We are their servants. "

"You need not be afraid of the world, Aoh."

I awoke, startled and terrified, only to be reassured of my safety, when I felt the hand of the queen wrapped against my chest. I winced several times, as the blinding sunlight made everything seem white. Lowering my hands, the first thing I saw was...blue. Blue waters surrounded by green trees, by white and ivory buildings, and more blue upon the top of, what looked to be, a palace glowing in the sunlight. It was encircled by smaller palaces draped in greenery. My mouth opened slightly at the sight of a place I never dreamed existed.

Zurvan called loudly into the air, raising his flag. In unison, the rest of the group called out as the horses began to run faster towards the city coming ahead. Aoh's body rattled as the horse's charge strengthened. The loud sounds of horns coming from the city boomed overhead. Zurvan and the rest of the group let out another mighty roar. Passing green, luscious fields filled with workers and shepherds, the horses continued towards the gates of the city. A large wall, rising perhaps taller than the palace of Egypt, towered over her like a mountain.

Through the large gate, Aoh winced as the sunlight pierced her eyes from between the top of something she couldn't distinguish in the distance. Almost every structure painted white was as tall as the other, built in layers of endless stone steps similar to the pyramids in Egypt. Balconies were covered with overhanging plants of different shapes and sizes. Vibrant shades of red outlined every door frame.

The horns continued as the gates were opened and the fresh

scents of wild flowers consumed Aoh all at once. The sharp clacking of the hooves against the stone road, surrounded by people and statues at nearly every corner. Aoh's eyes watched the people dressed in long, colorful garbs nowhere near as elaborate as the queen's or her men. Their black hair rested on their shoulders as their eyes glowed above their thin noses and lips. Working together, artisans and workers bartered using the objects they carried with them.

The noises of geese and and ducks exchanged for clothing and furniture blended in with the pleasing echoes of constant running water from fountains and drains over the rooftops of white homes. They stood out amongst the mud brick and reed weaved ones. The deeper they entered the city, the more wounds Aoh found in the glamorous city that seemed to thrive as one whole society within the protective walls.

Statues and homes were missing several pieces. Those still standing, cracked and crumbled, covered in burnt wood and black ash. Rocks were completely missing, the faint scents of smoke lingered... Large towers crumbled into nothing but pieces of painted and carved stone. Several groups of people were taking down the half damaged statues, working together with large ropes pulled by oxen.

Women washed clothes together in a watering basin as their children stayed with them, looking almost identical to each other. Peasants and nobles alike lived together wearing wool and animal skins on their backs. Fresh eggs were carried from the nests to the baskets as the vivid green colors of vegetables grasped the attention of many waiting to buy them. The horns fell silent, in the distance, allowing the sounds of running water to surround them.

At times, the laughing of small children grabbed Aoh's attention. She glanced at them running past the horses, disappearing into larger crowds of people when a heavy shadow fell over her again. Glancing upward, Aoh saw what she could only deduce was the palace. Her mouth opened slightly as her eyes remained raised trying to see the very top.

The queen lowered her voice and said sweetly, "This is where I live, Aoh. Welcome to my home."

7

The plate of fresh fruit was placed before Aoh, now surrounded by dish after dish of food from breads, to meats and vegetables. Goblets full of cool water and the smell of clear air surrounded her. The faint scent of burning sesame seed oil tormented her nose. Her small feet dangled just above the cool floor as the breeze swept through the room every time the sky breathed. Aoh's eyes hung over the food, staring at the unrecognizable dishes full of sweet and sour scents.

Across from her, the queen watched, sitting comfortably in her very loose, several layer flowing gown. Her long hair remained braided between her natural hair and the ends of a black wig, pulled behind her ears, covered in several golden earrings. In the silence, they heard the echo of exotic birds squawking to one another from across the room. Several female servants stood in a straight line several feet away from them, wearing the same dress with their hair done the same way.

The queen looked upon Aoh as she stared at the multitude of food quietly. Another loud squawk fell over the room.

"It's alright," she said calmly.

Aoh looked at the queen, seeing a warm smile painted across her face. Stretching her arm across the table, she lifted her hand, cupping Aoh's chin to look at her. Aoh didn't speak but stared back into the queen's eyes that reminded her of a precious stone that gleamed in certain light. The palm of her hands were so soft…unlike anything Aoh had ever felt before.

"Poor child. I can only imagine how long you've been in the desert all alone."

Her smile opened, partially revealing her teeth.

"You don't have to worry," she continued. "You'll never go hungry again. You'll never go thirsty again. I am going to take care of you," she promised.

Lowering her hand, she rose from her seat gracefully.

"Please, eat."

Aoh took the first piece of fruit in front of her and bit into its sweet center as juice dripped from around her small mouth onto her chin and lap. She ate it quickly, and soon moved onto another fruit but stopped when she saw the bread. As she was finishing, the queen called forth her servants. They followed each another in a straight line, as their dresses swished across the floor. Their eye makeup flashed with each blink, heads lowered and hands clasped together.

"When she's finished, provide her with a bath and clean clothing."

The three nodded simultaneously.

I had never seen water so clear before in my life. I could see my entire reflection as I sat in the basin, my legs drawn to my chest as each vessel of water was poured over my head. A servant would gently grab my arm, and scrub it to and fro while the other would run her fingers through my dirty locks of hair, massaging my scalp. I resisted but no matter how many times I did they never spoke. Their eyes didn't even show a hint of frustration or anger. They all had the same calm, almost soulless eyes as they bathed me.

From the bath they dried me, and I was welcomed with a clean linen dress that fell over my feet. I felt a brush run through my hair as I closed my eyes, gently enjoying each stroke. The bristles ran through my rough hair, turning it smooth like weaved silk into a dress. I trembled and wept lowly, dipping my head forward. The servant stopped brushing my hair and placed her hands on my shoulders. I quickly stopped, letting out a deep breath and blinked heavily.

"Aoh."

The heavy door was pushed open and the sight of an open room covered in multiple colors and scents welcomed her.

Aoh stumbled inside, unsure what to look at first. Statues as high as the ceiling and no larger than a small animal lined the walls. Incense burning smoothly, filling the air. Pristine furniture and intricately woven carpets were displayed across the floor. Near the large balcony was the most appealing bed that could sleep at least six people, covered in a multitude of sheets.

"This is your room, Aoh. All yours," Queen Huriye smiled, standing in the doorway as the servants entered and stood in a straight line.

Aoh stopped in the middle of the room, lifting her eyes to stare at the tall ceiling painted with a colorful trim. Layers of mosaics around stone accented even the smallest details.

"Aoh? Do you like it?"

Aoh nodded her head silently in response.

"Do not hesitate to ask for me. I will be in my quarters if you need anything. These servants are most devoted. They will serve you well."

Aoh continued to look around the room silently, rubbing her feet on everything from the cool floor to the fabric carpet, woven into intricate patterns. Her small hands ran across the sheets on the bed and to the dozens of pillows, trailing across the folds and indents.

Queen Huriye called over to her servants whom immediately exited the room.

"Have a good night, Aoh."

She pulled the door closed, listening to the solid thud and seeing Zurvan waiting for her attentively with both arms behind his back.

The moment her door closed, Aoh quickly dashed from her bed towards the desk like a startled feline. Finding pieces of parchment already there, she quickly looked for something to draw with. Her eyes scanned the room, lifting small statues and basins, looking underneath chairs, trying to find something to draw with while watching the door. She rushed to the other side of the room where she found dozens of bottles made from the same stone and, what looked like rounded, thin plates in her eyes.

I was dumbfounded by them… Taking each plate, some heavier than others made of stone and white marble, I rubbed my fingers across the smooth surfaces. With each touch, a pleasing sensation ran across my arms like tiny insects. My eyes wandered from the plate to other objects, including a large hairbrush. Lowering my fingertips gently over the ends, I winced at the touch. Seeing the reflection of my tiny hand in the mirror lying on the table next to the burning incense, I noticed something black. Near the brush laid a crushed black powder on one of the flat surfaces shaped like some beast I've never seen before.

Taking the black powder, Aoh rushed back over to the desk, worried that someone was going to enter her room at any moment. She dipped her fingers into the black powder, using it to draw lines and circles in several places. At the top of the parchment, she drew jagged trees in front of a tall structure she depicted making several square and oddly edged shapes.

Following the curves and rounded objects, she drew two more trees with different branches just before a line that extended upward on an angle across the middle of the page. Making two more circles she stopped, her fingertips covered in the black powder with traces of it on her arms and the desk.

I wanted to draw before I could forget how to get back home.

Aoh looked at the barely legible map she quickly drew, starting with the far right side and following the path to the far left. At the far left, her image was drawn slightly bigger than the others as she wrote one of the only words she knew, 'Home', above it. Quickly rolling the parchment with her ink smudged fingers, she looked about the room for a place to conceal it. She lifted her pillows and then under the sheets, trailing the black powder across the colors.

Unsatisfied, she went near the window and then, on the balcony, greeted with the cold night and a multicolored sky blending several shades of darkness with colors of fire. She found more than a few potted trees against the wall to her left. Picking the second to last one, she quickly dug into the potted plant, feeling the grains of dirt stick between the small space between her nails and skin, burying the map.

I drew what I remembered of my journey to this place. I hid that map so that when I would return home, I'd remember how to.

8

Bowl after bowl was placed on the long table that stretched in both directions. Within every small space, a bowl full of food was positioned before Aoh as she sat silently. The servants continued to serve the food until every last place on the table was full.

Aoh stared at the food as Queen Huriye watched her from across the table, wearing a new gown and a new hairstyle. The queen leaned back, twirling the long curls in her hair that fell to her waist, looking at Aoh sitting in silence staring at the food.

"Eat something," she said calmly.

Aoh didn't move.

"The queen told you to eat," Zurvan ordered sternly, standing next to Aoh like a statue.

"Zurvan, please. She's afraid," Queen Huriye consoled, immediately holding out her hand covered in rings. The bangles covering her arms lightly jingled with her gentle movement.

"She needs to eat, doesn't she?"

"Yes, but-"

She paused as a servant rushed to her side and quickly whispered into her ears, covering her mouth with her hand.

"Really?" Queen Huriye asked aloud.

The servant nodded deeply.

"Zurvan, watch her please. I'll return shortly."

Aoh watched the queen leave the room, disappearing behind a wall nearly concealed by the overgrown plants. Returning her eyes to the untouched food, she sighed heavily. Every moment her stomach would attempt to grumble in hunger, she'd place her hand there trying to mask the sounds.

Impatient, Zurvan bent downward and slightly lowered his cold voice.

"If you don't want to starve until evening, I suggest you eat something. We only eat twice a day here. I hoped you bathed before presenting yourself before the queen."

Aoh didn't respond, glancing at her hands laying in her lap and trying to feel comfortable in the thick linen dress that covered her from her neck to above her ankles.

"If you do not want to stay here, the queen will return you where she found you. But you can't leave if you're weak. If you don't eat, you will stay weak."

He picked up a plate of tiny pieces of already crushed fruit and bread, and leaned towards Aoh, slamming it onto the table.

"Eat," he ordered.

Aoh blinked heavily and picked out of the three closest bowls, what appeared to be, the most familiar of food in her eyes. Taking the pieces of already cut fruit, she took the smallest bite and chewed slowly. The thick piece of fruit had a slightly crunchy texture on the outside but tender on the inside. Realizing the taste wasn't horrible, she continued to eat it as Zurvan watched, keeping his arms at his chest. As she ate, she noticed an exotic bird with large feathers looking back at her from across the room, perched upon one of the short tree limbs.

It wasn't a large bird, but did have many large feathers and a particularly strange facial expression. Seeing the bird stare was a little unsettling. She looked back down at her food, hearing Queen Huriye returning by the pleasant sounds of her sandals across the floor.

"Wonderful, you're eating," she smiled, returning to her seat. "Take your time. When you're done, I want to show you something."

After swallowing the last piece, Aoh said quietly, "I'm done."

Zurvan glared down at her intensely. His eyes so heavy she could feel it on her shoulders.

"Really?" the Queen asked. "Are you sure?"

Aoh nodded.

"Alright. We will take some of this with us then. Come."

Zurvan grabbed a few pieces of fruit when Queen Huriye stopped him, gently touching his arm.

"No, you're not coming with us," she ordered.

Startled by her order, Zurvan handed her the fruit as she placed it into another bowl.

"My queen, may I ask, where are you taking her?" he inquired calmly.

"I want to show her our history."

"My queen, we know nothing about her," he said, biting into his lips.

"Yet, Zurvan. She's a child, left in the desert. No family-"

She paused, noticing Aoh still sitting in her seat silently, trying to avoid eye contact with the large bird.

"No family."

"And what of your family?" he asked.

"She will be accepted."

The gleam in her eyes triggered Zurvan's intuition.

His eyes narrowed slightly as he turned his head, "What news did you receive that has you in such a joyous mood this morning?"

Queen Huriye placed her index finger to her lips and whispered, "Shh… I will speak to you about it later."

He nodded and bowed deeply before leaving, taking firm and tightened steps.

"Come, Aoh," she called warmly, taking one of the fruits from the bowl and biting into it.

Aoh turned and looked at her.

"Come along, follow me."

Leaving the room, Aoh walked next to Queen Huriye down the hallway and outside, immediately greeted with vibrant colors and intense scents. Aoh's eyes followed every path, from stone structure to sounds of constant running water. Queen Huriye's robe trailed behind her, shining in the glow of the sunlight.

Cautiously watching her steps, Aoh followed close behind the queen, slightly terrified she'd miss a step and then fall. Outside, the warmth of a new day glowed over the city that looked so small compared to the magnitude of the palace. With each step Aoh took, she had to pause to observe how high they were in disbelief. As high as they were, the sky was far higher and out of her reach.

"Come, this way," Queen Huriye called, several steps down.

Aoh followed, rubbing her feet over the stone steps and slight greenery as they walked down the side to a walkway in the shade of the palace. Just before entering another hallway, Aoh noticed the overlapping balconies above and below her. The hallway was slightly larger and darker than the previous ones she had seen. She stopped, seeing the queen stand before a giant stone in a dark but beautiful gold and copper color.

"Do you know what this is?" Queen Huriye asked, glancing down at her.

Aoh shook her head in response.

"Hammurabi was a great king who made this city as glorious as it is," she answered. "His codes and laws changed the course of our world. Sadly, when he died, we weren't the same. We managed, until one after another they came. First it was the Hittites, then the Kassites, and finally the Assyrians. It has been a most difficult struggle but the gods shone down on us. Every day we were under siege by these horrid people. They loved us, and with that love, the Assyrian ruler was killed. And now we are recovering…"

Looking at the tablet, Queen Huriye continued, "Hammurabi's code consisted of 282 laws written in our ancient language, Akkadian. He talked about trade, slander, theft, even marriages and relationships. The Assyrians changed our language slightly since their occupation but they will not conquer us."

She raised the fruit back to her mouth as she bit into it fiercely, and the calm glow in her eyes soon turned dark and bitter. Aoh's attention was drawn to a statue of a man nearby. It haunted the corner of her eyes with a silent gaze. She walked around the queen to approach the statue only to be slightly startled by its depiction of a tall man with a long beard, standing on what appeared to be a boat. The boat looked strangely thin with the head of some kind of serpent at its bow. Stepping to the side, she looked at another image, seeing the same man this time with four wings on his back.

"I see you have found Marduk," Queen Huriye smiled with glee, shifting herself ever so slightly, swaying the bottom of her dress across the floor.

"Who?" Aoh asked, slightly afraid and feeling the glands in her throat swell.

"Marduk is our supreme god. We were created to serve him and the lesser gods. He became supreme god by making quite the deal with his father, to aid him in his war against the other gods. For his help in achieving victory, he took complete power over the other gods. He is associated with water, vegetation, judgment, and magic..."

Aoh felt a cold chill down her back that shook her slightly, running down to her small feet.

"Marduk will return to Babylon one day," the Queen mused. "It is said that he left our city to famine and pestilence, but would return when a new king takes the throne. He will bring salvation to our city and seek his revenge on the Elamites. I dream that one day, when I have a son, he will be the king the prophecy speaks of."

Unable to break Marduk's gaze, Aoh asked in a near whisper, "Do you believe that will really happen?"

"Oh, yes, Aoh, I do. I believe that within my womb I will carry such a son, such a king, and I will gladly watch Marduk seek his revenge, and perhaps...destroy what's left of Babylon's enemies, crushing them into the dust where they belong."

She finished the fruit quickly, licking the tips of every finger to absorb that last bit of sweetness. Aoh watched as the queen's smile slowly spread from glossy to shimmered cheek. Her expression shifted so swiftly from bitterness to ecstasy. Aoh's eyes returned to the god, puzzled by his appearance.

"Where do you come from?" she asked, noticing Aoh studying the statue.

I wasn't able to answer. My mind became empty of any thought or memory in that very moment.

"I don't know," Aoh answered.

"Your family?"

"I don't know about them. I don't know…"

Queen Huriye studied my expression as her thin fingers curled. She did not study me as Zurvan did. She studied me as a teacher would, discovering something new. I bewildered her.

"Come with me. I want you to meet my family."

Returning to the throne room, a little girl revealed herself behind large doors, dressed in a gown similar to the queen's with a timid expression captured on her young face.

The princess looked as though she were at least two years younger than myself. She appeared very quiet and almost shy. Not boisterous like the queen.

"Aoh, this is my daughter, Mylittia. When I pass on from this world, she will be the queen of Babylon, and you will have the privilege to serve her," Queen Huriye explained, looking at her daughter from the doors.

The princess hardly reacted. She seemed confused by me, as though she had never seen another child before. She was fair with dark eyes like her mother, but she didn't seem much like her. She was different. For days we were together, teaching one another how to read and write almost every language known in the world. I didn't know it at the time, but we were lucky. The other girls in the city were not allowed to learn how to read and write. They had far more important things to do, for one day they would be caring for a family of their own.

Princess Mylittia and I practiced every day, sitting across from each other in the most beautiful open space. The room was five times larger than any other, located on the far side of the palace so that when the sun reached us, we were not overpowered by its warmth. We used the silence to our advantage. The queen didn't want us disturbed; she seemed to always have the servants occupied so they let us be.

Very rarely did we hear anything but our own voices and the sounds of the tools tracing the ink onto the parchment. Of course, there was the sounds of animals talking. I never really minded. For some reason, those sounds made Princess Mylittia laugh every time she heard them. I would alway smell the scent of food towards the end of our studies. Food was never in short supply. Before we ate, we had to wash ourselves and wear new clothes and pray to the gods for the meal. Queen Huriye thanked them in such a profound way, as though she believed they were present in the very room.

The palace was unlike any place I ever dreamed possible. Every hallway and room was more elegant than the last. It reminded me of the mountains, so very tall, standing over the rest of the world where very few were allowed to enter. I had spent every night on the balcony outside my room, sitting on the ledge and staring out into the distance, wondering if my friend was going to find me, until I grew tired and went to bed. I can't recall how many nights I cried in my sleep, unable to think of anything but my family, wondering if they were still alive. If they were wondering what became of me.

9

One night, I couldn't sleep no matter how much I struggled. I vaguely remember dreaming of the gods of my homeland surrounding me with gifts before awaking to the eternal silence of my room. I resorted to walking the palace, never truly seeing it at night. I'd be lying if I said the statues of the Babylonian gods did not startle me during the day. At night, however, they were terrifying.

Aoh wandered the rooms, coming and going through places until she realized she was lost. Backtracking, Aoh took the wrong door, confusing it for another. She followed slight steps downwards and walked through a small space surrounded by large statues of beasts. Turning slightly, she heard a low hissing sound from the darkness. She remained in the light of the burning fires, hearing the sounds suddenly fade.

She cautiously turned at another corner, hearing the hissing magnify in volume and startling her. She hesitated at first, seeing nothing but statues of the gods standing on both sides of the narrow path towards another room. Keeping her eyes down, she continued forward into the room almost pitch black. Four burning torches created a slight glow, placed in a circular form around a stone pit.

A figure stood looking over the pit, dressed in a dark-colored gown with hints of white around the shoulders. From the pit, she saw the figure bend downward and pull out the cause of the hissing sounds. The creature wiggled and jumped, causing Aoh to gasp aloud. The figure turned, seeing Aoh hiding behind the corner, just barely peering forward. Her tiny hand clenched the corner of the wall; her left eye was revealed while her right remained hidden behind the wall.

"It's alright," Queen Huriye said, calmly.

The glow of the flames created a strange shine to her skin. Her eyes danced in the vibrating dim shadows as she grasped the creature in her right hand tightly with ease.

"Come, Aoh," she called, serenely.

Aoh took small steps into the dark room. The hissing sounds continued to grow as she stepped from the smooth marble floor to, what felt like, a multitude of different textured marble sealed together unevenly. The sound of her feet against the marble echoed off the walls around the domed ceiling. Approaching the rounded stone pit, Aoh glanced over the side, slowly, and found at least forty snakes hissing and biting each other at the bottom. She jolted backwards, hearing the snake clenched in Queen Huriye's tight fingers, covered in golden and silver wrapped rings.

"It's alright. No need to be afraid, Aoh," she reassured, looking at the creature.

Her eyes gleamed as she tried to tame the long, smooth body under her arm. It fussed, erratically trying to free itself.

"Do you know what this is?" she asked Aoh with a charming smile.

"A snake," Aoh replied lowly, looking upward.

"It's an asp. It's poisonous."

I took a step backwards, terrified at the prospect she was going to kill me. But…that was not the case.

"I'm not going to hurt you. I'm going to teach you," she reassured.

From around her waist, she gently tugged at a glass vial, tied to a long rope with her free hand. Freeing the empty vial, she held it against the asps' sharp, curved mouth.

"Not many know to do this."

Forcing the top of the glass into the mouth, the asp responded by fiercely biting into it. Aoh could just make out the tiny yet very sharp fangs clench onto the glass opening as a strange liquid slowly dripped across the sides to the bottom. Queen Huriye struggled slightly, keeping the asp's attention on the glass vial, moving it towards the light so that Aoh could see better.

"This is…the hardest part," she admitted with a slight grunt. "They are very temperamental creatures, asps. Very powerful. One bite from them…and that's the end of everything you know."

The yellow tinted liquid dripped very slowly, clinging to the glass. Each droplet slowly stuck to the vial, appearing thick like blood.

"My mother was bit by an asp that was placed in her bed," the Queen informed Aoh. "The bite killed her. Just as planned."

"How old were you?"

"I was eleven years old, recently wed and unprepared for the future. I could barely grasp the present. It is because she was killed that I told myself I would never share the same fate. I knew then what I needed to do to survive. For the past several years I have grown an immunity to asp poison by slowly consuming it."

Aoh's eyes widened drastically.

"Come on, now…just one more…" she whispered to the snake.

The last drop of the poison seeped from the fangs…very slowly. With a quick jerk, Queen Huriye freed the asp from the glass vial, and, with a swift gesture, returned it to the pit where the others remained, moving slowly across each other. Their narrow tongues slipping in and out of their closed mouths, their rounded eyes constantly staring into another's as they communicated through a constant hissing tune.

"Ah…what immortality awaits me now…" she gasped, staring at the glass vial, nearly half full of poison from one asp.

"It tastes horrid at first, but I grew used to it. I had to."

She lowered her hand and took a step towards Aoh.

"Care for a drink?"

Aoh shook her head violently in protest, furrowing her eyebrows and feeling her chest pounding against her frightened heart.

"You're too young, I'm afraid... Perhaps when you're older you can start building your immunity. It was the smartest thing I could do. I cannot allow the end of my life to be forgettable."

She paused, noticing the terror in Aoh's eyes as her body remained half in the shadow of the hidden room.

"This must all seem so terrifying for you, but this is something I grew to love. If I want to protect my kingdom, I must stay alive for as long as I am permitted. I cannot cheat death... however, I can delay it. It's my duty as queen."

She rotated the glass vial, watching the liquid twirl all the way to the bottom.

"They spared my life. I will not make the same mistake."

I couldn't imagine drinking poison. Not even with the chance of it saving my life one day. I guess I felt immortal myself. Untouchable. I was only a child. No royal blood flowed through my veins, so in my mind I couldn't image whom would want to kill me. Whom was I a threat to? It seemed that there were many things the queen did that I believed I would never understand. I was not born in Babylon. I did not desire a throne.

"Wait, wait...release!" Zurvan ordered.

Upon his order, Mylittia released the small arrow from the bow only to watch it fly barely a foot, dropping onto the ground. She sighed with disappointment, lowering her bow with a solid thud.

"Stop," Zurvan ordered harshly.

The princess looked at him, alarmed.

"Do not weep. You only fail when you stop," he explained firmly.

He picked up the arrow and placed it back onto the bow as Mylittia repositioned herself. Zurvan tugged her shoulders back slightly and pushed her forward. Her kicked her left foot back.

"Posture, concentration, and strength are not enough," he lectured. "You need to feel confident. You need to be confident. You are the princess to this kingdom, and one day it will be yours. You will need to stay on a straight path, like the arrow. Stay focused, concentrate, be confident, and then all enemies you face will fall."

Mylittia nodded innocently, letting out a slow breath in between the small part in her painted lips. She closed one eye, staring at her target of hay shaped into a figure several feet away. The arrow, rested perfectly, steady and prepared to be released, awaiting her command.

"You must look at this like everything else you come up against," he instructed. "Now pull back, tightly but gently. Take a breath, and release it when you're ready."

Following his instructions, the princess released, feeling the harsh pluck of the string against the skin of her fingers. The arrow moved slightly forward, not quite reaching the target but had gained more momentum than the previous one. She smiled slightly at her small achievement as Zurvan nodded, noticing the improvement.

"Zurvan," a servant said gently.

He turned and found the servant, approaching with Aoh at her side.

If there was one who preferred not to have me in their company, it was Zurvan. The queen's shadow…as I came to know him.

His frown deepened as he walked to get the arrow that didn't reach the target.

"The queen has asked for Aoh to learn archery along with the princess," the servant instructed.

"She did, did she?" he asked without a hint of surprise in his voice, touching the dull end of the arrow.

Rubbing his thumb across it several times, he looked down at Aoh who remained silently staring at him. Removing the arrow roughly, he glanced at the target clean of all puncture wounds.

"Aoh will learn with the princess under my close instruction as the queen commands," he stated, walking back towards Mylittia.

"Come."

Aoh followed Zurvan, standing next to Mylittia looking at the bow and arrow in her small hands. Stepping in front of her, nearly blocking the sun, he cleared his throat, folding his broad arms over his chest.

"Do you know what this is?" he asked coldly with a light scowl.

The moment my eyes caught sight of the bow and arrow, horrid memories of the slaughter of the people I once knew flooded my mind. I remembered how the dark sky became pitch black by the rain of endless arrows, striking and killing everything man and beast alike before they could flee. I remembered every scream and howl. My heart raced like a wild, untamed horse, hurting my lungs to the point I thought my ribcage was going to shatter.

Aoh blinked but once, and replied, "Yes."

"Tell me what this is."

Aoh inhaled deeply, trying to swallow the pain in her chest, responding, "It's a weapon used to kill."

"It is, also, a tool for discipline and concentration. We are given very few things to control. This is one of them. This arrow…is controlled by you."

Aoh listened as he waved over a servant whom was waiting in the shade with the basin of fresh water. Alongside the basin were several more bows and arrows, separated by size and strength. The servant rushed forward with a small bow and arrow, handing it to Zurvan as the princess watched silently.

"It is with discipline and concentration that decides whether the arrow kills or spares," the Queen's Shadow instructed. "Do you understand me?"

Aoh nodded, staring at the bow and arrow in his hands and feeling sick to her stomach.

"Then, I want you to do as the princess does."

Zurvan stepped aside, handing Mylittia another arrow.

"Princess," he said calmly, moving away.

She nodded, swallowing hard as her breathing hastened under her small chest. She positioned herself as Zurvan instructed, drawing the bow, looking down the arrow and at her target that she had yet to strike. Her small fingers gripped the string as her nervousness began to control her.

"Breathe, princess. Breathe in and out," Zurvan ordered firmly.

A peaceful breeze graced them as the princess patiently waited for the air to settle and released, only to have done so a moment too soon. The wind carried the arrow high, and just over the target. Missing, she sighed heavily, feeling guilt choke her. Her eyes glistened a wet dew that did not slip past her eyelids.

Placing a hand on her shoulder, Zurvan spoke, "You did much better that time, princess. Much better."

She nodded in disbelief, rubbing her fingers over her eyes as Aoh watched her walk towards the water basin, disappointed. Zurvan turned his attention to Aoh, who looked up at him in response.

"Repeat," he ordered.

He handed Aoh the bow and another arrow. As he watched, Aoh followed the same steps as princess, pressing her head to her shoulder with her arm drawn to her chest.

My feet remained planted onto the firm ground, as the breeze gently rolled across the bottom of my dress and through my hair. I gripped the bow made of strong wood and looked at the arrow with a blunt tip. Drawing the arrow back, I could feel my back straighten and my chest strengthen. The tight string stung my small fingers as I winced, trying to look down the arrow and at the target several feet away. As another breeze swept through, I ignored its smooth touch, staring at the steady target.

Lowering my face, I could feel my body tighten unintentionally; however, I was not tense. I was focused, able to dissolve the sickness in my stomach. When I released that arrow without thinking, it soared through the air and struck the target in the lower torso perfectly.

The solid sound of the arrow piercing through the hay figure alarmed Mylittia, as she looked and saw the arrow in the target. Zurvan's eyes hardly shifted as he immediately stormed his way to the target to see for himself. Upon studying the target, Aoh's arrow was there. The entire metal tip was inside the hay as the rest remained visible without bending nor cracking. Mylittia watched with the servant as Zurvan ripped the arrow from the target roughly. He held it in his tight grip, coming back to Aoh, blocking the sun once more.

I don't think Zurvan liked me, simply for the fact that I was not one of them.

"You struck the target on your first attempt. It happens to even the most novice of archers. Princess Mylittia!"

The princess quickly rushed to follow him upon hearing him call her.

"That is enough archery for today," he ordered. "Hurry along to the stables. You'll spend the rest of your afternoon there."

"May I bring Aoh with me?" she asked.

"Aoh?" he asked in response. He looked at her still standing with the bow and arrows in the sunlight as though she were waiting for further instruction.

"Yes. May she come with me?" Mylittia repeated.

Zurvan hesitated from answering at first, the replied, "I'm sure it is what the queen would want. Bring her."

"Aoh! Aoh! Come! Come with me!" she called loudly with excitement.

Princess Mylittia sat on her horse as her instructor stood next to her, with Aoh next to him. He explained thoroughly to both how to stay steady on the saddle and how to grip the reigns. He was an older, shorter man who had been teaching those of the palace of Babylon for years. He was patient and wise, explaining to both the mannerisms of horses, rubbing the face, ears and neck. High in the balcony, under canopies of blue hues, Queen Huriye watched, sitting in her seat draped with cushions as both of her hands were gently massaged by devoted servants.

She smiled contently, soothed by the soft touch of the servant's hands rubbing lotions across her fingers, around her palms and wrists. She leaned back gently, intrigued by Aoh. Aoh was always quiet, as though baffled by nearly everything she saw at the palace. Zurvan's heavy steps stretched the length of the hallway as he approached, holding a scroll under his arm with a troubled face.

Keeping her eyes on Aoh, the queen asked, "Zurvan, to what do I owe the pleasure of speaking with you about today?"

She turned around gently just as he reached the balcony, bowing immediately. Upon seeing him present, the servants stopped massaging her hands. They rubbed a clean cloth over both hands, folded the cloth, bowed in unison, and left silently. Zurvan stepped underneath the blue hues, as his long, black hair gently dancing about over his left shoulder in the breeze. The cool air did not soothe his grimace; however, it did bring him a sense of sincerity.

Taking a deep breath, he handed her the scroll firmly.

"Ah, Zurvan, what is this?" she smiled, until noticing the seal on the scroll was opened.

"You opened this?" she questioned with surprise.

"For your sake," he replied.

Able to read his expression, the letter was anything but good news. She ripped it into several pieces.

"You will not read it?" he asked.

"Your face tells me all I need to know about the letter. What was their reason?" she asked bitterly, clenching her teeth.

"Fear of Assyrian re-"

"Curse the gods…I wish Marduk would return, we need him. I wish I was…carrying a son," she spat, desperately moving her hands to her flat stomach.

"Will everyone fear them?" she mused, angry. "Will no one stand against them? What am I to do? Am I to fight them on my own forever? Am I to carry the weight of Babylon on my shoulders forever?

She shifted her body towards him as he stood at attention, keeping both arms behind his back. Queen Huriye rose her index finger to her mouth, staring at the floor and feeling the weight begin to pile over her shoulders again as she shook her head.

"Queen Huriye, the Assyrians cannot stay in power forever. You have already seen the damage they took when we rose up. They are fading," he explained calmly.

"Yet, I can convince no one of this?"

Putting her hand to her mouth, she shook her head again in disbelief.

"Am I to have my daughter, my only daughter, marry one of them, Zurvan? Just so that this kingdom can survive a moment longer? I'd be free from the burden, but what of her happiness? If I do not solve this problem, they will gain momentum from another ravaged kingdom and put an end to Babylon," she asked, worried. "They'll ravage her…and then what? What then? We live in such a beautiful place, and yet everyone wants to destroy it."

"My queen, what if you sent another to marry one of their princes?" he asked.

She looked at him intensely as his eyes shifted to the right quickly. Queen Huriye rubbed her mouth, feeling the breeze tickle the tips of her ears. They were decorated in earrings which dropped beading down to her shoulders.

"Oh, goodness, no. No. I could never do that to her," she quickly objected. "You would gladly do that because you aren't fond of her. You didn't want her here."

"My personal affairs have nothing to do with my suggestion."

"Ah, but I can see they do. She's an orphaned child, left in the desert with no means to survive. What makes her so threatening to you? She's just a child. She's a good child. My daughter likes her-"

"That I have already seen."

"And she would make a most reliable protector one day. They act like sisters born to different families. Insurance, Zurvan, protecting my daughter. My only daughter who…acts so much like-"

She stopped speaking, afraid to spew the words to follow. Clearing her throat, she frowned at Zurvan deeply.

"You can trust my judgment. If she does anything disloyal or harmful, I'll be the first to send her away, back to the desert where she came."

He nodded, though inwardly disagreed with her reasoning.

"Admittedly, it's not a bad idea. But she's not my daughter."

Zurvan took a deep breath and explained, leaning forward intently, "They do not know that."

"For now, leave her be. I'll have to think of something else. Something will come into the light, the gods will not leave me in this darkness. They never have. For now, I need to control what I have. Let me at least have that, Zurvan."

"Very well. As you command, my queen," he responded with a sincere bow.

10

Aoh walked the long halls as the nighttime hours began to draw near. The flames flickered gently, burning powerfully against the wood. The crackling created a slight echo as each step Aoh took slapped against the floors. Her eyes wandered from the torches to the ceilings where, at the very top, she'd notice long wooden flags decorated with the same images of what looked to be Marduk. His upper body was in the form of a man with wings behind his back. The wings stretched the length of the flag, made of solid gold.

She had seen his face before on the gigantic stone monuments at the entrance of the palace. Only there, the man would have the body of some large animal and the wings would be tucked to his sides. The images were unlike the gods she had seen.

The gods of my home embodied the heads of animals with the bodies of man. Strong and wise gods, watching over us day and night.

The abrupt sound of a door opening, and then the sweet sound of a woman's giggle prompted Aoh to stop. Tilting her head, she listened. She could hear the woman, and then what sounded to be a man's voice nearby. Following the sounds, she walked over to the left side of the hall where the open spaces would continually breathe fresh air into the palace every day. The fresh scents of water and rain consumed the air.

Looking over the side of the opening, she could hear the woman's giggles change to slight moans. Aoh couldn't see who it was at first. Only that her long hair was unraveled, running down the length of her back. Her skinny arms covered in bangles and cuffs jingled as she continually kissed the man she was wrapped around. His face was constantly consuming hers as every so often he would wrap his arms tighter around her. When the couple turned around, using the back of a pillar to hold themselves up, Aoh saw whom the woman was.

"She does this once in a while," the princess said lowly, looking over slightly in the shadow of another pillar. She hid from the moonlight, her small hands grasped to the stone, fingers digging into the carved images. "It's always with the guards. I'll catch her tiptoeing away from her chambers just as the moon reaches my window."

Aoh glanced back down at the queen and the guard. The queen giggled and bit her lower lip as his eyes burned a fierce shade. His mouth would move from her lips to her cheeks and neck. She'd run her longer fingers through his curled, black hair, enjoying the sensation of the smoothness against her skin.

"One day I hope to be in love," Mylittia smiled with hope and desire.

"Does she love him?" Aoh asked, looking at the princess.

"She loves all the guards. I thought at first that it meant I was going to have a father again but she hasn't married them. Not one of them."

"What happened to your father?"

"Mother says he died when I was a baby. She won't tell me when it happened, but she was hoping to get out of Assyrian clutches by marrying an Egyptian prince. Egypt refused because they were afraid of them, too. I think everyone fears them. She blames Egypt for everything she was put through. She blames them for abandoning her."

Listening, Aoh looked back down, watching the queen and the

guard move between the moonlight and shadow.

I caught the queen fleeing her chambers as Princess Mylittia told me, to be with a guard. Love was an endless bottle of hunger she couldn't fill. No matter how many times she rushed for it.

As the days passed with each sunset, the more Queen Huriye grew attached to me. Any activity her daughter participated in, I followed upon her order. Without realizing it, I was becoming her very shadow, and the queen's. Much to Zurvan's displeasure. There came a point where any meeting of any matter was brought to my attention. Nights were silent, except on occasion when many awoke to wander the halls and rooms.

I received similar luxuries. Having servants to do as I bid. Surprisingly, I adjusted to their constant aid. And so, every day for the next six years I lived in the palace with Queen Huriye and those worthy of her favor. I wore the best clothing, ate the freshest foods, and lived in the most holy of places under the constant watch of the Babylonian gods. I had learned about the new world I was now a part of. I watched many climb the social ladder. I have seen many obtain slaves brought in from another land, bought to tend to gardens and prepare meals. I witnessed the priests and priestesses in their temples read omens from broken animal bones, breathing in smoke and healing the sick.

Most of this I had seen from the palace, watching as the city thrived through vigorous routines and patterns. I wore cotton for the first of many times, and slipped my feet into mosaic-walled baths. I buried my past like a secret I didn't want anyone to know until it seemed…I had nearly forgotten it entirely.

11

Aoh ran the dull blade up and down the wood carefully with each stroke, peeling away strips and pieces that fell around her smooth feet. Each time a breeze swept by her, she'd hear the gentle chimes dance as though the wind wanted to watch her work. After each stroke of the knife, her hands rubbed the wood, slowly feeling the prickled and cut ends flatten. The thick piece of wood slowly became thinner, as a curved shape began to take form.

"I can have a bow made for you. I really can. All you need to do is ask," Queen Huriye said coming into the room with her three servants following behind. The layers of her long dress slipped across the floor behind her with each step.

Aoh lifted her head, "Thank you, but-"

"You want to make your own. I know. I know. But why waste your time with it?" she asked, touching the healthy large leaves from the potted trees.

She made her way over to a chair where larger leaves laid. Two of the servants picked them up, and began to gently wave them up and down as the third servant waited to the side for further orders. Queen Huriye released a heavy sigh, sitting comfortably in her seat made from the most talented craftsman. She watched Aoh work endlessly on the bow, studying each detail, picking away at tiny stubs and constantly checking its durability.

"It looks beautiful," she commented.

"Thank you," Aoh acknowledged, pausing for a moment.

She swiped the ends of the wood away from her feet, and turned the bow gently to the side. Her dark eyes followed the length as she rubbed her thumbs at the top and bottom knots. Running her hand across the wood, she felt the smooth texture, seeing several hints of brown within the strong wood.

Aoh released the arrow, sending it straight into the air and striking the sackcloth full of sand, ripping it and spilling its contents. Zurvan watched, hardly changing his expression as he often wouldn't reveal his thoughts. Aoh knew him all too well by then. He was impressed with her. She did not need to be validated.

As Mylittia prepared her bow, a faint flutter of frustration made itself very present. Her hands grasped the arrow, forcing it against the bow, keeping it in place as she tried to position herself. She constantly shifted her feet, feeling the tips of the grass prick the skin on her heels.

She struggled to pull the bow all the way back against her constantly red fingers, attempting to keep her other hand sturdy on the bow. She could see her target and wanted to strike. Releasing the bow, it flew fast and hard; however, it just barely hit the target. Zurvan closed his eyes and rolled his lower lips under his upper lip, looking to the other men who noted that she still struggled.

Simultaneously, they wrote on parchment, dressed in the same long robes. Aoh lowered her head, clutching her bow tightly around both hands.

"Between Aoh and your daughter, Aoh is the better archer in every manner possible. I've been keeping record of her progress since she first picked up the bow. She's hit every target, every time. She's blessed with this talent for precision. Whereas, the princess manages to hit her target half of the time, and even then, it would not be an instant kill. It would wound the enemy, even his horse or chariot but by comparison, she could learn from Aoh."

Queen Huriye looked at the report and listened intently.

"Seems my daughter's talents lie with her dancing and beauty, then. Aoh's lies with archery. I can tell she is dedicated."

Taking both reports, she read through them, noticing how she never realized how impressive Aoh truly was. She knew that she grasped the bow quickly, but never to the extent of that of an archer in her army. She smiled, rubbing her fingers over her glossy lips as two servants continually massaged her feet and lower legs with oils and cloths.

"My daughter is of age and will be able to marry any man she chooses. Now it is certain. Aoh will be able to protect her. Aoh can be the very soldier I've been needing in my palace."

Zurvan nodded, taking the reports, rolling them back up delicately. Queen Huriye picked up another scroll from the table next to her, resting in between two heavy statues on a silver tray. Her flowing eyes were glued to the parchment as several others covered the small stone table next to the servants. One laid on the floor, just before Zurvan's feet, slightly torn and wrinkled.

Picking up the piece of parchment, he read it quickly with his cold eyes and asked, "Tell me, what is it Egypt wants?"

"Only history will tell us that," she replied, focused upon every piece of parchment her eyes could find.

"The pharaoh is dead, and it seems his eldest daughter has married. Egypt, once again, has a new king."

"He died from his wounds in battle. We will send our deepest regrets that we cannot attend his funeral."

"You never intended to attend his funeral."

"And if I don't?" she snapped, wickedly.

Zurvan didn't answer, rolling the scroll up and tucking it under his arm in one swoop. Like a hawk closing its wings against its body.

"Since Egypt will never be an ally, perhaps Aoh can provide another option. She-"

"My Queen, I'm so sorry to interrupt!"

She and Zurvan looked up and saw their political vizier rush into the room with an excited expression across his face. The servants immediately stopped massaging her feet and sat on their own. Their toes curled against the pressure of the floor as they watched.

"We have received a message from King Khi with orders that it is read as soon as it's received."

Queen Huriye snatched the scroll from his fragile hands and read every word quickly. Her expression changed as soon as she completed reading.

Leaning forward she exclaimed, "Wonderful news gentlemen. He will be arriving within the week for my celebration as planned!"

"I will begin the preparations for our royal guests," the vizier replied, with a bow.

"Make sure they are given the newest accommodations. I want their stay to be as pleasurable as possible. Make it so they don't want to leave."

"Yes, my queen."

"Zurvan, send my daughter and Aoh. They will be needing to do their parts as well. Years of preparation will be presented."

Ever since my skills in archery presented themselves, I've had an overwhelming amount of guilt. Princess Mylittia was not talented in anything but dancing. Even that was something she would hesitate from presenting. By all accounts, I should have been talentless. I was a peasant with nothing more than the talent of surviving with my family

in a town. Mylittia was from thousands of years of royal singers, archers, horseback riders, musicians, and speakers. It was no secret that she was withdrawing into her chambers to hide for several hours before feeling strong enough to present herself to the rest of the palace after another failure. She wanted to prove herself. To show that she was worthy.

Knocking on the heavy door, Aoh heard it open a crack. Pushing the door open, she found the princess pulling her long hair back and then attempting to wrap the woolen fabric over her head, gently, to hide her hair and the sides of her face. She was wearing her longest dress that nearly covered her feet. Aoh quickly looked behind herself. Not seeing anyone, she closed the door until she heard the solid wood shut.

Seeing a woven bag on the bed, Aoh asked, "What are you doing?"

Tying the sides around her face, the princess she replied, "I'm going into the city for a few hours."

"Why?"

"Because I want to, that's why. My mother has invited King Khi here and we both know he will accept. This means she's going to finally begin making preparations for me to marry one of his sons, if not all of them."

"All of them?"

"And once I'm married, I will be living in their palace and never see the outside world again. I can't let this opportunity pass me by. This may be my last chance to take in Babylon before beholding another city."

In all honesty, Mylittia wanted to leave to avoid the palace gossip about her most recent failure.

Aoh watched Mylittia pull the bag over her head and onto her shoulder.

"I have some time in between my mother's preparations and another guard to feed her desires. Would you like to come with me?" she asked.

"I don't have a choice. I can't let you go alone," Aoh replied.

"It's not like I can defend myself. That much shows, no matter how hard I've tried. But that's why I'm fortunate to have you. You will always protect me, right?"

Aoh lowered her eyes.

"You will, won't you? Right, Aoh?"

I wanted to tell her no. But...

"I will."

I didn't have the heart to. I didn't want to leave her alone. However, I didn't want her to feel as though she needed someone in order to feel safe. But I didn't want her to be in the city alone. For the past year or so, the Assyrian occupants had been a little bolder than usual and because of this, tensions were high. There were countless riots and the hold the Assyrians had kept getting tighter.

Aoh wrapped fabrics around her head and led the way out of the palace and down the steps towards the lively and loud city. They avoided the guards by remaining behind the large statues and trees, peering through the overgrown vines and hanging flowers constantly dropping petals with each swift movement. Escaping the sun, both watched the movements of the guards and listened to the conversations before moving on and entering the city.

I felt scared and worried at the same time. I was so worried that I couldn't stop turning around, expecting to see someone behind me following us.

"What are you looking at?" Mylittia asked, noticing Aoh's quick movements.

"I'm making sure no one is following us," Aoh answered.

"What are you so terrified of?"

"You! I'm terrified of you getting hurt! If you're hurt, or taken, or killed I will never forgive myself for it."

"Not one person has looked at us since we left. Not one, Aoh," the princess reassured, calmly.

"That's because no one knows who we are," Aoh sighed heavily, unable to keep her fears at bay.

Side by side, they walked in between larger groups of people bargaining for items outside of shops and food in the carts pulled by large oxen and horses. Dancers and street performers presented themselves, collecting gold from onlookers. Children splashed each other at the fountains, following each other to their classes taught by the strictest of teachers.

Slaves were gathered again to be sold and the sharp, enjoyable sound of beads being exchanged ran rampantly. In an hour or so, the temples were going to be open for people seeking treatment and guidance in their lives. Aoh noticed how the windows to the temples were always open when no one was inside, only closed when the priests and priestesses called to the gods for aid in their works.

Several conversations overlapped each other as they continued deeper into the city, towards the quieter parts where many provided water for their animals and themselves. The water flowed through troughs and walls, clear and fresh over mosaic slates. The mosaic images sparkled in between shadows of onlookers waiting to play a game of dice before working again. Children rushed to splash each other before they were pulled away by their mothers, scolding them and carrying clean clothing. Aoh's eyes remained alert, noticing a few men watching nearby. She saw them once before and was worried they may have been following them.

"Wow…can you believe this city thrives on such large watering holes?" Princess Mylittia asked, smiling widely. She stopped at the next water basin, lowering herself to touch the water and noticing it was almost as clear as her baths. She looked at her reflection, curling her lips and touching her ears.

"Do you think they live in a palace like ours?"

Aoh sat down on the edge of the water basin and replied, "Probably."

"I wonder if they have fountains? Fountains of gold?"

Aoh looked up at Mylittia in disbelief at her question.

"Just a question," Mylittia replied.

"No. I don't think they will have fountains of gold. I doubt any kingdom does."

Aoh's fingers tugged at the pleats of her dress, keeping focus on the men in the corner of her eyes. They conversed with others with similar features, carrying dice and a rounded bowl under their arms.

"Have you been to other kingdoms?" Mylittia asked.

"No," Aoh responded.

Mylittia nodded and whispered, "I've heard Egypt drowns in gold. They use it for everything."

Aoh's anxiety reached its peak as her heart began to race.

"I wonder if that's true," the princess pondered aloud.

"I'd be more worried about whether or not you'll be one, or one of many wives," Aoh stated with a hint of frustration, trying to contain her nervousness.

Mylittia took a drink of the water, surprised by how cool it was. She rolled her lips together, enjoying the taste, and went for another as a small herd of sheep passed them with the shepherd behind them. Aoh watched him pass, while he whistled and called out to them with a heavy accent.

"I shouldn't get myself excited..."

Aoh glanced at her and asked, "Why?"

"I don't want to be let down again. That's all."

"Mylittia what-what are you talking about?"

"This would be the third time-"

"Third time?" Aoh questioned.

Mylittia fell silent, immediately regretting the words that so loosely slipped from her mouth. She twirled the ring on her index finger, given to her by her mother as a gift. Not hearing a response from her, Aoh turned to her friend.

"Mylittia what are you-"

From the corner of her eyes, Aoh saw a man run at them with a roar and wild eyes. Panicked, Aoh threw the princess to the ground and tripped him forward and into the water. He rose, swinging the blade from under his arm when Aoh ducked and, picking up a ceramic jug from on the ground, struck him in the face with it. The pieces scattered and red blood profusely spouted. He dropped the blade; Aoh lunged for it and swung, slashing his throat as two more men came rushing towards her like wild animals.

Mylittia ran to hide behind a pillar with the rest of the citizens screaming at the top of their lungs. Without thinking, Aoh grunted, killing the first man to her right and then the second by stabbing backwards as he lunged forward, grabbing the back of her head. Wrenching herself free, Aoh fell over, nearly hitting her head against the water basin. In a frenzy and ignoring his mortal wound, he grabbed her by the throat. Aoh struggled to scream, trying to release the blade still attached to his midsection. She strained her lungs, feeling the pressure against her throat intensify, suffocating.

Almost grasping the handle, she was slammed into the side of the watering hole, choking loudly, barely able to keep her eyes open. Ripping the blade free, she stabbed his chest repeatedly, until he finally let go and collapsed onto the ground. Aoh's coughing turned violent, her face beat red, and, upon each inhale, her lungs burned wildly.

She spat onto the sand, trying to focus her attention on her breathing, hunched over the ground, noticing the trails of blood forming into tiny pools. Rising to her feet she saw the dead man in the watering hole, face down.

Coughing loudly, she grabbed him, pulling him out of it with an angered and frustrated grunt. His blood tainted the fresh water like dye in a goblet. She swiped her hands into the water untouched by the blood, splashing it onto her face, unable to stop coughing. Aoh bent downward, trying to inhale without feeling the pain attack her to no avail. Spitting several more times she felt the pain beginning to cease and violent strains on her neck fade. She rubbed her neck gently, feeling the ends of her hair cling to her forehead.

That was when I realized I couldn't hear a sound. There was silence... Deep, silence. Unlike any silence I thought was possible to exist.

Forcing her legs to stand up, Aoh found herself surrounded by men, women, and children, looking at her silently with concentrated eyes and solemn expressions. She rubbed her eyes with her arm, momentarily seeing everyone looking at her quietly. Their gazes frozen like that of tombs. Permanently driven to Aoh's presence. Mylittia stumbled from her knees forward from behind the wall, barely able to walk noticing everyone looking up at Aoh.

Everywhere she turned, she found more eyes. Looking down at the blade in her hand, Aoh felt the dripping wet sensation from the blood and noticed the bodies of the three men lying dead before her, unable to comprehend what just transpired.

12

Aoh walked down the hallway, followed by Zurvan and several guards heading towards the throne room.

Every step was a struggle. I could barely stop my hands from shaking, trembling as my dry throat kept catching the back of my tongue. I've walked those halls countless times before, but today my steps sounded as loud as thunder.

The doors were pushed open for Aoh as she approached, taking the first steps inside as the rest of the company followed behind her. She stopped several feet away from Queen Huriye sitting on her throne, waiting for Aoh to arrive. She was dressed in her best gowns, as though she were anticipating the arrival of Marduk himself.

The moment we made eye contact, I closed my mouth tightly, feeling my lips burn intensely. I hid any trace of fear, forcing my arms to rest against the sides of my body. My feet continually fluxed in and out of numbness as my fingers continued to shake uncontrollably.

Queen Huriye remained silent, rolling her fingers to and fro against the arm rests. The burning incense crackled gently sounding like insects in the night.

After what felt like several minutes, she finally spoke.

"Everyone, leave us."

Without question, the room emptied, closing the doors behind them.

I'll never forget the expression on Zurvan's face as it disappeared behind the doors. My heart was in my throat. I couldn't bear myself to even look at Queen Huriye, and yet I could not look away from her. I felt ensnared in her beautiful eyes while she hesitated from speaking again until she wanted to. She was so patient and calculated. I believed she always was.

"I was told by several what they saw today in the city. Is all of this true? Did you save my daughter?" she finally asked, firmly.

"Yes," Aoh replied, lowering her gaze.

"Look at me."

"I…can't."

"Why?"

I lowered my head further, and bit into my lips tightly. I forced myself to remain silent, trying to keep any lingering thoughts of my mother away like I had been doing ever since I arrived. My mother's love would not leave me, not even in this state.

"Look at me," Queen Huriye repeated, boldly.

"I…can't," Aoh answered, desperately.

"Tell me why? Why will you not look at me?"

Aoh's mouth slipped open and replied, "Because I am terrified."

Queen Huriye's eyes softened, "Terrified?"

"Yes."

"Aoh, look at me. Look at me right now," she ordered with impatience, and sudden worry.

When I did, I didn't see anger nor rage. I saw gratitude and respect.

"It was Assyrians, wasn't it?" she asked with woeful eyes, afraid to hear the answer she already knew.

Aoh barely nodded.

Smacking her left hand on the armrest, she snapped, "They won't stop, will they? You saved my daughter…I could never…never thank you enough for what you did. You know what would have happened if they killed her, don't you?"

Aoh nodded again, trying to hide her face with the longer lengths of her hair not tied back with beads and fabric.

Queen Huriye trembled, gasping aloud as though her heart suddenly wept. Rising from her throne, she wrapped her arms around Aoh, embracing her in the warmth of her robes.

"Thank you, Aoh. Thank you for saving her! Thank you for protecting her! May the gods bless you for all eternity!"

Aoh nodded, feeling the numbness returning to her feet, causing her nervousness to grow. Queen Huriye gently pushed Aoh's hair away from her face with the palms of her hands.

"Are you alright?"

"The physicans tell me so," Aoh replied lowly. "The instructed me not to...purposely get in harms way again. And I...won't unless it's protecting you."

Moving strands of hair between her fingers, Queen Huriye voiced, "Your hair, on the other hand, is quite disobedient. What am I going to do with it?"

Aoh released a genuine chuckle. Turning her face gently, the queen studied her features.

"Yes, if we pull this back and then apply some makeup over the corner of your eyes and on the tips of your lips. Every man who arrives will be looking at you. Pining for you."

"Pining?" Aoh asked, confused.

"King Khi has accepted my invitation, and he will be arriving to celebrate with us."

Queen Huriye's smile widened, stretching from ear to ear as she stepped over to the several bowls of fruit displayed near the throne. She plucked grapes carefully from the stem, placing them in the palm of her other hand.

"He's bringing his sons," she commented, biting into the first grape slowly.

The sweet nectar inside flooded her mouth before she started chewing the remnants.

"Mylittia will be ecstatic to hear that," Aoh replied.

"Which is why I want you to help prepare her for their arrival.

Help her pick the best clothes, make sure she wears the more alluring perfume. Teach her their ways."

"I know-"

"You know. I've seen you spend days in my library, reading."

Aoh sighed heavily in response and continued, "But I'm not a teacher, I-"

"Will begin immediately. Yes? Take as many books as you see fit, and make sure she pays attention. The survival of Babylon will be on her shoulders. Those Assyrians need to be stopped and I cannot achieve that on my own. Our family needs to expand and quickly. Time is not our ally, Aoh. It never is."

13

For weeks, I had been studying with Mylittia everything I could find about our arriving visitors. I had frequented the library ever since I grasped reading. Reading was a privilege I wanted to surround myself with as many written texts as I could.

I wanted to spend time away to feel secluded in my own sanctuary of knowledge where I felt I could be myself without silent eyes watching me and the devoted servants. They were a kingdom I was unfamiliar with, but seemed to have had a vast history. I wondered if they would look as depicted. I lost count how many robes and dresses princess Mylittia looked at, how many pieces of jewelry she requested, and how many scents of perfume she wanted. She struggled remembering key information, was indecisive with the clothing and, at times, wore two perfumes at once hoping for a greater outcome. In all honesty, the perfume did grab the attention of more guards.

Being able to focus all of my thoughts and time with the princess helped me forget the events in the city. However, I noticed since then that she was holding back from speaking freely like she used to. Admittedly, there were days I was so occupied with Mylittia that I hardly ate the food on my plate nor slept a full night.

"The King Khi, who sits on the throne presently, has ruled his kingdom for how many years?" Aoh asked the princess, sitting on a chair with the open air behind her.

Across from her, three thin, large dogs laid on cushions watching. Near the far back corner, two women played harps, attentively stroking the strings with their nimble fingers.

Mylittia paced, constantly folding her hands, wrapping her fingers around each other.

"Twenty?" she replied with a hint of doubt.

"Of his sons which is married?" Aoh quizzed.

The princess shook her head in response.

"Their kingdom stretches as far as the water?"

"Yes."

"To which waters?"

"The Red Sea?" she guessed with complete insecurity.

"No," Aoh replied.

"Ask me something else."

"Whom are their enemies?"

The princess shook her head, unsure. Aoh nodded, looking at the other questions she had written down but didn't want to ask as the dogs looked to her.

"I think we-"

"No! We didn't do enough, ask me another question," Mylittia objected loudly.

"King Khi will not determine if he wants you to marry one of his sons by how much you know of him and his kingdom, regardless of what your mother says."

Two of the dogs whined in response.

"But I need to know these things! I can't just stand there and look like some pathetic..."

"You're being silly. You just have to-"

"Aoh, I have to do this!"

"If you-"

"I'm sorry!" the princess cried.

Aoh's eyes rose to her forehead.

"I should have told you about the failed marriage arrangements. I just felt embarrassed telling you. I didn't want you to think less of me, the way everyone here seems to do," Mylittia admitted.

"Mylittia, I would never-"

"I'm sorry. I hope this time..., this time I finally have my prince."

The loud sounds of horns from outside turned their attention to the windows where, down below, they could see cause of the noise.

"They're here. That's them, Aoh! They're here!" the princess exclaimed loudly, rushing to the window.

Aoh took the questions and placed them on the seat as she followed, hearing the same horns being blown repeatedly and growing louder.

The princess pointed in the direction of the entrance to the city.

"Look! Look, Aoh! Look!"

We could see them arriving, coming on their horses, one after another, proudly entering the city and receiving many applauses from the citizens. Many bowed at their presence, others tossed reeds into the street for their horses to walk over. They came carrying flags and pulling carts of gifts covered in a variety of fabrics. The gleam of the gifts reflected the sunlight, glowing like stars in a night sky. They marched all together like a concise army, cheering loudly with flags in excitement of their arrival.

"Princess Mylittia, Aoh!" Zurvan said boldly from the doorway, startling the dogs.

The two turned around, seeing him approach, dressed in dark but attractive sleeveless robes revealing his small muscular arms and traces of his chest.

"The queen has requested your presence in the throne room to greet our visitors."

Mylittia, grinning from ear to ear, pulled on Aoh's arm so rapidly her shoulder cracked slightly. Their embellished feet slid across the smooth floors as they quickly ran out of the room and down the hall to the nearest stairs. Mylittia's grip around Aoh's wrist remained tight as her smile highlighted her face. She brushed her hands over the long drapes and flags carried by servants rushing into place, as the breeze swung the hanging Marduk banners from the ceiling in the direction of the throne room. The clamoring of both bare and sandal-covered feet vibrated off the stone mosaic walls, as the shadows raced across the images.

Reaching the throne room, all the servants were standing in their place as the priests gathered around each other, burning heavily scented incense and praying aloud in half whispers. Queen Huriye came to her throne, picking up both sides of her gown, dressed with almost every piece of jewelry she owned. Seeing the two emerge from one of the side doors, she smiled and immediately patted the empty seat next to her.

"Come, my daughter, you will sit next to me. And Aoh, I want you standing to the left of me. Zurvan you will be to the left of Aoh."

I had never seen Queen Huriye dress to impress anyone before. She always dressed for herself. And never before had she ordered me to stand by her side. Obeying her, I stood straight, fixing the bangles on my arms while feeling Zurvan's eyes on my back, bothered by the fact he was moved.

Taking her seat, Mylittia's smile only grew. Servants rushed to apply finishing touches of makeup to both of them with fine brushes and thin sticks, patiently moving their hands as though they were writing a poem. Queen Huriye turned gently and looked upon her daughter, noticing her straight posture and glowing eyes of confidence. She turned to Aoh whom remained calm, keeping her hands at her sides, looking in the direction of the doors with anticipation, curious as to whether they looked as depicted. The record keepers readied their writing utensils and parchment. Everyone held their breath…

The loud sounds of the horns and cheering grew louder as the first doors were opened. The servants finished the last strokes of makeup, hurrying away as a few others gently fixed the fabrics over Zurvan's shoulder and pulled the sides slightly back with a sash. The loud sounds of another set of doors opened as the loud music lowered slightly. Each second that passed dragged, until finally the doors were opened and a parade of men, dressed in uniform, marched forward with their king and his sons following behind them. The instrument players continued to blow the horns, spreading to both sides of the room as the uniformed men separated, parting the path for their king.

The king needed no introduction, as a heavy foreign scent descended upon the entire room the moment he entered. His dark eyes so intense, like the thick clouds of a storm.

With one gesture of his hand, the room fell silent. His company, both on their feet and knees, faced him and all together they bowed to Queen Huriye. In response, Queen Huriye and her room lowered their heads and bowed in respect.

"Welcome to my Kingdom, my honored guests," Queen Huriye greeted with open arms.

"Thank you for inviting us into your realm," King Khi replied with a deepened voice.

Gesturing his hands to the sides, his sons emerged, all equally as handsome as the next, muscular, fair skinned with deep eyes like their father. Their black hair falling just behind their shoulders slick with gentle waves.

"My sons."

Queen Huriye gestured to Mylittia and said, "My only daughter and-"

Smoothly moving her hand like a snake, "Her protector, and mine."

The king and princes acknowledged Aoh as the heat from Zurvan's eyes intensified.

"We've traveled through the desert into this oasis and await Babylon's gifts."

"Then, may I proudly present my daughter and protector, for they have proven themselves to be great gifts of Babylon."

Mylittia's smile grew as she nodded, admiring the king's eldest son whom looked onto her with a slight expression of curiosity, like a child trapped within his older age. She couldn't look onto him for long, as her cheeks flushed red and her stomach flipped each second he stood before her. She rolled her lips, lowering her eyes. Her long lashes fluttering like wings.

Wrapping the leather straps around her arm carefully, Aoh muted the sounds of the audience just outside the doors, concentrating on her preparation in the dim light.

Zurvan handed her bow from the side and said, "Think you can perform in front of a large crowd?"

"I will not miss, not even if I was blind and deaf," Aoh replied, facing him confidently.

"Then prove it."

Taking her bow, Aoh tucked the quiver over her left shoulder, strapping it tightly so that the leather rubbed against the smooth dress. As the doors opened, Aoh's throat fell into her stomach, feeling the heat of the sun burning the air. Determined, she stepped into the sunlight with Zurvan following her, coming to the center of everyone's attention.

The targets were lined up in the distance, marked, positioned across the ground with thick sashes. The arrows gently rocked inside the quiver with each firm step she took as the audience cheered for her loudly from underneath the layers of shade. All of Queen Huriye's palace sat and watched with the king's company to their left, enjoying the cool air.

Coming to the first position, Aoh stopped, staring at the targets watching her in different body positions. Zurvan stepped to her side, blocking part of the sun from her eyes. His defined face was within breathing room of her skin.

"Draw," Zurvan instructed.

Aoh drew her bow swiftly, like a cheetah's leap, keeping it close to her face while staring at her target several yards away down the length of the arrow. Squinting slightly, she waited, keeping her breaths through her nostrils still.

"Fire."

Upon the release of the arrow, Aoh released a slight breath, watching it soar across the air and striking the target with a solid thud.

"Again," Zurvan ordered, keeping both arms behind his thick back.

Aoh drew her bow again, keeping her eyes focused, ignoring all the eyes watching from their seats. Hands buried into the mouths and covering the sides of waiting faces frozen like statues. Upon the release, she struck her target again, this time several more yards further than the first one. Large amounts of sand exuded from the hole, piling onto the ground.

Zurvan glanced to Queen Huriye, unsure if she wanted Aoh to continue. She gave him a reassuring nod and smile. Her face was barely visible underneath the array of jewels and gems in her hair, and around the fabrics on the sides of her face. He stepped closer to Aoh, observing her silence and unreadable expression.

"I want you to shoot three arrows at once."

Aoh glanced at him, as a slight flutter of puzzlement was cast across her eyes.

"You heard me."

Taking three arrows, Aoh positioned them onto her lowered bow, struggling slightly to keep them in place. As she positioned them, her ears heard the slight mumbles of the audience, watching her as Mylittia slowly craned her neck forward, nervously.

Drawing the three arrows, Aoh's fingers cautiously wrapped the ends of each of them. The feathered tips tickled her skin as a slight breeze swept over her. Lowering the bow slightly, she aimed at three targets that appeared to have been placed the closest together.

Watching her stand, Zurvan glanced at the targets and quickly spat, "Fire."

Without hesitation, the arrows were flown from the bow, slightly parting ways and connecting to three different targets. The audience erupted loudly at the sight before quickly calming down again. The guests nodded to each other, impressed. Mylittia's hands, tightly folded and unfolded themselves as she sat two seats away from her mother, covered in a light gown. She surreptitiously watched King Khi lean to his side, whispering to one of his sons as their eyes remained on Aoh, watching her.

Rolling his tongue to and fro, Zurvan glanced at the arrows she had left and then the targets.

"Shoot all your arrows as fast as you can," Zurvan instructed firmly.

Nodding, Aoh prepared the first arrow, glancing at the crowd to her left and seeing the princess watching with heavy anticipation before following two servants away from her seat. Taking deep breaths, Aoh positioned herself, tugging at the quiver slightly and leaned. She waited patiently for another breeze to pass, concentrating on the targets and her hands. Without releasing her breath, Aoh fired one arrow after another. Swiftly, accurately.

As she fired her arrows, everyone watched in silence. She moved fluidly, perfectly, as though she were in a dream. Suddenly, the image of the princess invaded her concentration, distracting her thoughts. She continued to fire her arrows, until coming to the last few. Aoh purposely aimed too high, missing the target. Upon finishing, she received calm, yet astounding applause.

A large weight of guilt covered my body as I released my breath. I could feel it in my hair, sewn over my arms and wrapped around my legs. It wasn't fair.

"Aoh will be a most loyal protector of my daughter when she receives the crown," Queen Huriye said to the king seated next to her. She leaned over slightly, enough to allow the golden accompaniments across her dress to gently chime when rubbed into each other.

He nodded in agreement as they watched Aoh walking away from the archery station and towards the princess. Mylittia glared at her coldly from the doors Aoh departed from, dressed in performing clothing, with bangles across her arms and legs. Aoh looked away from her, handing her quiver and bow to the servant waiting to take them, bowing in respect.

"You're not going to admit it, are you?" Mylittia asked lowly.

Aoh didn't respond, taking the goblet of water from the side, rubbing the faint drops of sweat from her forehead.

"Are you?"

"Admit what?" Aoh replied, softly.

"That you purposely missed at the end to make me look a little less pathetic than I am already."

"She's strong," King Khi commented, placing his fingers to his chin.

"Yes, she is."

"You mentioned…she is not your daughter?"

"Correct, even though she has every bit of my strength within her. Her skills will one day be used against such fierce enemies. That is, if they dare enter my threshold again."

"What of acquaintances?" he asked, placing his large hand over hers, stroking her skin gently with his index finger.

She grinned, "Depends whom the acquaintance is that wants to cross my threshold."

Hearing the crowd cheer loudly, she looked downward seeing her daughter walking out into the sunlight slowly as the stringed instruments were gently plucked and tuned.

"Ah, see, there is my beautiful daughter. All of her grace and beauty. She's like the colors of a sunset after long days of peace. Vibrant."

"Her face does embody innocence, but does her experience as well?" he asked, raising one eyebrow.

Queen Huriye frowned slightly and turned her attention towards him as Mylittia began to dance before the audience, keeping her sights on the king's eldest son.

"My kingdom has had experience in dealing with several situations for the past hundreds of years, and though we want to thrive, we want to be sustainable. With leaders of experience on our thrones. Leaders who have seen their fair share, and know how to handle any situation if the need for it should arrive once more."

"Babylon has seen its fair share," she informed him, "as I'm sure you have seen upon your arrival. We are no stranger to suffering."

He nodded slightly, however, unconvinced.

"We…will…never…allow such things to happen again," the Queen continued. "I swear it on my life."

"I only speak out of concern, Queen Huriye. I believe your daughter, in time, will become a quite powerful and just queen. She will become a most loyal wife, and conquer many. However, her time is not now."

Queen Huriye looked at Mylittia as her performance enthralled the audience watching, silently, with wide eyes and curious flames burning in their chests.

"Please understand," King Khi explained. "Your daughter is young to the world of palaces. I want my eldest son, my heir to my throne, to marry someone with experience," he continued smoothly, stroking her skin as she listened and then leaned over to view the row of seats occupied by the king's sons.

The eldest sat at the very end with the youngest sitting directly next to King Khi. They watched the princess dance silently, captivated by the performance. Queen Huriye stared at the eldest son, who was the tallest of all the sons, and appeared the most handsome even though he was not the strongest. She grinned and then leaned back to watch her daughter dance with a slight redness on her cheeks.

"I understand your honesty, King Khi. It makes me all the more pleased that you came into my realm. I do believe we can come to some sort of agreement. After all, the day is still young, and so am I," she said sweetly between her glossed lips.

14

Since arriving to Queen Huriye's palace as a child, I've seen my fair share of royal parties. In the beginning, I was too young and too timid to go, so I often watched where I knew no one could see me. When I decided to attend as Queen Huriye's confidant of sorts, I'd still watch as drinks overflowed from goblets and open mouths, exchanging juices from one another wildly, as though they were feasts of love. I wasn't one to partake. This time I wanted to watch where everyone could see me.

The princess would socialize almost as much as her mother. She knew everyone, even the lowest of servants too timid to approach and even the most handsome soldier no matter how desperately her eyes wanted them. This time not even prayers to gods would help her tame the nerves inside of her. Once she saw the eldest prince, there was no turning back. Her heart claimed him.

Aoh lifted the cup of wine to her lips as she looked at the large crowds of people across the room, drinking and conversing amongst each other civilly by one of several columns. There had yet to be a drunken performance, and the love between several was rather subdued. Some ate, attempting to sneak some of the luscious fruits by hiding them underneath their cuffs and between their robes.

Several men gambled together, surrounded by statues, tumbling dice in a mosaic jar against the floor. Pieces of jewelry, beading, and cotton were placed as bets as inner secrets of their lives were shared. Others watching placed bets against those gambling. Aoh watched as exotic birds, perched on shoulders of guests or columns, gained a lot of attention by the visitors pointing at them with intrigued eyes. They gently rubbed the feathers, studying them like subjects from books, unfazed by the outburst of squawks. They screeched, spreading their large wings, revealing an array of colors.

Aoh slowly walked behind rows of potted trees, glancing at the visitors remaining in their groups, observing every detail of the palace while others remained tight-lipped, and muttering between the goblet and the wine that filled it. Taking another small sip of the wine, Aoh glanced behind her as two young women were playfully being chased by one man. He wasn't quite drunk, however, just enough that he fell over once or twice before getting back up and continuing the chase.

Aoh remained behind the potted plants, hearing the sound of a platter collapsing onto the floor, followed by the sound of shattering. Aoh looked and found Princess Mylittia stunned, as the red wine covered her beloved dress dripping down her arms.

She frowned and sighed, swiping the dark red liquor off of her arms, seeping into her dress, desperately trying hard to keep the tears within her eyes. She gasped, feeling Aoh's arm around her.

"Come, come on," Aoh said, trying to gently grab her arm.

"Look at this. What am I-"

"Come, let's clean you up."

The princess and I were in the same realm in the sense we respected and loved each other. Our bond wasn't quite as sisters, but stronger than friends. We were different in many ways, like the wind and the current of the river. The smallest things seemed to have frustrated her as though she had this intense war within her she was constantly trying to control, but every now and again one side would have the upper hand and presented itself loudly.

Mylittia sighed, frustrated and angered, rubbing her hands up and down both arms as Aoh brushed the ends of her long hair, twisting the ends with her fingers to create longer curls. She glanced from the hair to look into the mirror, hearing the princess's bitter weeps.

"You look beautiful," Aoh reassured.

"But, do I truly?" Mylittia asked, looking at her in the mirror with cold eyes of doubt. "Am I truly beautiful when all eyes fall upon my mother when she enters the room?"

"She's the queen, a title you'll have one day yourself. If they do not look upon her as they do, Babylon will be in worse shape than it is already."

"You know what I speak of."

Aoh stopped twirling the ends of her hair.

"The prince Khian is here. I couldn't...take my eyes off him since he arrived. Even during my performance... I saw him look at me. He probably already knows how I made a fool of myself."

Taking the hair brush, Aoh aggressively replied, "Stop it."

"These bangles are quite musical, but -should I-"

"The prince will-"

"Aoh," she interrupted, looking at herself in the mirror and seeing Aoh to her side. "All I desire is to be desired. To be wanted. No matter what I do, it's not enough in the eyes of the gods. Do they not hear me? Do they not hear what I ask for? Is it...too much to ask?"

"Then, perhaps they are not watching," Aoh replied.

She tugged the silk cape over both shoulders, clasping the golden ends together. Slowly running her fingers down the sides, the cape flowed, falling to the floor. She twirled the sides of Mylittia's hair as though she were weaving them into a pattern.

"Perhaps the gods do not care what happens to you, or this kingdom. They already let it fall... But do not misunderstand me, princess."

Aoh crouched, lowering herself to Mylittia's side, fixing the bottom of the dress and ensuring the clasps on her sandals were tight.

"I care about you. So does your mother. You are desired. You are a princess. All of this will be yours. Speak to the prince, learn his ways. But be careful, he is still a guest of this realm."

"But…what if he wants nothing to do with me? What if he finds me ugly? What if he is already married?"

"He's not the only prince in this world. Even a shepherd can be seen as a prince."

"I am not marrying a shepherd," the princess chuckled, rising to her feet. "I am marrying a prince. It is my birthright."

Trying to force a smile across her face, Mylittia begged, "Aoh, come back with me, just to make sure I don't fall. Please."

"Princess, I-"

"Please. I do not want to go back alone. You'll protect me."

I could see the small tears bubble in her eyes. She was terrified. In a way, I could understand why she was. She was unlike the queen. Perhaps that was not the worst thing she could be.

"You need to calm down," Aoh whispered.

"I can't. My heart is in my lungs. I can feel something in my throat. I feel faint."

"Then only drink water. Do not drink wine."

The princess nodded, constantly bending her fingers, feeling as though she were about to pass out onto the cool floor before the crowd.

"Look, there he is now," Aoh said, gesturing slightly and tilting the princess's head.

There he was, a young man a little taller than the princess, laughing with whom Aoh could only assume were either his brothers or close relatives. He was handsome and appeared serious, even when laughing. The princess inhaled deeply, and slowly made her approach across the room as the group of young men halted their conversations. With one calm bow, Mylittia introduced herself. The eldest prince returned with a respectful bow and a small smile. Aoh smiled, slowly moving away from them to watch from behind a large dark statue of Marduk.

Wandering from the princess, Aoh heard the genuine laugh of

Queen Huriye not far away. Peering around the light blue curtains, she found her finishing her drink. Aoh moved away from the curtain, catching sight of Zurvan watching her from across the room near the balcony standing with two generals at his side remaining away from the celebration. Turning around, Queen Huriye caught sight of Aoh and smiled.

"There you are."

"Good evening, Queen Huriye," Aoh greeted, slipping through the opening in the curtain.

"Enjoying yourself?"

"Yes."

"Have you tried the wine?"

"Yes, I have."

"What of this one?" she asked, grabbing the goblet off the platter from a servant walking by them.

Aoh looked at the goblet full of wine and took it unwillingly. As she inhaled the scent, she felt the queen gently nudge her.

"Look, Aoh."

Aoh followed the movement of Queen Huriye gently turning her body towards the right.

"Across the fountain," she whispered.

There he was. A young man amongst other men all appearing similar to each other, looking directly at me. His eyes outlined in black make-up, his long black hair, braided and tied, hung behind his back dropping just below his shoulder blades. The other men with him all had their hair braided and tied, in a variety of lengths. Their facial features were broad and firm. Everything was defined, including their muscles. Not one of those men hid that fact. They wore skirts, some donning vests, and vibrant linens making sure that the structure of their muscles were visible.

Golden cuffs and bracelets decorated up and down their arms and legs. Their near- pale skin decorated with black tattoos enhanced their strength. They were strong men. Strong willed. Strong within. They were as described in one of the several passages I had read from the queen's library. They, too, existed for hundreds of years, in their own world away from others.

As I looked at them, I tried to avoid eye contact; however, the one young man in particular made it impossible not to. He was incredibly handsome, and yet I was not attracted to him. I would be lying, however, if I said he didn't make me blush. I could feel my cheeks flaring as I pressed my fingers against my skin.

"What do you think of him?" Queen Huriye asked, with a smile.

"I don't..." Aoh replied, unsure how to respond.

Queen Huriye's smile widened.

"He's looking at you."

"Queen Huriye, I couldn't-"

"Unsure about him?" she asked.

"He wears more jewelry than I do. I do not think that is something I could overlook," Aoh replied, with a smile.

Queen Huriye laughed in agreement as she took another drink of wine.

"Very true," she puckered between her lips. "All of them seem to look that way, don't they? Do not let their appearance fool you, the Hyksos are very strong men. They've conquered more enemies than you've read about."

"Really?" Aoh asked.

"Yes. They wouldn't dare attack us since we were taken by savages. We are still underneath them... Even now as we celebrate. These walls are only as thick as we believe them to be. Babylon is a place the world envies for. It was centuries old when man was still young," she explained with a crackle in her voice and a slight trace of a tear in her eye.

Aoh listened, looking at the young man as he continued to look at her from across the room, attracted by her presence. At times, he was distracted by other men whom were talking with him but he always returned his attention to her.

"King Khi has a son your age, Aoh. Which makes him more valuable than ever before."

"What value would they have except in...killing other men? If they are truly that valuable, wouldn't you think your ancestors would have made it a point to intermarry?" Aoh asked, honestly.

"My, you have read a lot, haven't you, since you've arrived? That's because my ancestors were fools who never saw a single opportunity when it presented itself before them. We should have intermarried with them. If we had, we would be ruling Egypt right now," she replied bitterly.

Her last statement rattled me as my fingers curled a little tighter around the goblet of wine.

15

My heart fluttered when I saw him trying to approach me, moving around the statues and groups of people. I froze. No words were forming in my mind to say.

"I shall let you enjoy the rest of your night," Queen Huriye smiled, slowly walking away.

Now alone, Aoh stood with her drink, noticing out of the corner of her eye the young man drawing near. She remained still, unable to move, fully aware that he wanted to speak to her.

"Aoh, yes?" he asked with a slight accent.

"Yes," she answered quickly, taking a sip of the wine and frowning slightly at the bitter taste that made her insides crawl.

"I saw you today with your bow. You're quite gifted in archery," he complimented her.

Aoh smiled uncomfortably in response, feeling the heat in her cheeks become more intense.

"I wanted to speak with you then but you were occupied," he admitted, glancing at the goblet of wine in his hands.

Aoh nodded, taking another sip. Once again, she puckered her lips together, frowning at the bitter taste. The young man gently raised his hand toward the goblet.

"Are you forcing yourself to drink something you don't like to purposely avoid from speaking to me?" he asked kindly.

Aoh's decorated lashes lifted, watching him, hold the cup, surrounded by a warm aurora.

He had a sweetness about him that I didn't expect. He surprised me.

"May I?" he asked.

"Yes, please. Take it away," Aoh replied.

He took the goblet from her hand and placed it on the table next to him gently between two statues.

"As I was saying, your skill is very good. I doubt many trained soldiers are as good."

Aoh released an awkward laugh, shaking her head slightly in disagreement to his honest statement.

"What is your name?" she asked lowly.

"Don't you know?" he smiled, a little surprised by her question.

"No, that's why I'm asking."

"Tyrgnn. My father is the ambassador to King Khi. One day I hope I will receive that title."

Aoh nodded, suddenly reminded of her older brother and his life of work her father also lived. She lowered her head to look at the floor, noticing how reflective it was, seeing Tyrgnn step closer.

"Would you walk with me?" he asked.

Aoh didn't answer him at first, feeling a rush of nervousness drown her to the point where she felt she couldn't move.

"Or would you rather stay and continue to drink wine you distaste?" he asked with a playful grin.

Biting her lower lip, Aoh left the goblet on the table and followed him, walking past large exotic potted plants and several birds sitting and hiding within them, leaving Zurvan's range of sight.

Leaving the party, we walked up steps together outside to one of the largest balconies that overlooked much of the desert and city. It was a quiet and peaceful night. A night that reminded me of my home, when I'd sit on the rooftop and listen to the young boy play his flute until I couldn't stay awake anymore. The crackling of the fire cast our shadows against the nearest wall as I sat at the balcony, observing the world we lived in, left behind by the kings of past, long dead and buried beneath the sands.

Tyrgnn breathed the cold air, releasing a sigh of content.

"Before I arrived, I wanted to find something special to bring with me to give to someone," Tyrgnn admitted.

From within his belt, he revealed a rolled piece of linen, unvealing exotic flowers she had never seen before…

"The heliotropes turn to the sun… and irises thrive in the most beautiful gardens. Like you," he smiled.

I couldn't resist smiling. The purple irises struck me like lightning. The white flower buds on the heliotrope soothed me.

"You're giving these to me?"

"I believe that when I found these flowers, they were meant for you."

"What has Queen Huriye told you of me?" Aoh asked.

"She told me how she found you in the desert as a child. How she raised you in this palace. How you've grown here since."

She smiled in response.

"I can't imagine how you were able to survive all alone before she found you," he admitted. "You must be strong willed. The desert can be a very testing place. It's an entity entirely of its own. They say the gods rule it freely," he explained.

She nodded, looking at the flowers, admiring the beauty they beheld.

"The flowers are beautiful, but the princess is more desiring of this than myself," She explained.

"The princess is beautiful, from what I've been told before we arrived. Any king or prince would be blessed to have her as their wife. But for men like myself…we do not receive that second glance from someone in the palace often."

Moving her eyes from the flowers to his face, she whispered, "I believe you have me mistaken for a princess."

He smiled widely, and replied with sincerity, "You are a princess."

Aoh chuckled in disbelief, when suddenly she noticed a shooting star cross the night sky. She became distracted by all the tiny but bright stars and the shadows of the mountains.

Oblivious of Aoh's distracted mind, Tyrgnn continued firmly, "I have learned the most about myself wandering through the desert. It has tested me several times, and I believe the gods were watching my every step. The desert is our greatest teacher. Cold and warm, bountiful but just. It was a pleasure having crossed it just to come here."

"Do you know the desert, then?" Aoh asked, trying to listen but continued to be dazzled by the sight before her.

"I believe I do. Why do you ask?"

"Could…you tell me which mountain that is?"

Tyrgnn got up and looked in the direction Aoh was pointing towards. He saw in the darkness many mountains, jagged and rough, outlined underneath the dark blue hues of the sky full of stars.

"Which mountain?"

"That one."

Tyrgnn lifted his hand outward and pointed.

"Point me in the direction," he stated firmly.

Aoh's hands wrapped around his hand as she moved him to the left, stopping at the mountain she was focused upon. Tyrgnn looked, studying the mountain, wincing slightly.

"I am unfamiliar with that mountain. Although I do believe many a shepherd tend to their flocks out there."

Aoh nodded feeling a swift cool breeze encircle her for a brief moment. She noticed Tyrgnn move his left hand ever so gingerly towards hers, still holding the flowers.

No man had given me such attention before at the palace. No man seemed to notice me in such a way before. Yet here Tyrgnn was, seeing all of me, perhaps in ways I never saw myself.

After a long silence and Tyrgnn's lingering hand, he released a deep breath.

"I should return. Come with me?" Tyrgnn asked, holding out his hand.

"I'm going to retire. Thank you for the flowers."

"You're welcome, princess."

Aoh froze, watching Tyrgnn grin once more before leaving to return to the celebration that continued below. Taking the flowers, Aoh wrapped them with her dress, feeling herself growing tired. She wandered down the halls, following an irregular path, when she heard a feminine sound. Continuing down the darkened hallway, Aoh listened and heard it again, passing an open doorway leading through two rooms. Turning to look in the direction of the rooms, she froze.

I couldn't believe what I was seeing. Queen Huriye was with a man...her long hair loose and untamed. Her dress draped all about the bed as she repeated the name of a man with passion,

I left, embarrassed, unsure where to go, suddenly forgetting my way around the palace I had lived in for several years. As I hurried, I passed the statue of Ishtar and immediately lost my breath. Escaping the hallway, I recognized where I was again and rushed to my chambers as fast as I could to the safety of my bed.

As hard as I tried, I could not sleep. I was unable to stop thinking of my family as I wept into my pillows. The words Tyrgnn spoke to me reminded me so much of my brother. They were wise and ever so truthful. Thoughts of my brother soon transformed into thoughts of my family, Their love continued to stay with me, but to what end? To what end would I find myself able to think of them and not cry? The wet trails from my tears dripping like rivers. By now the celebration had long ended... Everyone was sleeping and the palace silent as the pyramids.

Leaving her bed that gave her no comfort that night, Aoh walked down the hall, remaining in the light cast by the dying flames from statues and torches. She heard a low voice say her name. Following the voice, Aoh walked into the room, seeing Queen Huriye draped across her chair. She was sitting behind her war table, surrounded by the glow of the flames. Entering cautiously, Aoh looked at the ornate table standing across from the queen.

I've seen that table more times than I could count. Queen Huriye had all of the known world depicted on it, cut from different stones, metals and materials. Although she used it to keep track of her enemies, constantly changing it when she received news of what kingdom fell or expanded, she observed it like I imagined Ra does. Keeping close watch over everything he created… Even though looking upon the table was displeasing, I couldn't help but feel that it consoled me of my homesickness. For right there, carved of black stone, was Egypt.

Panting, Queen Huriye drank from her goblet, keeping it in her hand with the large water basin full of fresh water beside her. She rubbed her hand over her mouth, gently using the faint glow of moonlight to read.

"What is keeping you up this late?" she asked with a wide grin.

"I couldn't sleep. I was going to try to please the queen by checking to see if all the guests have left and the visitors were in their chambers," Aoh replied.

"Keeping watch, I see," Queen Huriye let out a strange chuckle. "You think everyone enjoyed themselves?"

"Yes, I do. There was plenty of wine. Plenty of food."

"And what of our foreign friends?" she asked Aoh, reaching to fill her goblet with more water.

"Interesting," Aoh replied quietly after hesitating.

Queen Huriye stared at her looking for a deeper answer.

"Oh, come now, Aoh. What do you think? I want to know."

"As I said before, the men wear more jewelry than the women. How will that make me look?"

Queen Huriye laughed, which caused Aoh to chuckle in response, realizing that what she said was indeed funny even if she didn't intend to be.

"Well…aside from their looks, I did some digging. Apparently the King Khi's oldest son, Khian, isn't married. Thankfully… So, I did some further digging, well, I should say he did, and I think an arrangement has been made."

"What sort of arrangement? Don't tell me you're going to have your daughter marry him?" Aoh asked with a hint of excitement.

Oblivious to her excitement, she replied, "Oh, no, of course not. I will be."

I wasn't sure how to react. I wanted to laugh thinking she was joking. But she wasn't.

"You will be married to his eldest son?"

"Yes. We had a meeting and discussed a solution. He agreed to my terms."

"When was this meeting, during the celebration?" Aoh asked, confused.

"Yes. We met in private, and, as queen, I am very convincing."

It struck me like lightning. I knew then who that man was she was with earlier that night. It was the king of the Hyksos...and, as a queen, she convinced him the only way she knew how. If there was one thing she taught me, men are human and tire of gold, jewels, and war very quickly. There is only one thing they will forever desire.

"I understand that their looks aren't quite those of my people; however, they have what I want," Queen Huriye explained firmly as she leaned over to the table. She looked to Aoh, and then down at the ornate table wittingly.

Women are human and tire of men, riches, and titles very quickly. There is only one thing they will forever desire.

"Land."

Power.

"His Kingdom once ruled Egypt before they were overthrown. They reside just on the other side of the Nile River, stretching far into the north and south. When we marry, we will unite both kingdoms and have conquered the majority of our world, expanding where the Hittites reside..." she explained.

Her eyes glowed with such fire and desire. It was as though she was lost. Gone off to another world where Aoh could not follow.

"We will rule this world. All of it."

"Does that mean non-threatening countries like Egypt as well?" Aoh asked with suspicion.

"Why do you ask?"

"I only ask out of concern of what you are desiring."

Aoh paused, pointing to the table, trailing her fingers just above

Babylon and where the Hyksos ruled.

"Because won't all of this be enough? Won't it?" Aoh asked firmly.

Queen Huriye didn't respond initially as she listened, intensely watching Aoh's fingers slide across the table.

"You will have ruled this, this, this, even these mountains!" Aoh insisted, pointed to the different realms as she spoke. "You will have control of the rivers and trading routes. You will have control of all passages both in and out here, here, and here! Isn't that enough?"

Comprehending her tone, Queen Huriye asked, "Aoh, I want you to be honest with me as you always have. Haven't you ever desired something? Something, it could be anything, jewels, a man, kingdom, a slave of your own, something, anything?"

Aoh's lips remained sealed.

"My dear, enough will never be enough. Once we are married, the future will be this much closer to my grasp. Closer than it has ever been. I do not know what will happen. I do not know the future. I will not say I will attack Egypt, nor will I say I will not. Same for other kingdoms in my way. I will simply suggest that he take back the land that was once his. Take it all and leave none of it left…"

She looked at the table, focusing her attention on the map and where Egypt lied.

"Once we combine kingdoms," she continued, "the Red Sea will be our only opposition from conquering Egypt and the kingdoms following it."

Aoh listened, feeling the uneasiness inside of her grow intensely worse with every passing second.

"I haven't told you, and for that I am sorry. The Mitanni has their eyes on us, Aoh. And the Assyrians are not through with us either, that you witnessed yourself. They always had us in their sight, and they will not stop. They will never rest. I will not watch this kingdom fall into foreign hands ever again. I will never allow it!"

"What of the king's son? Won't he –, won't his people be taking this kingdom?"

She grinned widely and replied, "Like I said, I'm very convincing."

Queen Huriye's ambition gave me no rest. No matter how sweet the incense was burning. No matter how comforting my bed was. No matter how calming the breeze from my open windows… I worried about my homeland, my family, my king. What if I had to choose between Queen Huriye and my homeland?

The faces of the men I killed flickered in and out of my consciousness like flames. Remembering them made me sick to my stomach. The tense feelings went away when I forced them out of my thoughts. I couldn't believe I was capable of such an act.

Because I could not sleep, I decided to keep the night company. I sat outside, overlooking the kingdom and open desert in the direction of Egypt. I could not see its glory from where I sat. I could only see the desert stretching for miles and miles, surprising myself that I had traversed it alone and survived. I sat there in silence, ignoring any slight sounds from bugs or animals. I was consumed by the wonderful sight of a fading darkness, slowly changing colors in the distance. And while I watched, I felt a calming reassurance that everything was going to somehow be fine.

16

Sucking on the juices of the grapes she pierced with her teeth, Queen Huriye's mind fluttered like the wings of a bird, carelessly changing directions at the next colorful and delectable sight. Hearing the faint sound of a whine, she glanced at her dogs, watching her eat. She smiled at them and released a coo from her lips, lovingly running her decorated fingers over the nearest dog's head. Queen Huriye turned her attention back towards her meal, just as a servant delivered another plate silently. As she ate, she glanced upward at Aoh unraveling a long gown from a multitude of colored ropes and fabrics.

"You like it, don't you?" she asked with a smirk.

I became lost in the beauty and extravagance of the gown; threaded with fringe and a multitude of patterns, just covering my chest and falling to my ankles. The shawl wrapped within the gown matched in its lavishness. Queen Huriye never blessed me with such an outstanding gift before. She was generous to me often, but never to the extent of providing me with a gown that only a princess would wear.

"I know, I know. A gown from the gods," Queen Huriye smiled, taking another stash of grapes.

"This is beautiful, Queen Huriye," Aoh replied, exasperated.

Holding the gown in both hands, she pressed it against her thin body, watching as the patterns insinuated her form.

"I couldn't wear something like this."

"Of course you can. Truth is, you well deserve it."

Aoh rolled her lips inward and replied, "I don't deserve anything you have given me."

"Stop it and look at yourself. This is how you were destined to look."

The dog's eyes followed Queen Huriye as she lifted elegantly from her seat and placed her hands on Aoh's shoulders, turning her to face a mirror. Her thumbs tenderly rubbed Aoh's skin, feeling smooth from her most recent bath.

"See? This is you. This is who you are. This is who you will always be." She tenderly spoke.

Aoh turned bright red with embarrassment, unable to wash away the growing smile on her face.

Seeing her smile, Queen Huriye continued, "See? See how beautiful you look? Think of it as a gift of gratitude." She paused, nearly chuckling to herself. "Think of it this way, it won't stay on you for long once Tyrgnn sees you."

"What are you speaking of?" Aoh asked instantly.

"I know how men think, and what he thought of you when he saw you spoke louder than any words he could describe."

Queen Huriye released her grasp on Aoh and walked over to her open windows, allowing the wind to grace her body, lifting her hair and cape from her gown behind her gently. By now one of her dogs had fallen asleep while the other two playfully irritated one another. Their chatter echoed about the room.

Inhaling the air, she listened to Babylon coming to life. The sounds of men and women, working and talking in the distance, with the sounds of her own palace breathing – it all pleased her embellished ears. Aoh's hand wrapped the gown and shawl back together, slipping her hands between the smoothness of the fabrics like walking through cool water.

Turning around, Queen Huriye noticed Aoh's expression of utter torment, folding the gown and shawl.

"What's the matter?" she asked, concerned.

"Nothing," Aoh answered with a crackle in her voice.

Queen Huriye drew a hand to her mouth and chin, studying Aoh's expression and asked, "You were never intimate with a man before, were you?"

"No…Queen Huriye," Aoh admitted.

"Never? Not with a single man in my palace, my kingdom, or any kingdom?"

"No."

"Well…that is interesting. I'd had thought by now you'd be swept off your feet. But-"

She leaned over to look outside as Aoh's face burned red.

"I suppose you have always been quite shy around men. Not one to be bold, much like Mylittia."

Aoh ran her fingers along the fabric of the dress, already wondering if Queen Huriye's words were true about Tyrgnn.

"Oh, we better go. King Khi will be presenting us with his kingdom's gifts today. I look forward to seeing what these gentlemen can do," Queen Huriye explained as a servant quickly began to fix the sides of her dress that repeatedly slipped downward. Another servant brushed the ends of her long hair, preparing to braid them as two others cleaned the remnants of the meal from the table.

Titling her head to look at Aoh, she smiled, "The men of their kingdom are skilled fighters and wrestlers. I look forward to seeing this very much."

That afternoon in the same arena, next to Princess Mylittia, I watched two Hyksos men wrestling across the stone ground, scattered with grains of sand. They grappled each other, grunting, their faces distorted from the struggle of trying to conquer the other. Both men fighting to win while the audience encouraged them loudly, raising their fists into the air. After every match, more sand and flower petals were tossed onto the ground before different men began to wrestle. They screamed and groaned, using all of their strength to overpower their opponent, receiving continuous applause as each match seemed to grow increasingly more intense and violent.

When it was time for the eldest prince to fight the second eldest, I noticed how both Queen Huriye and Princess Mylittia leaned forward from their seats to watch. My guilt seemed to return tenfold. Both princes used all of their strength. With one move after another, they countered each other, escaping tight grips between arms and legs, sweat pouring from their pores and soaking the ends of their black hair. They roared like mighty beasts, refusing to pause for even a moment to catch their breaths... I'd be lying if I said I wasn't impressed. Their strength was truly profound.

In the end, the eldest, Prince Khian, next in line for the throne, was the victor. He had cuts across his back and chest, sweat shinning in the bright sunlight. He screamed from the top of his lungs a cry of victory.

That very night, Queen Huriye wanted to celebrate with our visitors. It was to be their last night before they returned home. I wore the gown and shawl she gave me while trying to avoid the princess at all costs. I dreaded her reaction to the news I knew was about to be told to her by a servant before hearing it from her own mother. Many men's eyes turned my way, admiring the gown, but did not approach me. The feeling of not wanting to be around the barrage of celebration grew stronger and I decided to leave early, to get away from the distractions. I instead returned to my room where I could find some peace.

Entering my room, I immediately laid on top of my bed, removing my sandals and listening to the light sound they made hitting the carpeted floor. Staring at the high ceiling, I looked at the night sky carved into the stone with images of creatures that always watched over me as I slept. My heavy eyelids slowly closed and I felt a calm flow over me, until I heard a strange sound behind me.

Rising from her bed, Aoh walked out onto the balcony, finding her kite friend flying in the night sky. Watching him circle over her, faintly in the darkness, Aoh lifted her arm, welcoming him to land. Floating gracefully downward, the kite landed on her arm, wrapping its claws gently, nearly pricking her skin. It squawked loudly, shifting its weight, turning its face towards her. Aoh released a gentle laugh, happy to see her friend again, unable to recall the last time she had seen him.

Delicately rubbing the soft feathers on his chest, she heard the sound of her door slowly opening. Startling the kite, he immediately rose from her arm and returned to the night sky. Aoh immediately looked in the direction of her bedroom door, alarmed until she recognized Tyrgnn walking from behind the long curtains.

"Why are you up here alone in the dark?" he asked confused.

"I didn't feel like attending," she replied.

"Why?"

"I don't know. How did you find me?"

"I just wandered about. I was concerned when I didn't see you."

"I'm fine. Just spending time with the night."

As Tyrgnn entered the balcony, he became consumed by all the wonder about him once again.

"Wow…everything looks so different from here," he admitted, constantly turning his head. Looking up, he saw every tiny star in the sky.

"This view is better than the king's. So, this is the company you keep?" he smiled.

"You shouldn't be wandering the palace. Zurvan won't like it," Aoh warned.

"He's nothing to worry about. There are far more important things to be worried about."

Aoh didn't respond, sitting on the balcony railing. She drew her knees to her chest and draped her arms over them, feeling her shawl drop slightly down her back.

"You think it wise that we left the celebration?" he asked with a small smile, playing with one of the gold rings on his fingers.

"You think anyone noticed?" Aoh asked in response, looking at the tattoos on the surface of both of his hands.

"I'm sure Queen Huriye did."

"If so?"

"She'll be wondering what we were up to, what we did, what we talked about."

"She doesn't need to know everything," Aoh replied coldly.

"My king doesn't either," Tyrgnn agreed.

He looked at Aoh, noticing her preoccupied expression as she looked out into the desert with contentment yet confusion. He stood next to her, leaning himself against the balcony railing, unable to stop himself from admiring her.

"You look so beautiful," he said with sincerity.

"Thank you," Aoh replied, unsure how to respond.

"Do you like it here?"

Aoh frowned slightly.

"In Babylon, I meant to say," Tyrgnn corrected quickly.

"I suppose so," Aoh replied.

Tygrnn's eyes remained on Aoh as a chill rushed through them.

"There is something else, isn't there? I can see that as happy as you must be, blessed by the gods, a great burden is weighing you down."

Aoh took a deep, slow breath, rising her chest and replied, "Queen Huriye desires his eldest son, not for her daughter but for herself."

"How does the princess feel about that?" Tyrgnn asked.

"She doesn't know," Aoh replied wearily. "I'm worried about how she will react when she finds out. She loves Prince Khian."

"He is a good man. I've known him all his life. We practically grew up together as children in the palace."

Aoh looking down at Tyrgnn and asked firmly, "How well would you say you know him?"

Tyrgnn turned to her and replied, "Why do you ask?"

"Do you think he will want to go to war with Egypt?"

"What of Egypt?" he asked with a slight chuckle.

"If the Prince Khian were to marry Queen Huriye, would he declare war on Egypt on her behalf?"

Tyrgnn paused before answering, "No."

"Why?"

"The prince is in many aspects unlike his father. While his father likes to show our strength through victories in battle, the prince would rather prove it by being more noble. He acts in ways of delaying. He sees the whole scope of things before acting. He's calculated and intelligent," Tyrgnn explained. "Why do you ask?"

"I'm worried that Queen Huriye's hatred for the Egyptians will end her own kingdom. Her ambitions are dangerous. She acts without delay, and sometimes without thinking."

"Which is why she trusts you," Tyrgnn added with a small smile.

"I don't know why she trusts me. I just told you something I shouldn't have told anyone. She shouldn't trust me."

"You told me because you are trying to protect her from destroying herself. You told me because you know this marriage is going to happen, joining the Babylonians and the Hyksos. And you told me because you trust me, don't you?"

Aoh didn't answer, rubbing her arms gently up and down, sliding the soft palm of her hands across her skin.

"Aoh?" he repeated.

"Yes?"

"What do you think of me?" he asked. "You won't come closer to me, yet you kept the flowers I gave you in a vase by your bed. You will not lay with me, yet you find comfort in speaking with me. Make no mistake, I did not come up here to ravage you but adore you."

"I think you are a rarity to this world, Tyrgnn," Aoh replied.

"As are you," he beamed.

He watched how her hair just laid against her body so perfectly, as though she were a living, breathing mosaic brought to life by the gods.

"We are leaving tomorrow."

"Yes, you are."

"I don't want this to be the last time I see you, Aoh. Whether your queen marries my king, prince, or another entirely, I want to see you again."

"If it is the will of the gods," Aoh replied.

"It is my will."

Tyrgnn raised his hand to touch Aoh's face but she rejected him, standing up and crossing her arms against her chest.

"You should go. I am tired and need to rest."

"If you wish me to go, I shall as asked to. But just know, no matter how hard you try to hide your affections for me…I can see them."

Tyrgnn walked over to the edge of the balcony and lifted his leg over the thick stone railing.

"What are you doing?" Aoh asked worried.

"Climbing down. I couldn't leave through your bedroom door. What will they think?"

Aoh nodded, watching him climb down ever so carefully, one step at a time, using the edges and carved images of the thick walls to place his sandals and fingers.

"Will you remember me?" he asked, reaching the lower level safely.

"I will," Aoh replied.

"Then I wish you good night and know that, whether it be in this life or the next, no man will ever love you as much as I."

17

A few days passed without incident. The Hyksos left, returning to their homeland, and Princess Mylittia was still convinced she was going to be marrying Prince Khian. He became the only subject she talked about, day and night. She was happier than I've ever seen her before and as much as I wanted to tell her the truth, I couldn't.

"How are you, my friend?" Aoh asked the kite, stroking his chest with the knuckle of her hand.

With each stroke, the kite whistled happily, slightly moving its feathers as it remained balanced on her arm. She looked into the eyes of the kite, noticing how, over time, the feathers had become less vibrant; some were missing entirely. The claws looked older and worn from the constant perching and snatching meals. The eyes, still powerfully large, looked somehow weaker. The beak had a slight crack up the side that never healed. With all these changes from time, it still remembered her and always returned to comfort her.

It wasn't just the fact that the princess would have her heartbroken that kept me worried. It was the fate of my homeland that hung before me, like bait in front of fish in the Nile River. I came to the only conclusion that became clear in my mind, as I beheld my feathered friend. Even though it did not guarantee Egypt's safety…it was the only option I had.

Without warning, the kite lifted from her arm and flew into the sky, screeching loudly, as it spread its wings and hovered in the cool air. Aoh watched the kite fly, first circling over her and then turning towards the large desert. As she watched it fly away, she noticed something moving in the darkness.

I saw them in the distance. The queen's soldiers dragging at least twenty men in chains through the desert, coming towards the city hastily. I couldn't see who the men were; however, I recognized their movement. They were shifting side to side as Babylonian soldiers remained both in front and behind them, constantly shouting.

Aoh quickly wrapped her shawl around her head and shoulders, pulling it from over her chair. Passing through her room, she tip-toed down the open halls, listening to the sounds of her feet and watching her shadow move across the walls. The curtains danced each time the wind swept through them, rising and falling each passing second as the guards on duty remained at attention. She remained in the shadows, moving between columns, avoiding them easily, following one hallway to another, passing closed doors.

Following a set of stairs, she continued to tip-toe across the cool floor, hearing the sounds of the doors opening with a low moan and whistle from the wind. She moved towards another set of stairs, hearing the sounds of the soldiers' boots against the floor.

"Awaken Queen Huriye."

Coming to the bottom of the stairs, Aoh peered carefully behind a potted tree and grasped the outer rim of the stone pot with her fingertips. She watched a number of men storm inside. They met the queen in the hallway, as she tried to fix her long hair by pulling it over her left shoulder and tying her robes together at her neck and chest.

Aoh heard one of the men speak to the queen with a thick, brash voice. Her eyes followed them, quickly walking down the other side of the room towards the front of the palace.

"We have them. Egyptians trying to infiltrate the kingdom,

staying at our borders."

"How many?" she asked.

"Twenty. We have them rounded up outside, about to be placed at the compound until provided with your further instructions."

"Keep them there. Do a head count again. Give me their names and watch them. Keep this quiet. I do not want anyone to know they are here."

He bowed, and the men behind him bowed to her in unison before leaving. Aoh's eyes followed Queen Huriye as she moved through the shadows to return to her bed, braiding her long hair quickly. Seeing her disappear into the night, Aoh followed the direction the soldiers went. She found them outside the palace, gathering the captured men, all chained at their wrists and ankles to each other, dirty and ragged in their armor.

The chains rattled each time they moved, struggling to free themselves to no avail, pushed and shoved towards the compound on the farthest side of the city.

The moment the sun rose the next morning, I left the palace to see them.

18

Aoh wrapped herself, covering her face except her eyes, unrecognizable as moved amongst the people. Upon seeing a soldier, she would constantly shuffle her feet in the sand. She lowered her eyes to avoid eye contact and to steady her steps, passing them as nothing more than another woman.

Following the path upward, she climbed the hill, passing women carrying the thick coats from sheep and water from the canals. Two children rushed past her, bumping into her legs, nearly knocking her down. Aoh watched them run down the slight hill, noticing how high she was climbing as she came to the compound where the Egyptians were being held. Immediately, she noted the guards positioned at every opening of the area. All of them were stone-faced, arms folded, muscles protruding from their bodies, sweating before the sun reached its peak in the sky.

I expected nothing less, given the queen's hatred of the Egyptians.

Aoh's eyes quickly moved, studying the scale of the compound made of several layers of stone, wood, and metal trimming around the gates. It appeared very old and in need of repair as evidence showed, several walls were replaced with only wood. She avoided the main entrance of the compound and, instead, moved towards the far right, near the edge of the steep side that faced the desert. She hesitated, looking over the edge and noticing the slight drop before another opening in the wall and then the desert.

Backing away from the edge, Aoh could see the captured Egyptians through the gaps in the fence. They were all sitting on the ground, chained to each other, burning by the hot sun with no shade. Their only water was provided in a small hardened cup, barely enough for a meal let alone a day. All of them sat, resting their arms over their bent knees, some dipping their heads towards their chest, aching and sore.

I saw dried blood on their faces and in their hair. Their skin tainted with dried dirt. Their armor and weapons stripped from their bodies. From their appearance alone, I immediately recognized them as Egyptian soldiers, once bearing the protection of the gods to serve the pharaoh, now stripped down to nothing but rags. My eyes quickly looked onto each of them, tired, and angry at having been captured.

Aoh took another step, suddenly feeling something hard and misshapen under her foot. Lifting her foot, she looked down and saw, what appeared to have been, a carved piece of stone. Picking it up, she could just make out the symbols, spelling out a name she couldn't quite read in a language she wasn't familiar with. It was charred and scrapped, tied onto a thin piece of a leather strap.

Picking it up, I suddenly felt eyes on me. Turning towards the direction of the captive men, I saw a man whose face was covered the most in blood looking back at me. His hair was darkened gold, like sunlight in shadow. His skin was unlike mine. He did not look Egyptian, nor did he look foreign in my eyes. He looked at me in silence, sitting on the hard ground, resting his strong arms over his knees, dirty and dry.

"Keep your head down," the guard growled, stepping up to the man and, by using his fist, shoved the man's head downward.

Aoh quickly pocketed the small object, standing up to leave when she heard a guard open the gate behind her.

"You there, what are you doing over here? You should not be here."

Aoh didn't turn around.

She tugged the sides of the drape closer to her face and replied, lowering her voice, "My apologies sir. I'll be on my way."

"Do not come back here, understand? This is no place for anyone but prisoners. If I see you here again, Queen Huriye will hear about it."

Aoh nodded and apologized once more. Walking away, she noted the guards watching her leave from both inside and outside the compound, holding spears with swords at their waists. Removing the leather bracelet from her pocket, she wrapped it around her wrist, tucking it under the sleeve as she glanced one last time at the captured men before returning to the palace.

Upon her arrival, she encountered several servants waiting for her. They instructed her to follow them to the queen's chambers, immediately. Concerned, Aoh quickly removed the wrap from around her hair and face, and undid her robe. She handed it to the servants, who gladly accepted her clothing without saying a word.

Entering the chambers, Aoh found the princess already present, sitting at her mother's side holding one of her hands. Every window in the room was opened as servants constantly moved the giant tree leaves up and down to create more air by the bed, with doctors continually pouring multiple liquids into large basins, stirring and whispering to each other. Zurvan stood by Queen Huriye's bedside, looking over her with heavy eyes, constantly rubbing a hand over his mouth. The doors behind Aoh closed, alerting Zurvan and Mylittia to turn around. Seeing Aoh, Queen Huriye smiled weakly beneath her pale complexion.

"Aoh, where were you? I didn't see you this morning," she asked.

"Just went for a walk," Aoh replied, remaining still.

She watched the doctors shaking their heads slightly and began to feel worried. Books were brought in and placed on the table next to several crushed ingredients and used glass vials.

"What happened?" Aoh asked, concerned.

"I refuse to believe how weak my body is in comparison to asps," she laughed.

Princess Mylittia rose from the bed and allowed Aoh to sit there.

Aoh slowly approached the bed as Queen Huriye continued, "Not enough to kill me; however, I will not take any chances."

She smiled warmly for Mylittia as she left the room, wiping the tears from both eyes roughly. Aoh listened to the priest praying loudly near the bed, where a statue of Marduk was placed, and then glanced at Zurvan who stared back at her with harsh eyes.

"I want to proceed with the marriage arrangements as soon as Zurvan permits me."

Queen Huriye struggled to clear the phlegm from her throat, wheezing. Aoh quickly handed her the water by the bed, holding the cup up to her lips. Queen Huriye swallowed the water slowly. Upon swallowing, she noticed the stone around Aoh's wrist.

"What is this? A gift from someone?" she asked lowly, smiling.

Aoh looked at the stone, turning it to face the inside of her wrist and replied, "It's nothing."

"If you think that is nothing, I wonder what you will think of the necklace Tyrgnn sent you."

Aoh frowned slightly, confused. Queen Huriye waved over a servant who carried the necklace looped within her slightly parted thin arms. Every step the servant took, the large necklace glistened. Aoh's eyes widened seeing her tiny reflection all over the large gemstones.

"This came for you. A very generous young man, don't you think?"

Aoh couldn't answer, mumbling words in surprise.

"Your silence speaks for itself," the queen muttered. "Let me see it on you."

Aoh lowered her head slightly as the servant clasped the golden chain, pushing her hair away from her neck. The necklace had a slight weight to it, as Aoh felt herself lean forward.

"Oh, my…" Queen Huriye smiled faintly.

Aoh's lips mirrored the queen's.

"Beautiful. Absolutely beautiful. He must be thinking of you constantly. Perhaps he will be with King Khi when we invite him back."

Aoh nodded, suddenly feeling her arms grow numb.

"What's wrong, Aoh? You look troubled," Queen Huriye asked, reading Aoh's face.

"I'm worried about you," Aoh replied.

"This is nothing. You and my daughter have nothing to worry about. You'll be fine regardless of what happens to me."

"I wish that were true…"

"You don't believe me?"

Aoh shook her head in response, "Lately I don't seem to understand myself."

Queen Huriye strained her hand and cuffed Aoh's hands together at her waist.

Tightening her grip, she said, "I have no doubt that you will always protect my daughter. You will not fail. It's not in your nature to."

A staff hitting the floor twice and a loud shout grabbed Aoh's attention. She turned around and noticed a head priest enter the room from another door. Queen Huriye rolled her eyes seeing him enter and nodded to Zurvan. He gently nodded in response and approached the head priest, watching Aoh intently.

"Now, they will pray for my recovery for hours. You should go. Do not worry about me, Aoh."

Aoh nodded, removing herself from the room, slowly closing the doors in front of her. She was able to see Zurvan return to the queen's bedside but not before looking in her direction once more, intensely.

"Aoh."

Aoh turned and saw the princess standing up from a cushioned chair near the open windows, wiping her face clean from the tiny tears. In her small hands, decorated with several rings, wrapped with linen, was a rolled piece of parchment.

"Aoh, this is for you. It came with the necklace," Mylittia explained calmly.

Aoh inhaled deeply, taking the scroll, pulling the thread free, and unrolling the message written in smooth, dried ink.

The sun rises for you and you alone
Singing your name through the air
Golden like the shine in your eyes
The moon rises for you and you alone
Weaving your name across the stars
Glowing like the color of your eyes
My goddess
You are the face I see when I sleep, when I wake
When I walk, when I eat, when I pray
An immortal echo that follows me
Like a spirit of scented wind
You are my purest love
You are my Aoh

Mylittia read the poem silently, next to Aoh, astounded by his words.

"Glory be, that is beautiful," Mylittia gasped.

Aoh faked a smile, feeling her body tremble. Clearing her throat, she rolled the scroll back up and walked over to the nearest table to find something to tie it with, even though all that decorated it were statues.

Puzzled, Mylittia asked, "Aoh? Did you hear what I said?"

"I did," Aoh replied, looking at the statues and feeling her heart race, pounding in her chest as her necklace jiggled gently with each slight movement.

"Will you not write back to him?" she asked.

"I may."

"A man writes something truly romantic and moving and…you do not seem moved."

"I've hardly known Tyrgnn," Aoh defended, still struggling to find something to tie the scroll with.

"He seems to know you quite well. The gods smile upon you, constantly."

Aoh blinked heavily, biting her tongue from saying what was on her mind, closing her eyes heavily and rolling her tongue gently between her teeth. Letting out a slight shriek of frustration, Aoh gave up trying to find something to tie around the parchment.

"Do you love someone else?" the princess whispered.

Do not ask me why I hesitated. It wasn't my choice. There was something out of my control that made me do so.

"No. I don't," Aoh finally answered.

"He gives you a beautiful gift and writes you a magnificent poem. Not many women can say they have received as much. You should write back to him. Say something to him."

"I don't want to steal his heart just to steal it. That would make me no better than a common thief," Aoh snapped, viciously slamming both of her hands on the table, shaking the smaller statues slightly.

Mylittia frowned deeply, only adding to Aoh's frustration.

"I would die to have someone love me as much."

Aoh turned around, clutching the scroll in her hands and replied, "I have to go."

My nerves rose higher and higher with each step I took. Exiting the hallway I followed aimlessly as though I was lost, I found one of several fire pits burning fiercely in a bowl of broken wood.

Carefully, Aoh held the scroll over the open flame, preparing to burn it. However, as she hovered above the flames she suddenly stopped. Her eyes fell under the spell of the wild, bright flames watching their dance against the parchment. Lowering the scroll to her side, she looked at herself in the mirror just near the fire pit, touching the large necklace. Tingling sensations ran up and down her arm, prickling her fingertips like pulses. Dropping the parchment, she wrapped her fingers to the clasp of the heavy necklace and took it off.

Hearing sudden loud sounds outside, she followed them to the nearest balcony, alerted. In the distance, random Babylonian citizens shouted in distress, surrounding the compound where the Egyptian men were captured. The shouting carried on loudly, as guards pushed them away…slurs upon slurs were spewed from their mouths, ferociously angered by the Egyptian presence, throwing stones and small pieces of marble at them.

19

With Queen Huriye recovering in her chambers, I spent the next five days in the palace watching the entire compound. I recorded how many guards were present, when they left their posts, and for how long. I even observed the layout, drawing it to my best ability while remembering the man's face. The way he looked at me covered in dried blood...so intensely. In between that, I could not avoid my practices in archery. My one and only addiction that had me in its grips.

Aoh prepped herself, in the heat of another day, staring at the distant target. The servants were constantly moving the it's position and extending the distance. Remaining calm and patient, Aoh listened to the wind and the vibrations from the ground, keeping her eyes focused on the target staring back at her.

For the first time, something within me awakened. I felt this sudden sense of strength I never knew I had. With every arrow I fired, I imagined a dying soldier... I imaged them, falling to the ground. Silent... Gone... As they burned my home...I imagined the screams, the flames. One after another I fired my arrows, striking the target every time, moving my bow with grace and precision. The arrow soared...the screams. Another arrow...burning. Another...men falling to the ground. Another...bodies laid on top of each other. Another…fire. Another…screams. Another… cries.

On my last arrow I hesitated, for only a moment, releasing my breath slowly from my lips as the memory of my brother yelling at me to run returned. Releasing the last arrow, I watched, listening for the snap at the end of the field.

Zurvan didn't speak but stared at Aoh as she breathed heavily, lowering her bow as she thought of her brother, seeing the whites of his eyes as he ordered her, with fury, to run. Zurvan shouted to the servants, pointing in the direction of the field as they rushed to retrieve the furthest large target of straw and sand.

As they carried it back, struggling slightly, Zurvan watched as she removed the empty quiver from over her shoulder slowly, wincing slightly, and leaning to retrieve her water. Bringing the target back, Zurvan noticed that several of the arrows were split in half by another arrow. Some arrows were split at least three times down the middle. He studied her remarkable skill, unable to comprehend why she had such a talent.

"How are you able to do this?" he asked firmly, as a flicker of disbelief flew across his eyes.

"I have a lot of bad memories," Aoh replied, after swallowing a large amount of water.

Moving her hand towards the top of her bow, she winced and gasped loudly, feeling a burning pain across her hand. Several of her fingers were cut across the skin, revealing red flesh trailing streams of dark colored blood. The droplets falling onto the grass like red rain with throbbing intensity.

"Ow… Ow. OW! Stop!" Aoh screamed each time a medicated swab touched her hand.

She placed the knuckle of her other hand in-between her teeth, trying to bite down each time the pain struck. The silent servant stopped each time Aoh cried, gently holding her lower arm with one hand and keeping the medicated swab in between her fingers. Dipping the swab in the oil again, slightly soaking it, she hesitated while barely touching Aoh's skin, trying to the clean the intense wound.

"OW! Stop! Stop it!" Aoh cried.

"Stop," Queen Huriye ordered, coming into the room very slowly.

The servant stopped, removing herself and allowing the queen to take her seat. Aoh turned and saw the queen approaching, rubbing her face with her hand, briefly trying to avoid eye contact.

Queen Huriye sat down and looked at the cuts across Aoh's fingers, shaking her head.

"What have you done to yourself now?"

Taking medicated swabs, the queen soaked them, tossing the old ones to the side. Aoh held out her hand, noticing the bleeding had stopped but the redness remained. Even the slightest movement irritated the wound.

"Aoh, what am I going to do with you?" Queen Huriye asked with a heavy sigh.

She applied gentle pressure to the wounds, while using her other hand to squeeze Aoh's wrist. The pain struck full force, causing Aoh to bite into her lips, wincing deeply.

"Zurvan told me how well you did today," the queen announced, changing the topic.

Aoh didn't speak, watching the queen gently rub the oils across her wounds. The squeezing around her wrist seemed to have lessened the pain, but only slightly. As she cleaned the wounds, Aoh could hear her wheeze with each breath. Glancing at the queen's hands, barely visible under the fabric, she noticed the color of her skin had returned.

"What are these bad memories that you have?"

Aoh looked away, staring at the large mosaic image across the room that stretched the length of the wall. Queen Huriye tightened her grip on Aoh's wrist as the pain began to strike up her arm to her shoulders.

"You shouldn't be out of bed so soon," Aoh replied, staring at the mosaic.

"I'm fine now. Thank the gods," she replied calmly. "Marduk's return will be coming once again just as soon as I can be wed. But Aoh, please, be open with me. Are these memories about what happened to your family?"

Aoh didn't speak, but allowed the mosaic to distract her, bringing out her imaginations.

"If something is bothering you, you can tell me," the queen prompted.

Aoh exhaled and replied lowly, "I can't tell you this."

"Well…if you change your mind, I will listen. I will always listen to you."

The door suddenly opened as a flushed guard came forth, holding a scroll tightly in his left hand.

"So, there are twenty of them," she stated with a heavy wheeze, reading the names off the scroll quickly. Her eyes shifted as she took small steps to the side, trailing her finger over the names. "Tell me something good. What have you found out from them?

He hesitated for a moment and then answered, "They claimed that they were following a small group who were sighted within their city. They lost the group somewhere in the desert."

"No doubt they wouldn't admit to spying. Any of them generals?"

"Unfortunately not, my queen. In fact, less than half are soldiers."

"Of course. Fortune can't smile upon us too often now, can it?"

She rolled up the scroll quickly.

"Have you heard them talking amongst themselves?"

"Regrettably, no. They remain silent. How do we proceed?"

"Yes, that is the question, isn't it? What to do with them? Egypt will realize they're missing even if they are not worth a trade, however…"

"Should we bring them-"

"No. I don't want them removed."

"Perhaps they mean us no harm," he suggested.

"How would you know that?" she snapped.

"I would think if they did, they-"

"Why wait until they have studied the palace from afar long enough to, then, prompt an unexpected attack after they escape? They are not dimwitted."

"My queen, even if they were to somehow breach the palace, they will never get to you. They don't know a way in or out. It's a giant labyrinth, in their eyes."

"I don't want to risk that happening, regardless how slim it may seem. I would rather die than allow that to happen. I do not want a single unwanted guest in my walls ever again."

She hesitated, looking out her window, rubbing her fingers over her mouth as she exhaled deeply.

"We could let them go," he suggested.

Queen Huriye shook her head silently in disagreement.

"It would lure Egypt into a false sense of security," Zurvan spoke, walking in from the corner of the room.

"I was thinking of making a statement," Queen Huriye agreed.

It was obvious she was not going to let them go. She wasn't going to let them live either. Which meant I had no choice…

20

I knew what my decision would cost me. Just as I knew what would happen if I didn't make this decision.

I waited until nightfall, when I knew I would be able to leave the palace without being caught. Taking my bow and quiver of arrows from my room, draped in dark fabrics to cover my head and mouth, I escaped from my balcony following Tyrgnn's steps.

As I climbed down, I allowed my mind to free itself to the night as each breath I took was through instinct. The only thoughts that repeated in my mind were getting to the compound and freeing the Egyptians.

Aoh remained in the shadows as her quiet steps slipped across the ground. She was hunched over and constantly moving her eyes around the entire compound and up the side underneath the large overhang. It was made mostly of wood that had seen many prisoners and needed severe repair.

Staying low, using both hands to move forward, she listened to the heavy steps of guards above her. She moved in unison with their movement, carefully shifting her weight around the thick poles, as she followed the wooden fence and came to the side.

Glancing upward, she noticed the guard was not at his post as expected. She quickly made her way through the small tunnel where she could see at the metal gate the group of Egyptian men. Some slept on the floor while others remained awake, pacing silently. Startling Aoh, the man whose face was previously covered in dried blood walked in front of the gate, leaning downward, clutching the metal bars with his rough hands.

"Who are you?" he asked firmly.

Removing the cloth from my mouth, I looked at the gate and recognized the lock as the same ones used in the palace. I grasped the lock with both hands, turning, wincing slightly at the long groans from the metal. The rest of the prisoners slowly emerged, baffled. With a shove, I felt the lock open fairly loudly, like a grunt.

"I'm a peasant from Egypt. I'm going to free you," Aoh responded hastily.

His firm eyes narrowed, watching Aoh strain herself to pull the door open. Moving both hands he grunted, using his strength to pull the door free from the locks.

"What is going on?"

"Who is she?"

Hearing the sounds of several footsteps above them, Aoh quickly shushed them, remaining still.

"Who is she?"

"What is going on?"

"All of you, be silent," the man ordered between his teeth.

"You do not tell us what to do. It's because of you we got into this situation."

"They are going to execute us, Laggus."

"The fact is, you should have not been trusted by the pharaoh. You know nothing of tactics. General Sefkh would not have-"

"Do you want to get caught?" Aoh snapped, viciously interrupting them.

The sounds of the footsteps suddenly stopped. All the men raised their eyes to the ceiling and listened, quieting their breaths. Removing her hands from the gate, Aoh slowly stepped back and heard a slight shift in the movement above her. Taking another step back, she prepared her bow, crutching low. The moment a guard looked down and saw her, she whipped around and released the arrow…striking him in between his eyes. He fell dead before the horn could reach his mouth.

The Egyptian men watched, stunned at Aoh's precision. Hearing the sound of another guard rushing towards her, she grabbed another arrow, waited only a second, and released…striking him in the neck.

"All of you need to follow me," Aoh quickly whispered.

The men looked to each other, confused and unsure, whispering over each other with confusion. Their voices gaining volume, complaining and pointing fingers angrily.

Aoh turned and noticed they weren't following her, and repeated firmly, "Follow me. Now."

Using the palms of her hands, she balanced herself through the small space in the narrow tunnel, feeling her toes cramp every time she tried to reposition her feet.

"Enough," the man who had been addressed as Laggus grunted, just loud enough for the rest of the group to fall silent.

"We don't listen to you," one of the Egyptians argued.

"Pharaoh put me in charge."

He looked at Aoh waiting for him, and quickly spat, "Do as she says."

One by one, the men followed him as Aoh led them outside. She waited for a brief moment, seeing that the top of the towers was were empty of any guards, which could only signify that they were on their way down the stairs to the lower levels.

Noticing Aoh stop, Laggus whispered, "Which way?"

Aoh hesitated from answering, unconvinced that all the guards were away from their current post. As the man attempted to move slightly forward, Aoh shoved him back. Her intuitions were correct and one guard walked over to the edge of the tower, looking in the direction of the quiet desert. He pulled his sword from its sheath, looking at his reflection in the blade and rubbing his hand over his face, feeling the scars across his skin. Aoh remained still, keeping her hand against the man's defined chest, staring at the guard as her heart rose to her throat.

"Will you just leave like you're supposed to?" Aoh said impatiently under her breath.

I don't know how long the guard lingered at the tower before he grew bored and left to join the first round of guards in the lower levels. Once the top of his head vanished from sight, I ordered the captives to keep low and follow me. We dashed underneath the ledge following the curve to where the horses were tied to posts.

Entering the stable, a guard came rushing towards us. I drew my bow, killing him instantly, and prepped my bow a second time as another guard came. I killed him as well. Each man took a horse and, without hesitation, we turned towards the direction of the desert, following the slope downward, kicking up the sand and dirt into the air.

Riding away from the compound a safe distance, Aoh pulled the reigns of the horse violently, alarming the beast and slowing it down dramatically. Seeing her pull back, Laggus whistled over to the other men as they pulled their horses back in response.

"No, you need to keep going," Aoh ordered.

"I'm not leaving until you return my stone," Laggus said firmly.

Aoh winced, confused, "What stone?"

"The stone you found outside the compound belongs to me."

Aoh looked down at her arm, rolled up the thick sleeve, and found the stone tied around her wrist. Untying it, she held it gently between her index and middle fingers trying to read the name on it, unable to decipher it.

Handing it to him, Laggus said calmly, "Gavril. My brother's name. He died protecting me."

Taking the small object, he tied the loose ends around his right wrist.

"I carry him with me. His memory gives me the strength to fight."

"His name does not sound Egyptian. And you are Laggus?" she asked, able to study his appearance carefully for the first time.

"Yes."

She nodded.

"I am Aoh."

"Egyptian blood flows through our veins as with our father's. For we are and we are not Egyptian, as are you."

Aoh looked down at the reigns wrapped around both hands, unaware of the blush that had spread across her face.

A strange feeling came over me. A feeling I hadn't felt before but knew one day would find me unsuspectingly. Laggus barely gave me time to process what I was feeling, already prepared with a question I saw coming.

"What is an Egyptian peasant doing in Babylon?" Laggus asked, curious.

"What are Egyptian men doing in Babylon?" she asked in response with a quip.

Laggus refused to answer her. It was as though he didn't know how to react to being questioned. Tired of waiting and feeling her blush grow a deeper shade of red, Aoh bit her lips together and pulled the reigns back on her horse, startling it once again.

"What are you doing?" Laggus asked immediately.

"Going back."

Aoh turned her horse around, wrapping the reigns around her hands several times, feeling her body shift with the horse's movement.

"You won't return to Egypt, yet you free its people?" he asked coldly.

"I can't leave. Not yet," Aoh explained.

"Why?"

I couldn't tell him the truth. Even though my mind kept commanding me to. Just as it was commanding me to look at him. Looking at him lit my body afire and froze time all at the same time. I found myself unable to speak, my tongue suddenly solid as stone and my heart pounding as loudly as a drum.

"If you keep stalling, you'll all be caught before the sun rises," Aoh explained. "Keep going, you'll find several landmarks. Stay to the left of all of them and you will find your way back. As soon as I am finished here, I will return to Egypt."

Pulling her horse, Aoh continued towards the direction of Babylon. One by one, the Egyptians ordered their horses, loudly kicking up the sand and dust behind him. Laggus watched as each man followed the other, waiting for the last man to follow behind. After the last man controlled the wild horse forward, Laggus glanced at Aoh one last time, watching him from her horse, still in the breeze sweeping around her, twirling the sides of her clothing and loose strands of her hair.

There was something unspoken in his lips. A gratitude of some kind as he nodded ever so slightly and left, following the others. I watched them as they fled into the desert, disappearing into the night and unable to stop myself thinking of those intense eyes that spoke so clearly to me.

21

Turning back, Aoh caught sight of several men on horses rushing towards her, loudly. Pulling the reigns back, the horse stopped. Rubbing her fingers over the leather, she watched as they came to a halt before her, dressed in armor and weapons at their waists.

Aoh followed the soldiers down the hallway, hearing their hard steps behind her. In the midst of their steps, she could hear Queen Huriye's frantic voice echoing off the walls. The throne room doors slammed open, startling the queen at first. Half dressed, her long hair was tied loosely over both shoulders. Upon sight of her, Aoh's heart sank, remaining still as the soldiers roughly pulled her forward.

"Aoh..." Queen Huriye gasped, with worry painted across her face.

She rushed to embrace her, burying her heavy perfume into Aoh's shoulders and chest.

"What happened to you?"

"She has been caught and brought to you for a serious act," the tallest of the soldiers explained, as the sounds of another door opened and closed.

Zurvan and two of the queen's record keepers entered the room, donning loose robes. Upon seeing what was occurring, Zurvan ordered them to leave.

"For what?" Queen Huriye asked, confused.

"She released the captured Egyptians from the prison compound and killed several guards in the process."

Queen Huriye's eyes flickered like lightning across the walls. The bold color in her eyes shrunk into the pits of her black pupils. She released her embrace and took a step backwards, nearly tripping over the long train behind her.

"My queen-"

"Get out," Queen Huriye interrupted coldly. "I want all of you out! Out, now!"

The soldiers bowed and turned around, following each other out the heavy doors as Zurvan took a side step backwards.

"Not you Zurvan!" the queen ordered.

Turning around, he entered the room, walking between the fading glow of moonlight, drawing his arms behind his back. Aoh remained silent, listening to the queen chase the soldiers out of the room and slamming both doors behind them. The echo hovered over the room like a fog.

Aoh's eyes watched Zurvan as he continued to the right side, hearing the sounds of Mylittia's feet tiptoe across the smooth floor. She peered from behind the largest pillar silently, seeing Aoh in the center of the room. Chills ran up and down her body, trembling as she placed her fingers to her tender mouth.

"Aoh..." Queen Huriye whispered. "Please...tell me this isn't true. Tell me this is some sort of mistake or plot to be rid of you."

"I'm sorry but I can't," Aoh replied.

Queen Huriye walked past her, quickly pulling her long train behind her, constantly trying to keep her hair smooth. However, the more she ran her fingers through her curly locks, the more unsatisfied she was with its outcome.

"You purposefully released Egyptians from my compound and killed my people?"

"They were not all Egyptian," Aoh corrected.

"They fight for Egypt," Queen Huriye barked.

She began to pace in front of her throne, tears starting to hover over her eyelids as she clasped her hand over her mouth.

"Please, try to help me understand why you did this?" Queen Huriye begged. "What was going through your mind? What happened to you?" she asked.

"Because…I am Egyptian," Aoh replied.

Now the truth was out. And I could tell that nothing could have prepared any of them for it. Not even Zurvan.

"So, you mean to tell me after I cared for you these six years… you found it within yourself to hurt me like this? You had no problem breaking my heart after everything I have done for you?"

"Egypt-"

"Egypt… Please, tell me you were not some spy all these years. Please, tell me all these years were real. Please, Aoh."

"Egypt is my home. I was born there. It always will be my home no matter where I go…"

Zurvan's eyes glanced from Aoh to the queen as he watched her weep.

"I love you, Queen Huriye," Aoh gasped. "I love you. And I love Mylittia."

Mylittia wept aloud, wrapping her arms around the pillar.

"Please, tell me this isn't happening. Please…please, tell me this is some sort of a horrible dream. Some nightmare. Some punishment."

Queen Huriye rubbed her eyes dry, and then her mouth.

"And now…what do you expect me to do?" she asked.

"I will gladly leave Babylon and never return, for my actions are unforgivable," Aoh answered.

"No," Mylittia interrupted, entering the room. "Mother don't send her away. Please."

The queen began to growl as her hands tightly gripped the knobs on both ends of the throne.

"Mother-"

Queen Huriye released a horrid scream, interrupting her

daughter from speaking. Zurvan watched as the princess gently raised both hands and took two steps backwards.

"When I took you in, I did so because I believed that you were more than just an orphaned child of the desert. More than just a child... But I can see now that I was wrong. So very wrong. Zurvan was right about you from the beginning. I shouldn't have brought you here and now...I must do something I never dreamed I'd ever do."

"I'm sorry that my actions upset you. I'm sorry that I disappointed you, but-"

"Don't speak!"

"Your hatred for Egypt has no just cause," Aoh explained. "They have done nothing to you, or your kingdom."

"They are vain, cruel people with nothing but greed and self-love!"

"Every kingdom is vain, full of greed, self-love, and cruel people. Just because Egypt did not choose you to be their queen those years ago, does not mean you have to wipe them from the surface of the Earth."

"How do you know about that? Who told you that?"

Mylittia's wet eyes shifted to Aoh immediately. Aoh glanced at her, and then quickly withdrew her sight, choosing to stare at the Marduk statue hiding in the far left corner of the room.

"I found out reading...in the library. I put the pieces together... It wasn't that hard to," Aoh lied, feeling her stomach turn sour.

"They could have spared me years of pain. And they chose to look out only for their own."

Queen Huriye looked at Mylittia, barely able to stand straight. She leaned forward, wet-eyed, constantly struggling to breathe.

The princess slowly moved her lips and silently begged, "Please."

Queen Huriye glanced to Zurvan who hadn't muttered a syllable. Her eyes pierced through him.

As though reading her mind, he rolled his tongue over his dry lips, "Spare her, my queen."

I could not believe what I was hearing.

"If it weren't for her, your daughter, the princess, Babylon's future would not be here. Spare her."

"Alright," Queen Huriye whispered with a nod.

She released a heavy sigh, rubbing her hands over her eyes again, looking at the trails of tears on her thin fingers.

"Aoh is forthwith banished from Babylon. She must leave immediately."

22

I survived the desert once before and I had to do it again.

Aoh gently tucked the scroll she dug up from the potted tree into the small bag. The directions she drew as a child remained legible. Seeing the bow in the seat, she tucked it over her shoulder and packed her quiver with several arrows, mentally counting each of them.

She glanced over her shoulder, seeing the soldier at her bedroom door keeping watch. The last thing she grabbed was a blanket from the bed, with a lingering sweet scent. Tying everything together, she made her approach to the door when the soldier moved and Zurvan appeared.

Slightly startled, Aoh moved a step back. He did not speak to her but, gently moved aside and allowed her to exit safely.

"Thank you, Zurvan," Aoh acknowledged. "For everything."

I left the palace feeling nothing. I wasn't sad. I wasn't happy. I wasn't mad. I was leaving a world so few would ever see to return to the desert. My last thought was Mylittia and what would become of her. This time I wasn't going back alone. I felt an invisible weight pulling me with each step. My friend returned flying above me, as though making sure I didn't stray far from the pull. I was returning home. I was going back home.

Even if I didn't carry water, I knew where to find it. Even if I didn't carry food, I knew where to find it. A heavy amount of guilt overcame me during the first night alone. I huddled under a quick shelter I made with tree limbs and heavy rocks. I couldn't close my eyes. I slept with my bow and arrow prepped under my arms, tucking my hands under the side of my face, looking out from inside the tight space. I breathed heavily, thinking about what I did, somehow able to accept it while hating myself for it. I knew that if I didn't help them escape, they would have been killed.

I wouldn't have been able to live with myself knowing I could have done something and refused to. This, I know I can live with. Time assures me that I will be able to live with it. Queen Huriye may never forgive me for it, but I forgave her. I did the moment she banished me. She didn't understand, she couldn't understand. Forgiveness isn't something she was going to learn.

On the second night I was unsure how long I slept before being awoken by a noise. I heard a loud shrieking echo, like the sound of a dying animal. Taking my bow, I rose to my feet, listening carefully. When I heard it again, I left the protective hole. Listening, I heard it once more, followed by a loud roar. I followed the direction I heard the sounds, walking slightly uphill. I climbed the small peak and, upon reaching the top, I saw nothing but miles of fire.

In the midst of the large wall of flames, I heard the screaming. I bore witness to men in uniform slaughtering an entire town of people, burning every last bit of them. I left...refusing to sleep that close to such horrors, traveling all night and into the next day until my eyes couldn't stay open anymore and I succumbed to sleep.

The map I drew remained with me, bringing me back to memories I had tried to forget. I was counting the days it took me to cross the desert, reaching the very landmarks I remembered several years ago. By the sixth day, after crossing the first small mass of palm trees where I first drank from, I could just see the outlines of Egypt behind the Nile River.

I wished I could have seen the smile on my face. It must have been so bright that the sun itself was jealous. The first thing that overcame me was not the sight or sounds, but the smell. The smell of animals... For, as I entered my homeland, I was welcomed by a shepherd and his flock of goats. He was no more than ten years old, carrying with him a large stick, calling out to the goats who trotted together in their group forward.

Where I once lived, was now a larger part of a new home with a new family living inside. I could just hear the muffled sounds of children on the other side of the door. Across from my old home, I noticed the same thing.

One home was now extended into two. I didn't recognize one face I saw passing them, like a foreigner in an unknown land. All of them were people, working and living, but no one I knew. I was taken aback by them. I hadn't seen people who looked like me in years. They were unlike the faces of Babylonians. I noticed the temple remnants contained cracks in the walls, but the priests remained dedicated to the gods.

Noticing the sun was going to set in an hour or so, Aoh knew she had to find somewhere to sleep. Seeing two women of similar age coming by with baskets full of bread, Aoh stopped them, asking for where she could spend the night. Both pointed in the direction of the lodge not far from a group of women hiding in the shadows. Two men passed with drinks, stopping to look at her before moving on, with their dogs following behind.

Aoh went to the lodge, trying to keep her mouth covered. Her sense of smell was being overpowered by the odors of so many living so close together. Having been away for so many years, she was no longer used to it, and breathing it in was making her sick to her stomach. She didn't need to knock on the wooden door as it was opened immediately by an elderly man, standing all gray and white with dark eyes over skin the same color as hers.

"Excuse me, sir. May I spend the night here?" she asked.

He didn't answer me. He raised an eyebrow, unfazed by my request, looking down at me quite curiously.

The inn keeper studied Aoh, confused by the bow she carried on her back and how clean her hands were that she tried to hide underneath the wool cloak.

Eventually he answered, raising a hand, "Yes. If you can afford it."

Aoh tugged her pouch of coins from her side, trying to hide the bag from his eyes and emptied it into his wrinkled and worn hand. A hand that had easily held dozens of tools throughout his lifetime. Seven coins slipped out, shinning in the fading sunlight. He looked at the money, noticing it was not common instantly.

Picking just one piece from the pile, he showed it to Aoh and asked, "Where did you come across this?"

"It's all I have. A kind man gave it to me while wandering the desert," Aoh replied.

With a nod from the inn keeper, she entered, greeted by the smell of something sour cooking over the fire in the corner of the room. Closing the door, he pocketed the money inside a pouch on his left side.

"You must be hungry if you've been in the desert. Help yourself," he instructed, showing Aoh the table where some kind of unrecognizable meat was just prepared.

Aoh nodded, taking off her cloak and bow, putting her bag near her feet and sitting down. He watched her as she took a small piece of the meat and began to eat with a slight struggle. Her cheeks rolled and her teeth tugged with each bite.

The meat wasn't tender, but very rough and chewy. It was slightly overcooked and had a horrid smell to it. Perhaps it was from a spice he used.

"Where did you come from?" the innkeeper asked.

"Down there," Aoh replied, pointing in the direction of her old home.

He looked with confusion.

"My family used to live there. I got separated from them when the town was attacked."

"That was easily six years ago when that happened. Have you been alone all that time?"

Aoh didn't answer him, trying to swallow the meat without choking.

"Uh huh…" he murmured, noting her persistence in refusing to answer him.

"Did - do you know what happened? Did anyone survive?" she asked, softly.

"There were many families who escaped just before the attack, fleeing into the city where the pharaoh's soldiers were ready. We don't know how many we lost that night. The families that fled to the city stayed there and people from other towns came here to start anew. This was just one of several that were attacked. Since then, the pharaoh has been preparing in case a need for war would arise. For six years we've kept them at bay, but they have been lingering at our borders, destroying smaller towns in the desert."

Aoh nodded listening.

"When you're finished, I'll show you where you'll be staying the night," the innkeeper continued. "Then tomorrow I suggest you find a way to pay for another night."

23

The next morning, Aoh awoke early from the sounds of goats and sheep followed by shepherds and children. Opening her eyes, staring at the hard, low ceiling, she glanced to her left and at the window, seeing shadows passing in the small cuts and holes of the shutters. She sighed heavily, forcing herself up off of the straw bed, feeling her back crack with the slightest turn and movement of her arms.

After getting dressed, she tucked her belongings under the corner of the uncomfortable bed. Walking the streets of the town, she felt overcome by the amount of people present. Men, women, children, farm animals, guards. All of whom bumped into each other gently, greeting each other, and continuing on their way.

She noticed charred remains of several homes, new paths dug while old ones forgotten. The heavy odor of animals was enough to chase her away. Following the long paths out of the town, she entered the capital city and immediately was welcomed by a more familiar world. She looked around, smelling all kinds of different spices and perfumes pleasing to her senses.

The foul smells of animals and workers could not reach the realm of the rich city. Everywhere she turned someone was trying to sell her something, presenting what they owned in their hands and organized in woven baskets. Men and women alike wore white clothes over their skinny, healthy bodies and leather sandals on their feet. Some women donned expensive wigs and perfumes, and others simply painted their eyes. Some men wore only skirts with animal skins while others dressed in robes, presenting gifts to the priests for the gods.

The walls of every building were white, glowing in the bright sun. However, the more Aoh observed the city, the more she realized her appearance didn't match those who lived within it. Her garb was far more common among the peasants than the women of merchants and soldiers.

She found a small group of women, gathered together, carrying with them empty woven baskets, just barely under their arms. They were dressed in older linen dresses, nearly covered from head to toe. Attracted by their appearance, she followed them as they walked together in their group, smiling and talking to each as they headed to one of several large wells.

Aoh stopped just at the last home before the well, watching the women work together. Simultaneously, they placed their baskets down and one grabbed the ropes hanging slightly above her from a secure wooden frame. She laughed, unable to grab the ropes in one try as one of the other women helped her. Working together, they pulled, raising the wooden bucket, full of water, to the top of the well.

They worked, filling each basket full of cool water, unaware that Aoh was watching close by. One laughed when she accidentally spilled a little bit of water over the shoulder of another. The water was cold and the other women flicked water back in retaliation with a hardy chuckle.

Aoh heard one of them mention something about shepherds and before she knew it, the group of women had filled all of their baskets with water. Together they left the well, making their way down the hilly path, kicking up the sand and dust with their ragged, over worn sandals to meet the shepherds tending their flocks.

Several men gathered round their flock of soft and adorable sheep. The sheep called out to each other in their animal language while two to three young boys, no older than ten, sheared some with care. With one swoop of a sharp blade, they cut away the warmth of sheep's wool that would later be sewn and made into cloaks. Using similar tools, they cut away the hardened clay and mud from the hooves with hard taps.

The children worked together, diligently, as the sheep resisted each time they were taken. The men called out to the women by name with smiles on their sweated faces. Taking wooden cups, the men drank the cold water as the women filled their jugs made of animal skin, hanging just over their shoulders.

One of the men, speaking with whom – in Aoh's opinion – was the prettiest of the group, nodded towards her. The woman turned around and saw Aoh watching them; both exchanged a confused expression. Aoh started to leave when they called out to her.

"You there! Turn around! You there!"

Aoh looked back and saw the two of them waving their hands forward. Pulling her long hair to her left shoulder, Aoh walked forward, passing the other women and shepherds, trying to make her way through the large flocks of sheep. Aoh stopped just on the other side of the flock, nearly stepping on the smallest lamb that continually ran in between older sheep.

Stopping, she looked at the man and woman who had the same colored eyes and intrigued smiles. Up close, she saw that his body had fading scars revealed between the linen fabrics, and her neck and shoulder had never fully healed from a horrible animal attack.

"What is it that you need?" the man asked, drinking some more of the cool water, and then wiped his mouth roughly.

"Nothing," Aoh answered.

"It seems to me that you need something, why else would you be watching?"

"I was only…wondering if I could perhaps help these women in gathering water for you and your flocks."

"We also give water to workers in the fields and the city," the woman explained with a half amused chuckle.

"I don't see why someone as young as she would want to be a water maid," another women commented, as she and two others filled the watering trough for the sheep.

"She looks as young as yourself," the woman next to her replied with a tender smile.

"Exactly why she should be elsewhere. Like…on the lap of some general."

Her snarky remark dug into Aoh like a knife. The woman glanced to the shepherd and shook her head side to side, trying to pull rough ends of her long braided hair away from her eyes. He placed a hand on her shoulder and looked to the other shepherds who refused to acknowledge the situation.

"We could use the help. Two more hands will spare us two more trips to the well," the kindest and oldest of the women added, as she gently wiped the eldest shepherd's mouth dry with a cloth. He, in turn, smiled and kissed her upon her cheek.

"That is, if she can carry the weight without slowing us down."

Aoh looked at her as the grin on her rounded face spread. She was the only woman in the group who painted her eyes in attempts to distract the fact she smelt like the desert. Her eyes were tainted with a false sense of confidence that she could not fill, no matter how many cruel remarks she made about others.

"Don't be unkind. She's offering to help us," the older woman interjected, walking forward, rubbing both of her hands clean of sand and dirt.

"I'm sure your inquiring as to payment. Make no mistake, we are not going to offer what a mistress makes in one night."

It was no surprise that, although the women allowed me to help them, they did not welcome me with open arms. Even the kindest of the group had her allegiances with the rest of the women, but she did teach me some tricks, like how to walk steadily and hold heavy amounts of water without spilling any.

From what I could understand, they were all sisters by blood and marriage. I was of no relation to any of them. If anything, I was simply there to help and nothing more. At times, they hardly acknowledged my presence. Carrying on with their lengthy conversations, undeterred by how many times they were repeated while I followed close behind, mirroring their movements in silence.

I felt blessed to, at least, have something to do with my time. I was able to make a small amount of silver and gold that I had hoped would perhaps be the beginnings of my new life. That is, if it weren't for the rates of the lodge. The work was nothing short of difficult, considering I had never carried more weight in my life.

When I wanted to save the money I made, I'd spend the night trying to sleep under a nearly clear sky of stars while my back and arms ached in beats, simultaneously pulsating with my heart. When I couldn't sleep on the bed, I climbed to the top of the roof to look at the sky, staring at the stars like I've done since childhood, until my eyes would grow tired and I'd fall asleep.

The nights were unusually quiet in the town. Not a sound. Not even from the young man, now grown, playing the flute. Perhaps he, too, was lost, like my family that night. Perhaps they were watching over me from the skies after they made their way passing judgment and entered the eternal fields.

Her darkened eyes lifted from the back of the horse's head to the tall, overpowering tops of the white palace, now grey in the darkness. Raised by dozens of decorated pillars and columns painted with the names and stories of Egypt, it was the grand symbol of all power. The top of the palace looked as though it could touch the sky.

Her heart dropped as she became overwhelmed, shrinking in the presence of the palace with each step the horse took, coming closer to the marble steps and large stone doors. The roaring fire pits outlined the path, creating shadows against the walls, crackling the wood into ash. She could hear the calming sounds of insects hiding in the small gardens and the echo of bubbles from fish reaching the surface of the Nile River. Though, the clop-clop of the horses ridden by the stoic soldiers escorting her was a constant distraction from the serene ambiance.

From the nearest balcony, the pharaoh looked down upon her, watching her every shift and gleam as though she were a goddess entering his domain. His hands remained on the smooth stone surface, as he leaned forward, watching the doors behind her close, shutting out the rest of Egypt from his realm. A solemn breeze swept past him, gently swaying his cloak against his body, casting a shadow on the wall behind him. The wall depicted Egypt's victory over a barbaric kingdom, complete with an array of chariots and archers.

From the door behind him, he heard the sounds of rough sandals against the floor and the shuffle of leather armor rubbing against linen and skin. In the dim shade of the doorway, the man in the leather armor entered and came to the pharaoh's side, entering the faint light of the fires, feeling the warmth around his body.

From the hallway behind him, florists worked diligently, replacing the flowers from the day before with fresh ones, plucked tenderly from the bountiful land. Each flower burst in color and scent, ranging from cornflowers, chrysanthemums, and lilies, to lotuses. The scents swirled around him, as he became lost in her presence. He beheld a woman he saw as rivaling Hathor in beauty for the first time from his palace. A treasure, that no amount of flowers could overpower.

Without taking his eyes off of the woman, as she and her escorts disappeared into the grand entryway, he spoke to the man beside him.

"Laggus."

"Sir," Laggus replied.

"I need you to find someone to protect Daimina. I want them to pretend to be her personal servant. But by no means are you to tell Daimina, nor anyone, of this conversation."

Narrowing his youthful eyes, the pharaoh turned to the older man he trusted.

"This is our secret and we will take it to our graves," the pharaoh ordered. "You are a man who has seen Egypt from outside of these walls. I trust you to find someone like you. Someone loyal, strong, and devoted with a sustainable amount of compassion. Will you do this for me? Will you accomplish this task?"

"Yes, my king. If I can find her, I know exactly who can take this task."

24

The sun was hot the following day, as many sat in the shade of tents and hid in the corners of buildings. Commoners fanned themselves slowly with large palms and soaked cloths in water to apply to their faces and necks. Every face of every man was tightened in deep frowns of discomfort, hardly speaking as they sat behind their stands of food and small treasures.

Aoh wiped her brow continuously before wrapping the cloth over her head and tugging her hair behind her ears. Keeping her eyelids open was a constant battle as the fatigue grew stronger. She slowly consumed fresh fruit that she purchased with most of her earnings, feeling the sweet and refreshing liquid running down her throat, savoring each bite.

While she feasted, she heard two women just outside the door making their way to the well, prompting Aoh to quickly finish the fruit and follow them. Upon reaching the well, the rest of the women were already preparing to gather the water, sweating profusely underneath their wraps. All of them constantly tried to pull loose strands away from their faces, sticky with sweat beads, consuming most of the water they drew from the well.

As Aoh stopped just before the well, the shepherds and their flocks began to head towards the open land. Their small children followed, making sure the last sheep remained with the flock. Dragging their feet, the children slouched forward, unwilling to work in the heat. They used their sticks to poke the sheep forward, whistling to call their wild dogs to follow. Even the dogs rebelled, wanting to lay in the shade, panting heavily.

"Aoh, we'll need you to go into the city and provide water to the bread maker and incense seller first, and then the instrument maker."

If it weren't for the heat, I would have argued with her and insisted that I provide water to the farmers and well diggers by the Nile River. As frustrated as I was, I did not have the energy to refuse and agreed.

Aoh sighed a heavy breath as the rest of the women looked at her, relieved that they didn't have to go into the city.

"Here."

I looked and saw a small pouch in the incense seller's hand tied with a thin red rope. The color drew me instantly. It was so bold and beautiful, reminding me slightly of the wine Queen Huriye drank.

"For you," he offered kindly.

"I couldn't-"

"As a thank you for coming all the way up here just to give me fresh water. You are most dedicated," he interrupted with a nod.

Aoh hesitated at first, unsure whether or not to take the small pouch of spices but realized he wasn't going to let her leave without them. He was a humble man, even for a seller of spices. She had witnessed him giving spices to several starving children from the town before. Even providing gifts to the temples for families who had nothing to spare.

Hiding a frown of frustration, Aoh took the pouch and said, "Thank you for your kindness."

As she turned to place the bag into a small opening in her dress, she nearly collided with a taller man entering the tent for some quick shade, fanning himself with his hands. Passing him, she lugged the basket under her arm, making her way across the street to the last man before the basket was empty and needed to be refilled.

As she walked, she couldn't resist the sanctuary of shade. She quickly moved in front of a shop to stand under its overhang. Once under the cover of shade, Aoh took the moment to relax, pulling the cloth from over her head and rubbing her hand across her forehead.

Running her hand into the basket of water, she flicked droplets onto her face and wiped it again, enjoying the brief chill before pulling the fabric back over her head and continuing.

"Can you believe the pharaoh? He's allowing them to sneak across our land without doing a thing to stop them. After what they did to the towns, burning them to the ground, killing whole families."

Aoh stopped in her steps, as the basket suddenly slipped down her arm before stopping at her hands.

"Now, look at them. There they sit, across our waters, waiting and, plotting. I am forever grateful to the gods that my family and I were just far enough from the massacre. I don't know what I'd do if I had lost them."

"Massacre? The one six years ago, yes?" Aoh asked, interrupting the conversation.

The two men looked at her with slightly baffled expressions. Neither one answered her question as she looked at them waiting for an answer.

"Six years ago? Yes?" she asked quickly.

"Yes," the taller of the two replied.

"Did anyone survive? Anyone, anyone at all?"

"No one knows. From what I witnessed, they left nothing behind but ashes."

"Who?"

"The Hyksos. How are you not aware?"

"Not aware of what?" she asked.

"The Hyksos came and killed many peasants in several towns before pharaoh's army came and sent them back. They've been sneaking across the Nile ever since, hanging around the lodges and bars at night amid others not welcome," he explained, annoyed.

I don't know if it was the heat or the news that hardened me more. Hearing that name immediately made me think of Tyrgnn and King Khi.

"What is the matter with you?" he snapped.

"I-I-"

"Unless you're going to buy something, leave. You're blocking the only air coming this way today," the shop owner growled.

Aoh nodded several times, walking away, aimlessly, barely able to hold the basket in her sweaty arms and hands. She glanced at the many faces hiding under the only shade they could find, waiting for customers to grace their stand. Aoh blinked several times, feeling the sun constantly pound on her, feeling as though she was nearly glowing while walking down the street. Conversations of those nearby overpowered each other. All of them centered around the pharaoh, the Hyksos, and the travesty they left behind.

She easily avoided a group of guards marching towards her down the street, keeping her head down, while trying to carry the water. She glanced at them when they passed, avoiding eye contact with the prostitutes who seemed to remain at the same location all these years later. The same businesses ran as they usually did, with Egypt's prosperous society continuing without a moment of hesitation.

I couldn't stop thinking of Tyrgnn smiling at me and then the necklace he gave me. I couldn't forget his sweet smile and the glistening of the jewels. The declaration of his love.

Drinking some of her water, trying to refresh herself, Aoh saw an older man to her left waving to her. Shaking her head, Aoh approached him.

"Anything of interest for you today, sir?" asked the nearby tradesman.

"No. Just here for the shade," Laggus answered, unraveling the sash from around his neck.

Taking both hands, he dipped them into the water basin and splashed his face gently.

"On a hot day like today, the pharaoh should not have you patrolling the city streets. Hardly anyone in their right mind will venture into this scorcher today. If they're robbing today, they'll be robbing from their own."

Laggus shook his head several times, sending water droplets into the hot air. Taking the sash, he dried his face, allowing the water to rest in his thin hair.

"Unless the pharaoh has you out here for business other than patrol?" the tradesman inquired.

Laggus didn't answer him, wrapping the slightly damp sash back around his neck. Spitting onto the ground, Laggus asked, "You haven't noticed anyone unfamiliar in the city have you?"

The tradesman shook his head, "Nah. Not that I've seen."

Laggus nodded in response.

"At night that may be a different story."

Shaking slightly, rubbing water down both his arms, the elderly man turned, seeing Aoh standing in his light. Noticing him shake, she placed a wooden cup in his hands and filled it with fresh water.

"Here. Drink this," she instructed gently.

He looked at the wooden cup and then at Aoh. All it took was her nod to reassure him. Raising the cup to his mouth, he drank it quickly, feeling the cool water run down his chin.

"Thank you," he said graciously, keeping his eyes focused on the street, watching every vendor, still shaking.

Taking pity on the man, Aoh filled three empty bowls next to him to the top with water, carefully making sure not a drop hit the sand.

25

As Aoh filled the three alabaster bowls and water jug, Laggus watched her from across the way. He caught glimpses of her in between the fraying ends of the low tent, dropped to provide shade to the long table of fish. Lowering his head to more clearly see her, he watched her small hands keep the basket steady as her calm face remained focused on her action.

He frowned for a moment, observing her carefully as she raised her arms to fill the last water jug, holding the end of the basket near her face. She struggled slightly, the sweat on the palm of her hands loosening her grip on the basket. Just before her grip failed her, the jug was filled and the basket nearly empty.

The man thanked her with a soft nod, reaching to hold her hands. Taking the last of the water, she poured it into her mouth, just barely hydrating her dry lips. She swallowed, feeling the heat burn her outer body as the water soothed her internally. She released a heavy breath, dreading the walk back to the well in the hot sun.

Taking a few steps to the left, Laggus pushed the ends of the tent upward over his head. He noticed Aoh fixing the basket before tucking it under her arm and walking back onto the street, dragging her feet slightly. He gave the tradesman a gold coin for the water he used and followed her down the street, keeping himself at a safe distance.

Aoh sighed heavily as she returned to the well, happy to see more fresh water waiting for her to drink. Dropping the basket, she leaned forward, grabbing the heavy rope and using it to hold herself upward, feeling the fatigue growing worse. She looked out into the distance, seeing two of the women with the shepherds and assuming the others were probably in the fields nearby.

I couldn't help but feel a little jealous, wishing I was in the fields so that I could use it as an excuse to dip my feet into the cool water of the Nile River like I wanted to. I should have spoken when I had the chance…but if I had, then my life wouldn't have taken the turn I never expected…

After taking her third large drink of fresh water, she gathered the cool liquid from the well, waiting patiently in the sun as the rope tugged in her light grip, feeling the water filling the woven basket. She gently applied the knuckles of her other hand against her lips, drying the free droplets of water from dripping down her neck. She heard firm steps against the dirt, kicking up light sand and tiny stones, approach her and then stop before taking another step forward.

"Aoh."

Turning around, she found Laggus approaching her, dressed in his leather armor, carrying a short blade at his waist. Traces of his dark bangs fluttered about his high forehead as whispers of a soft hot wind traveled through them. Taking the heavy rope, Aoh walked over to the opposite side of the well and quickly tied it around the wooden pole, securing it safely. Blinking several times, she cleared her eyes of dryness, unsure as to whether she was looking at the same man she last saw covered in the dried blood of his enemies.

"Laggus…how did you find me here?" she asked, concerned, wincing slightly.

"You said you were returning. There are only two places you would be. I've come to find you for the most serious of requests."

Aoh looked around her, quickly noticing a few men speaking to each other near the well, oblivious to Aoh and Laggus' presence.

Frowning slightly, she asked, "What is it?"

"I need you to protect a young woman at the palace whom the pharaoh seems to have taken a strong liking to."

"What of his wife, the queen, surely she-"

"She knows and as you can imagine…isn't happy. There are many in the palace who will want her dead. The pharaoh has asked me to find someone to protect her by pretending to be her servant."

Aoh shook her head repeatedly, "I'm sorry but I cannot-"

"Betray your people? You've done that before," Laggus interrupted.

"I'm not a soldier like you, Laggus."

"You killed men from a distance with only a bow without hesitation. You are precise and just. No peasant could do what you did. Not one. The pharaoh trusts my judgment and I trust you will protect her. And I am not a soldier."

"No. I won't do it."

"By disobeying me you are disobeying your king."

"A king who should be faithful to his wife," Aoh argued calmly without raising her voice for fear others would overhear their conversation.

Laggus took a step forward, lowering his voice slightly as Aoh's breath trembled unintentionally.

"I'm not going to pretend to understand the lives of royals. I never bothered to because I'll never be one. My duty is to serve the king of Egypt. He has given me this task and I will not fail him. He asked me to find someone to protect her. What better person for it to be than a woman that no one will suspect to be anything more than a servant? Your days in the sun and sand are over. They've been long over."

I knew Laggus was right. I felt as though such since I took that first ride on the back of Queen Huriye's horse. My days in the burning sun, sprayed with the harsh sand, were over.

"Listen to me very carefully. You are to be her very shadow, following her steps. Be like the walls. Watch everyone. Listen to everyone. Know this: once you cross the threshold into the palace, you cannot trust anyone. With no heir yet to the throne, everyone will be clawing for it. Egypt loves their queen and they will kill to keep her queen."

Aoh walked with Laggus through the streets, towards the large palace that was so tall, when the sun began to set the entire city rested in its shadow. She noticed how many of the people in the city watched them as they passed, stopping in the middle of their conversations, their work.

Many nodded to Laggus before continuing with their activity. Some scowled upon the sight of him, grinding their teeth behind chapped lips. Coming to the large doors separating the palace threshold from the city streets, Aoh felt a cool sensation fall over her body. It gave her slight chills, even in the heat, as she waited next to Laggus, listening to the sounds of goats and chickens.

I remembered the last time I saw these doors and what lied beyond them…

When the doors opened, she beheld a sight of white and ivory surrounded by a multitude of bright colors. Every step from the large doors to the palace was off white marble. The entrance to the palace was at the center of two long paths made of white stone with two giant carved lions, laying down facing the city. On both sides of the path were fifteen soldiers standing at attention in their armor, with swords at their sides and spears in their left hand. They stood like silent statues, hardly a bead of sweat upon their skin, able to withstand the intense sun.

Taking a deep breath, Aoh watched Laggus step first into the sunlight, keeping one hand at the handle of his blade and the other on the leather belt around his waist. He winced when a sudden burst of wind whipped sand in his face. Noticing Aoh was not walking next to him, he turned around, finding her standing in the shadow of the large doorway.

Releasing her breath through the small part in her lips, Aoh gently straightened her back and kept her attention focused on the large, white doors ahead of her. She took her first steps, entering the sunlight, now in the realm of the pharaoh. Laggus waited until she stood next to him, gently wincing.

He nodded to her and said close to her ear, "You are about to enter a world very few Egyptians see."

Aoh nodded, responding, "I understand."

Together, they continued down the long marble path, passing both lions. They made their way up the long steps built in between rows of large pillars covered completely in names, images, and stories from top to bottom and painted in bold colors. Laggus pushed the doors open as a rush of scented air overcame Aoh.

Pots of incense hung from the large pillars closest to the doors, burning gently, releasing streams of white smoke into the air before disappearing. The pillars inside the palace were just as decorated as the ones outside, in bolder colors of red, blue, and green with gold embellishments. Walking inside, they passed two rows of the pillars assembled to depict the royal bloodline, passing several more attentive guards entering the center of the large room.

"Wait here," Laggus instructed.

His voice became a faint echo whisking around the multitude of carved faces on the walls. Aoh watched him walk to the left of the large room, disappearing behind the pillars and entering a hallway. Keeping both her arms at her sides, she was unable to control herself from lifting her head and studying the grandeur of the room. Hearing slight sounds of the city outside, she stared at the unimaginably high open ceiling, covered in drawings and carvings of the gods, telling stories and depicting the new pharaoh amongst them.

The colors were vibrant and beautiful, detailing intricate features on every face, including the horses. Each victory in battle unfolded with a life to it, drawn out across several places, wrapping around some of the taller pillars. She wondered if her father was the man behind the exquisite work.

The open room was eerily quiet. She couldn't hear a sound apart from the faint city noises and the wind whispering from outside. It shook the leaves from the tall potted tree tops and swept curtains to and fro like a brush through hair. The jolt of the closed doors opening startled her, causing her to turn to face them.

The young pharaoh emerged, frowning deeply, as he took bold steps towards her, with Laggus following behind, carrying a faience in his right hand. Aoh quickly lowered her head and body to bow, feeling an overwhelming amount of anxiety rattle her nerves. Her long hair dropped over both of her shoulders as she remained low to the floor, staring at the gold sandals wrapped around his feet.

"From this day forth, when you address me or when I enter the room you are to kiss the floor," he instructed seriously.

"Yes, great pharaoh," Aoh responded, forcing her nerves to calm down.

"Now rise," he instructed.

His voice wasn't childlike nor that of an older man. It was strong. Confident.

Aoh rose to face him, noticing he was only slightly taller than herself. The domed crown upon his head reflected every plant and tree surrounding them. His brown eyes were outlined in thick black make-up. His tanned skin matched her own tone, covered in gold cuffs, rings, and smothered in smooth silk. The Eye of Horus attracted her attention immediately, hanging just underneath his collarbone.

"Follow me," he ordered.

Aoh followed the pharaoh with Laggus behind her as they walked to the end of the room and entered three antechambers, where she finally saw, for the first time, the Broad Hall. The ceiling appeared lower than the previous rooms, enclosed and privately hidden. The walls around them were bright and bold in the light, but dark and mysterious in the shade. Rows of plants were placed around the columns made of several variations of granite and quartzite. Three cats laid under their shade of the trees, curling their tails, blinking slowly and purring.

After they entered the room, the doors behind them were slowly closed, leaving Aoh alone with the pharaoh and Laggus. The movement of the doors closing sent a light draft through the room, lifting the bottom of the pharaoh's long robe and cloak, fluttering the tips of the large leaves.

Coming to the back of the room, Aoh saw two thrones, noticing the one on the left was smaller than the one on the right. An array of animal skins laid on the floor before the thrones next to unlit vessels of incense. The endless rows of columns disoriented Aoh slightly as she kept expecting someone to emerge from behind them at any moment. The pharaoh took firm steps towards his throne, keeping the faience against his chest.

Placing his right hand behind his back, Laggus remained positioned to Aoh's left silently, tugging the armor against his chest.

"Laggus told me that I could trust you. I trust he is not wrong," the pharoah explained firmly with calmness in his voice. Aoh glanced at Laggus who simply looked at her and then returned his attention to the king.

"I want you to answer me truthfully. Did you save him and my men?"

"Yes," Aoh replied without stammering.

"Your actions not only saved their lives, but mine as well. They have been ordered to not tell anyone what truly occurred, for your own safety. You have proven yourself strong, and a true servant of Egypt, even if you did not realize it at that moment. I doubt many would have done what you did."

Aoh lowered her head slightly in response.

"What is your name?" he asked.

"Aoh, my king."

"Aoh, whatever your life was before will be no more. The moment you entered this realm you have entered my world. You will now serve me. You will do as I say. You will come to me when ordered to."

He glanced to the left side of the room at the doors she entered, frowning deeply as he cleared his throat.

"You will come to find that Daimina is not Egyptian. I wanted to tell you so that when you saw her you would not be surprised nor judgmental. I believe that under different circumstances she would have been born an Egyptian, but the plans of the gods are never written in stone. Or, so I am told."

He glanced at Laggus, turning around. He took a step closer, not to overpower Aoh, but to speak lower. Every word that came from his young mouth was clear without any signs of confusion or doubt. He clasped his hands firmly to each other behind his straight back.

"I need you to protect her from anyone who intends to harm her. Whether it's my guards, my soldiers, my priests, my vizier, or my wife. You are to protect her while pretending to only be her servant. Nothing more. You are not to tell her anything of this. I do not wish her to know. Therefore, you will be dressed in servant's clothes, act as a servant to all in this palace, and be treated as a servant. Make no mistake, Daimina is very important to me. I will do what is necessary to keep her safe. I expect you to do the same. Understood?"

"Yes," Aoh replied firmly.

"You are to tell me of any improprieties that occur at all costs, and understand that I am trusting you with her very life. You are to trust no one but myself and Laggus. He will protect you if need be, for be warned that, although you are not a threat to anyone, you will be the closest to Daimina aside from myself. Many will be curious by your sudden presence. They may want to know who you are, threaten you even. But always remember you are to only obey me. At tonight's dinner, you will be introduced to everyone as Daimina's servant. They all know who Daimina is. As much as you feel that this is not a service but a decision that has been made for you, I am grateful for your duty."

"Thank you, great pharaoh. I promise to be her shadow and protect her for as long as I live," Aoh replied, bowing once more.

"Good. Laggus, take her to Daimina's room. There you will find your new clothes and belongings."

"Yes, my king. Follow me," Laggus replied, nodding over to the closed doors.

Aoh bowed once more to the pharaoh and followed Laggus,

keeping her hands folded at her waist. They exited the room and began the trek down the first of many long hallways. As they walked, they passed several guards and other servants whom were tending the gardens and carrying food in large baskets over their shoulders or balanced on their heads.

Laggus lowered his voice, "The palace has two main sections. The outer wall has courts and porticos where Daimina likes to walk through, and the inner contains the king's apartment and the chambers."

Aoh nodded silently in response.

"You will manage to memorize the layout with time. Its best that if you become lost, to not reveal a thing. Not even with your eyes."

Laggus's advice chilled me.

Both the male and female servants wore black wigs, covered in white linen dresses and skirts, with the same expressionless faces and black around their eyes. Aoh studied the hallway, breathing in the fresh air from outside as her steps nearly matched Laggus'.

Every wall and column they passed told stories. Tempted to read them, Aoh watched them for as long as she could before returning her attention to the end of the hall. In silence, they traveled down two more hallways in unison until they stopped at a room.

"This is Daimina's chambers. Your room is in the back. You will be staying in here with her. Your things have been prepared. Remain here, Daimina should be returning shortly," he explained, standing at the open doorway.

"Thank you," Aoh replied quietly.

Laggus nodded and waited until she entered the room before leaving.

26

Entering Daimina's chambers, Aoh found it to be unlike any room she had seen before. The large bed could have easily slept five people, covered in the finest silk bedding. Large incense burners hung near both sides of the bed, surrounded by translucent curtains. The floor had animal skin carpets placed around the bed and at the doorway. Small mirrors, brushes, and hair pieces made of gold and gemstones rested on her desk. The large windows on both sides of the bed let in the hot outside air each time the sky breathed. The small chair against the end of the bed was covered in a clean, sheer dress already prepared for Daimina to wear.

Aoh ran her hands across the bed, feeling the smooth texture in between her fingers, slipping freely like water. She gently picked up the dress, holding it in front of her, amazed by the near nonexistent weight to it, with extraordinary details upon every stitch. Putting the dress gently back down, she moved towards the makeup resting on the golden bureau before moving to the end of the room, finding a narrow doorway to her room.

The room was nothing more than a bed and chair at a table with one mirror and a mid-sized statue of Horus against the furthest side of the room. Though, the walls were made of the same stone as the rest of the palace and there was a narrow window that she could see one of many side entrances to the palace and into the Nile Roaring flames filled a brazier and a curtain covered the doorway. Laying on the bed, the clothing was folded smooth. Just beneath it, a pair of sandals lay waiting for her that already looked used. Aoh quickly changed into her new clothing, placing the semi-worn white linen dress over her body, noticing it to be too long.

Taking the worn sash next to the sandals, she tied it around her waist, picking up one side of the dress just enough for it not to drag across the floor. She slipped her feet into the sandals, tying the straps around her scarred ankles and feeling the irritating material rub against her feet. In the light of the flames, she delicately applied the makeup around her eyes looking into the old mirror.

I could hardly recognize myself.

Aoh couldn't take her gaze off of her reflection in the mirror staring back at the unfamiliar eyes; darkened, beautiful, and mysterious. With no brush at hand, she lifted her hands and rummaged her fingers through her hair, attempting to tame sections left untidy. Her hair still had a sense of smoothness since the last time she washed it in Babylon. The strands were soothing to her palms as she stroked clumps of her hair over and over again.

From outside the window, she could hear the dogs barking amongst each other and then the screech of cats trying to escape them. Turning slightly, she tugged at her sandals, frustrated at the loose straps when she noticed something by the end of the bed. Standing up, she found her bow and a quiver full of arrows.

I felt a strong sense of joy seeing the one thing I owned there. Touching the bow, I felt empowered. A rush of relief. I noticed immediately that most of the arrows were not mine. They were professionally made. Stronger. Durable.

Tucking the bow and arrows under the bed as far as she could, Aoh heard a sound from outside her room. Taking a deep breath, she heard someone enter Daimina's room. Lifting her head, she looked and could see a figure swiftly move towards the bed. Rising to her feet, Aoh lifted the thin curtain and peered into the room, finding a young woman no older than herself with thick black hair, rounded eyes, unfamiliar skin tone, and larger bodily structure standing at the bed.

Aoh stepped out of her room and immediately bowed, startling the young woman.

"My name is Aoh, and I will be your servant," Aoh introduced firmly.

The young woman looked upon me with utter confusion. She was unaware I was present. She raised her tamed eyebrows and attempted to look behind me as though she were expecting another person there.

"My servant?" she spoke baffled.

"Yes. Upon the orders of the pharaoh, I am to be your servant."

She released a disgruntled sound, and shook her head slightly.

"I don't believe I'm deserving of such a gift," she admitted.

Aoh didn't answer her statement, but instead replied, "Would you like me to help you prepare for dinner?"

"Not tonight…thank you."

I remained in my room waiting for Daimina to finish preparing herself for the dinner. I could tell she felt uncomfortable having someone help her, which could only mean that she was not of any royal bloodline. She almost seemed overwhelmed to be receiving a servant, as though she didn't know how to respond to the pharaoh's generosity.

Now prepared for dinner, Aoh followed close to Daimina's side, talking small steps as Daimina's stride reflected that of a graceful ibis. Every so often, when she moved her arms, a slight jingle sound was made from the exquisite bracelets she wore, glistening in the light of the flames. The dress fit her perfectly, fitting her every curve and gently flowing across the floor when she walked. A light sweet scent of flowers trailed behind her.

Following down the long hallway, we could hear the multitude of voices speaking to each other growing louder. The clatter of food being placed blended in with the purring of the cats. My eyes remained in front of me at all times, watching as the back of Daimina's hair bounced when she walked, passing wall after wall of stone and astounding carvings. The long strands of beads in her hair clicked slightly, like her woven jewelry.

Turning at the next hallway, the voices grew louder as it was apparent a legion of men were present, speaking proudly in high tones.

"Laggus," Daimina suddenly said aloud.

Aoh turned her head and saw him standing ahead of them, outside of the dining room as though waiting for her to arrive.

"Daimina. Good evening," he greeted, nodding gently forward.

"Good evening. Has the pharaoh mentioned, that I received a gift?" she asked.

Turning to the side, she revealed Aoh standing with her hands folded at her waist.

It seems Laggus couldn't recognize me either. I could just see this slight shift in his rather stern expression from strict to stunned.

Nodding, he replied, "I'm afraid he did not. You are very lucky to have one. Seems he spares no expense. You are most welcome in the palace."

Aoh nodded in response with a cascading bow.

"I told him many times that I did not need one. I wish he'd listen to me like he does to you. It's not that I'm ungrateful, but I don't want to make things worse. I didn't ask for this..."

"The last thing he would want would be to make things worse for you. Come, he'll be happy to have you at his table tonight. Eat and enjoy yourself," Laggus reassured.

He held out his arm, gesturing for Daimina to walk first. Aoh followed slowly, keeping her face as expressionless as she could, revealing nothing but tightened lips and dark, emotionless eyes.

As she followed down the first of five steps inside, she noticed Laggus remained at the top of the steps from the corner of her eyes. Aoh refused to even take the slightest turn of her head to look at him, following Daimina as she took her seat at the long white table. Aoh remained standing completely still against the wall behind her, feeling all the eyes in the room suddenly turn to face them.

The conversations occurring with several dinner guests slowly began to cease as each person at the table looked at Daimina, who hadn't spoken since entering the room. Her breathing remained steady, underneath the luscious fabrics, linens, and gold, keeping her eyes forward at the wall and focusing on the images between two silent male servants.

Upon seeing her enter the room, the queen bit into the gold goblet she was drinking from at the end of the table, frowning deeply with a stare of wrath. The king's vizier next to her whispered something, barely able to take the goblet from her fingers tightly wrapped around the handle. The very muscles in her throat and head revealed themselves as she focused all of her attention upon Daimina.

The table seated at least twenty people, all of whom nearly looked identical to each other. Priests were garbed in white. Their bald heads reflecting every shiny object in the room. Their skin wrinkled, yet lively as most of them were nearing the end of their lives, except for two. Their eyes were dark like the rest of the ones in the room, including other servants standing against the walls or sitting on their knees, holding trays of food and drink waiting to serve the guests.

Three of the pharaoh's generals broke up the constant white in the room. Even while retiring for the day, they wore their light armor as though anticipating their enemies to somehow leap from under the floors. Their muscles were barely contained by the armor covering their arms, waist, and legs.

At the very beginning of the table, next to the empty seat and to the pharaoh's older vizier, was the queen in all her anger and hate, dressed in a light blue gown, covered in gold and gems from her neck to her bust. Her long hair was weaved with golden strands, braided, and tied. Her makeup was painted so perfectly from the corners of her lips to the last eyelash. She was skinny and tall, a few years older than her husband, with long fingers like spider legs. She never took her eyes off of Daimina. Not once…

A sudden sound, followed by steps revealed the pharaoh as he entered the room, walking to his seat. The entire table rose at his presence as the several cats that were scattered about the room retreated to the dark corners with their pieces of food. Every servant dropped to the floor, kissing it at his presence, alarming Aoh who followed their actions, slightly embarrassed.

The moment he reached his seat, he held out his arms and said loudly, "Please, enjoy the feast I have prepared for you all in announcement of our newest guest."

The silence in the room became as heavy as mud.

Looking to Aoh, he waved a hand forward, "Step forward. It's alright."

Every head and eye in the room turned and, before I could react, I was surrounded by the faces of people I didn't know.

Stepping forward, Aoh nodded and bowed, feeling her long hair fall over both of her shoulders.

"Now, I invite you all to eat and converse. I want no upsetting discussions at my table tonight," he ordered, addressing the room.

The eyes and heads slowly returned to their king in a swift motion. Taking his seat at the table, the servants carrying food rose to their feet and began to serve the room. Each plate and vessel was full, as drinks were poured into the goblets and food disappeared as fast as it was served. The sounds of the plates clattering against the hands and jewelry created a loud atmosphere, nearly drowning out the pleasing sounds of flutes and stringed instruments playing behind the pharaoh.

White smoke from incense burners hovered over the silent guests. No one spoke to each other, taking their meals in their hands. Everyone ate, chewing, swallowing, and tasting such delicacies of fruits, meats, and vegetables. Eyes shifted left and right each time they lifted their goblets as though waiting for someone to be brave enough to begin a conversation. But no one did…

As I watched from the back of the room, I observed the woman I was to serve and protect. Daimina was plain compared to the Queen of Egypt. But in her features, I could see innocence and this sense of unexpected courage. She had this outpouring of kindness and natural love for the king as she'd look at him sweetly between swallowing. He'd sneak glances at her when his queen wasn't looking. The queen's slender hand would crawl across the table to touch her husband's. Daimina was not oblivious to the fact she was an unwanted guest.

For nearly an hour, the room was silent aside from the soothing music and eating. The pharaoh's dark eyes shifted from the right side of the room and then the left... Noticing how no one was speaking. Not one person. Hands rummaged through the baked breads, desiring the consistent fill of red wines and slurping up the pieces of meat they ripped by hand. The lack of conversation lasted far too long...as a result, the pharaoh alarmed the room, slamming the bottom of his goblet onto the table and startling the musicians and resting cats.

"Why is everyone so silent? Why?!" he shouted. "I only asked that no upsetting discussions were to take place at my table. I did not ask for no one to speak at all or...is it that one no one speaks because the words that will spew from your mouths will be upsetting to me?"

No one dared to answer, glancing from their plate to their hands, or glancing from perhaps the table to the wall across from them. The vizier exchanged a look with the queen, who slowly bite into her lower lip and clutched the piece of bread so tightly her fingers were beginning to pierce the insides. Her knuckles turned white and her lower lip began to trail light blood.

"I will not allow such disrespect in my presence any longer! I want to hear some conversations and I want to hear them now! Now!"

Immediately, one of the priests rose from his seat and said, "The feast of Nephthys will be approaching with promise of a glorious full moon. Much to our correct prediction, she will enable you to see in such darkness. Her protection shines brightly on us."

"We have preparations drawn to have the celebrations take place under such light. It will cast shadows of your statues over the rest of the kingdom, reflecting not only your power but influence," another priest chimed in calmly.

"We have debated on the wine and beer, but regardless of the decision, we believe that we will be in full supply."

As the priests continued to address the entire room, excited about the preparations, Laggus leaned against the wall, watching the room as he ate his meal slowly. The largest of the three generals drank heavily from his third goblet full of wine, shifting his eyes onto Laggus like a lightning strike. Both men made eye contact and, when the general broke the bond, his throat swallowed the liquid slowly as he rolled his tongue to the side of his closed mouth as if he were displeased by the taste.

The priest next to him whispered something, glanced at Laggus and then called over the nearest servant. The general mumbled something as he wiped his mouth, smacking the small hands of a servant boy away trying to pour him more wine and scowled him for beer instead. The priest said something between his firm lips, and the general answered him with a roll of his tongue to the side of his mouth again.

"I look forward to what Nephthys will tell me. Perhaps she can inform me how our soldiers are faring in their training. Sefkh!" the pharaoh called from the end of the table.

Sefkh turned to the pharaoh's attention as he was given a goblet of beer.

"Tell me…how are our newest additions to my army doing?"

Taking one large gulp of the beer, he replied proudly, "They are doing very well, my king! They have succeeded in many of the tasks and show great promise!"

"How are my archers?"

"As ordered," Sefkh hesitated and nodded to Laggus, "he and I have selected the most capable men to be archers. They have been given their own bows and arrows, and will be learning how to fight on horseback."

Laggus nodded to the pharaoh silently, in agreement.

"I would like to see them in action. Assemble a practice; I'd like to see what they can do."

"Yes, my king! I will prepare that for you immediately."

"Good. And what of my city? I have heard from several in this room that there have been some problems with thieves as of late," the pharaoh asked, looking again at Sefkh.

"Well…yes, thieves will always be a problem, my king. They are like rats, bearing other thieves constantly for sport."

Several of the priests and the two generals chuckled in response.

Noticing the pharaoh did not share his amusement, he continued, "My skills are for war and training, you see, not for patrolling the city streets."

The pharaoh nodded in response and glanced at his vizier.

"Senmet…"

"Sefkh, the king is aware of what your skills are, but insists that you should be making sure proper men are patrolling the streets and that any reports of thieves be addressed by you to our king. Truth is, many incidents have been going unreported including violence against innocent women," Senmet explained calmly, slowly peeling the skin off of the strip of meat.

Sefkh let out a chuckle along with the generals and replied, "Yes, you are right. We already have the names of several thieves. They will be charged as accused. Truth is, many of the women have not approached us on these matters. However, I do have a suggestion. Perhaps…I could assign someone to watch over them, someone who was familiar with living on the streets? I could then…put a better handle on the situation."

"Are you suggesting someone in this room for such a position?" Senmet asked, intrigued.

"If you know someone who is capable, please, advise me so I can speak to him. I'm sure…he would agree to the task without question."

Another low chuckle followed as Sefkh eyes raised from his drink to Laggus again, like a sharp dagger before returning to his conversation with the generals. The rest of the dinner remained quiet with few conversations taking place. Once the dinner was finished, everyone slowly left the room except for the pharaoh and his queen, whom he ordered to remain with him.

Stomach full, Laggus' steps down the hall stopped when he heard the sounds of someone following close behind. He listened to the light clanking of a sword handle against armor and the shuffle of heavy sandals against the smooth floor. Turning to the right, he saw Sefkh standing behind him.

"Laggus? That was your name, wasn't it?" Sefkh asked, slightly unsure with a crooked smile.

"You know who I am," Laggus stated in response.

"Sorry, it's just that I've seen many soldiers and guards come into my midst. Many come and go, especially after such dinners with royalty. While some are so strong they can soar with Horus, others, unfortunately, aren't cut from the same cloth. You once patrolled the streets, yes?"

"Yes. I did."

"And now you are in here, in the palace. The pharaoh asks you for advice in subjects you are not familiar with. You eat his food, drink his wine and beer. Lavish yourself in his glory. Irresponsible, is it not? Pardon, but what do you possibly know that I do not?"

Laggus watched Sefkh walk over to the wall depicting the pharaoh and his queen. The next one depicted the pharaoh going into his first battle on a chariot with Sefkh as his rider. The images continued showing Egypt's victory over their enemy as the chariots rode with mighty horses, firing arrows and raising their swords. Their enemy lie dead on the field. Many captured and later sold.

"If you are unhappy with my presence, then perhaps you should be doing your duty instead of drowning yourself in pharaoh's spoils," Laggus suggested firmly.

"But that is my duty as general. We bathe in the spoils of war. We…earned…it," Sefkh bit into his words with spite. "You wouldn't know anything about such duties if you couldn't even become a soldier for the crown. You tried and failed how many times?"

"Yet here I am."

Sefkh took several steps forward as Laggus remained still, preparing his hand ever so gently over the handle of his blade. Rolling his tongue in his mouth, Sefkh lowered his eyes and noticed Laggus' rough hand above the handle.

"Even you know that if you were to kill me, you could never

take my place. I have the entire army on my side and they will never follow you into battle. Their actions in Babylon said as much."

Laggus didn't respond to the insult, but stared into Sefkh's eyes coldly. Sefkh smirked widely, purposely slamming his shoulder into Laggus as he passed him.

Suddenly stopping just underneath his image on the wall, smiting Egypt's enemies next to the pharaoh, he commented, "You know there is nothing more pathetic than a street cat who thinks it's a palace cat."

He released an irritating chuckle, continuing down the hallway as Laggus watched him leave.

27

The flames left nothing but destruction in their path, as the bodies of the dead laid across the ground littered with arrows. Their blood flowed across the sand like rivers…

The sounds of people screaming echoed into the night. The sky darkened with arrows, falling like sleet and hail, left nothing breathing in its wake. They came like an unstoppable flood. Killing every man, woman, and child. Their blades soaked in blood… Their hands covered in the dust and sand, throwing stored food into the growing, hungry flames. Their war cries stretched the length of the desert, shaking the Earth beneath their feet.

"Go now! Go! Don't turn back!"

Aoh awoke from her uncomfortable bed the next morning to the sound of a cat meowing by her face. The skinny, long legged feline looked at her, begging for something to eat. Aoh rolled from her side to her back, staring at the ceiling and then at the statue of Horus against the wall.

I couldn't remember the last time I had that nightmare. It was so vivid I could barely prevent myself from crying. If it weren't for Daimina asking for me, I would have cried for countless hours alone in my own misery. My heart nearly broke.

That morning, the heavy scent of the desert swept through the palace, unable to be concealed by the variety of perfumes. The palace was peaceful, as many who were awake silently began their day. Entering the kitchen, separate from the large volume of traffic throughout the palace, she found servants preparing meals. The display of food stretched the length of several tables. She beheld a sight of endless fish freshly caught from the Nile River, roasted goat, and pigeon. Fruit was peeled tenderly and placed in a variety of bowls.

The servants only nodded to Aoh, continuing with their duties in silence. Gathering what food she believed Daimina would enjoy, she left, seeing the servant salting fish in the open windows.

She carried the tray of food up the steps as carefully as she could, watching her steps as she went. Walking, she felt overwhelmed by the high ceilings and endless walls that surrounded her, suddenly visible in the natural light that came in from the open spaces and windows. She paused, touching the wall, while keeping the tray steady with her other hand and allowing her fingers to grace the carved images.

The limestone wall ran smooth against her palm as she trailed her hand across the large story. It unfolded through several images that continued above her. She read the name silently to herself, following the paths of kites taking flight and fish moving in the Nile River. She stopped on the image of the pharaoh standing before craftsman, looking at each one standing next to each other holding their tools. Fixing the tray in both hands, she realized she had gotten lost on her way to retrieve a meal for Daimina and now feared she was becoming even more lost trying to find her way back.

Seeing the outline of a shadow, she took the first few steps forward when the bottom of her dress began to slip and drag slightly again with each step. She stumbled as her feet moved awkwardly slow.

"The new servant."

Looking upward, Aoh saw a tall, thin, bald man dressed in white with darkened linens draped over his shoulders standing in the light that cast his shadow over her. The make-up he applied around his eyes made him look like some sort of luring creature from another world of powerful beings. His voice rose and fell several times as he curled his ring- covered fingers before resting his hands upon the sapphire colored sash around his waist. The white robes flowed about his arms and legs like a winged spirit.

"Yes, you are, aren't you? Having trouble finding your way around the palace, are you?" he asked, studying her appearance.

"It is rather vast," Aoh replied, taking several steps upward.

She wobbled on her last step, feeling the bottom of her dress slide into the small space between her heel and the rough sandal.

"Indeed. There are many rooms, many open spaces, so many places to get lost. You will find your way poor girl."

His eyes fell upon the food Aoh carried on the tray and commented, "Daimina seems to be eating fairly well."

Aoh didn't respond to his comment, continuing forward.

"I should have properly introduced myself last night, however…" he paused, plucking two grapes from the branches and placed them into his mouth slowly one at a time. He bit into the skin, swallowing the sweet juices first.

"Speaking with the gods is most important, for without them there would be no pharaoh."

Aoh watched as his grin grew exponentially wider as his eyes swallowed hers in his stare.

"Aoh? That is your name, yes?"

Aoh turned and nodded silently.

His grin widened as he continued to speak, "A beautiful name for a beautiful servant. Yes, compared to the others I've seen… I wonder where the pharaoh dug you up."

"Thank you," Aoh replied, feeling unsettled to the point that her skin crawled.

She continued on her way as quickly as she could, glancing behind her, noticing the high priest remaining, watching her leave.

The look from that man was a look I never wanted to see again.

Upon returning to Daimina's chambers, she placed the meal on the small table near the bed. Pulling the curtains back, she found Daimina wrapped in the comfort of royal blessings. She stirred, hearing Aoh return with the food and rubbed her eyes repeatedly. Aoh gently tugged the curtains more, pulling them open.

"Thank you, Aoh," she acknowledged with a groan.

"It is my pleasure. I did not want to wake you."

"I didn't want to wake. After the dinner last night…"

Daimina paused, reaching for the grapes. As she did, Aoh held the goblet of water in her hands, waiting to serve it to her. Daimina ate silently and held out both hands when she wanted the water.

Swallowing another grape, Daimina asked, "The queen is going to kill me, isn't she?"

My insides flared as though a fire was lit from the pits of my stomach.

"I'm sure the king will never let anyone harm you," Aoh reassured her.

Daimina turned, shaking her head in disagreement.

"I shouldn't have come here. Why did I agree to come here?"

"You love him," Aoh answered.

Daimina's rounded eyes met with Aoh's instantly.

"You do anything for love. It's the way women are."

"Have you ever been in love?"

Aoh shook her head, pouring more water into the goblet, wincing from the endless itching across both of her feet.

Suddenly, there was a loud, panicked scream as the sounds of men running echoed off the walls.

"My king! My KING!" they screamed repeatedly, rushing towards the throne room, disturbing the pharaoh and his queen as they spoke with Senmet.

The doors flew open, scattering several papyrus scrolls across the floor. The swift air smothered several incense burners. The soldiers emerged…their faces white with terror and panic. The whites of their eyes outshone their color of their skin.

"Something terrible has happened."

The bodies of dead sheep, goats, cows, and donkeys filled the fields. Their blood seeping through the ground, slipping into the water, covering the area with a red unlike any shade seen before. Farmers and shepherds wept like widows over their dead animals. The crops planted in the water, now poisoned, drowned in the blood that expanded across several fields.

A rotten smell of decay hung over their bodies.

"What caused this?" the pharaoh demanded, standing at the sight of widespread death.

"I believe the question you should be asking is, who caused this my king," Senmet stated, standing next to him.

"No one could have done all of this," Laggus added, looking at the sight.

He slipped the cloth from around his neck, over his mouth.

"No? Is it hard to believe someone would be capable of this slaughter?" Senmet asked, in response. He waved a servant over, holding a cloth to place over the pharaoh's mouth.

"Look."

Senmet walked into the knee-deep polluted water to the nearest cow. Turning its head to the side with the lightly damp red cloth, he revealed a long slash across the animal's throat.

Raising his wrinkled hand to reveal the red color, he proclaimed, "This was done not by the gods, but by man."

"Still looks to be the work of a bad omen," another commented, surveying the dead animals while holding a feather and papyrus paper. The pharaoh looked at him as he continued, "This is catastrophic."

"Have you seen anything like this before?" the pharaoh inquired, lifting the cloth from his mouth.

"The last famine on record wasn't this terrible," he noted, with woeful eyes.

"Perhaps the high priest would like to come and explain to

pharaoh how something like this happened without him being told so beforehand?" Sefkh boldly queried, removing himself from the chariot. "My apologies for being late to the slaughter."

The pharaoh stared at the dead animals, noticing the flies beginning to swarm.

"Laggus," he commanded.

Laggus nodded and walked over to the cow next to Senmet. Observing the wound at the throat, his fingers slipped across the blood as the water thickened, becoming heavier and wrapping around his legs. Turning the head, he gently traced the slash with his fingers.

"It was done by some sort of blade, my king," he admitted, lowering his head.

"There is your proof," Senmet interjected, standing back up.

"How could someone have killed all of the animals with no one noticing?" another asked, worried.

"Can you tell the kind of blade it was, Laggus?" the pharaoh asked.

Before Laggus could answer, a farmer called out to the pharaoh, trying to run in the knee deep red water while, holding something in his hand. Laggus took the cloth from the man's hand and turned it, trying to decipher what he was holding. His eyes squinted, holding up the cloth to the sunlight, noticing smudged lettering and symbols.

"The Hyksos, my king," the farmer informed him, shuddering. "The Hyksos."

Laggus stared at the cloth, unable to discern if it was the language of the Hyksos.

"Bring it to me," the pharaoh ordered.

Laggus walked through the polluted water, handed him the cloth, and said as he spoke from behind the sash, "He seems to believe it's the Hyksos."

The men gathered next to the pharaoh to look at the cloth, obviously ripped from some form of linen and written in the language of the Hyksos. However, the writing was incoherent.

"Where was this found?" he asked, firmly.

"My cattle, my king. With my cattle," the farmer wept.

"I want all of this cleaned up. Take the dead animals, burn them, burn the lost crops, I want a supply count and I want it done immediately. If need be, the people will feed on papyrus reeds again until we recover. If we must, we'll double the trade amounts of grains," the pharaoh ordered as he began to walk back to his chariot.

"My King, what are we to do for the people?" Senmet asked, dripping blood onto the ground.

"Feed the people. And I want more men patrolling the streets at night. If the Hyksos did do this, they might not have left. Spies could be lurking in the shadows," the pharaoh stated, staring at the cloth.

He turned it to the side, rubbing his hand on the black ink, seeing it bleed lightly onto his skin. Standing next to his chariot, the pharaoh watched the farmer dig his hands into the soaked ground, pulling up the poisoned plants while weeping loudly. The lingering sounds of men shouting and crying in the distance grew.

"Laggus, what does your sight tell you?" he asked him sharply.

"I would consult with the high priest."

The faded cloth, tainted red from the blood, was handed to the high priest. He stood outside of the temple with his priests standing at attention behind him on either side in the sunlight.

"What is it?" Kha'y asked, frowning.

"You tell me," the pharaoh asked in response.

"Looks like nothing more than a written note of nonsense. The words are written in an older form, not…used anymore as far as my studies have shown."

He raised his painted eyes and read the pharaoh's.

"Where was this found?"

"On one of many dead animals decaying in the farms and fields.

Sheep, goats, donkeys, cattle, – all slaughtered, left to bleed out in the fields to ruin the crops," he explained, coldly. "I've come to you, like you asked me to many times before, to ask why this happened and why we weren't informed?"

"You believe this could have been prevented?" Kha'y asked with a small smile. "The gods show me everything, they do, my king. They did not show me this."

"Ask them why this happened."

Kha'y looked at the cloth, feeling the ink rub onto his fingers. He rubbed his fingers together and turned his head slightly towards the entrance to the temple.

"I shall ask them, my king. The gods will tell me what caused this," he explained confidently.

Entering the temple, the priests followed, immediately beginning to pray aloud, walking in two separate lines with their heads raised to the sky. Taking the cloth, Kha'y began to pray in between his loose lips, entering the darkness of the temple to the large display of statues over an altar. Taking the flames from the fire pits, he burned powerful incense. Throwing seeds and powder, plumes of thin smoke were released…slightly sizzling.

Taking vessels of wine, he poured it into fire slowly, watching the flames burn brighter. Taking a handful of food, and throwing sand onto the fires, he breathed in the smoke while watching the colors change with each powerful glow… The priests lowered their heads, opening their arms and hands, inhaling the scents.

Kha'y rolled his head, rocking to and fro, taking the cloth and lifting his eyes to stare at the statues. With one bold outburst, he dropped the cloth into the fire as the smoke rose to the ceiling, releasing a high pitched burning sound. The humming and praying of the priests surrounded him as he bowed repeatedly before the statues, calling out to the gods, screaming and crying… His eyes rolled to the back of his head, his body covered in pins and needles, spreading like lightning up and down continually.

"What happened?" Daimina asked, entering the throne room as the pharaoh returned with Senmet slightly sweated.

Ignoring her, he rushed to the servant approaching him with water, splashing it onto his face and taking the cloth from the servants arm to dry himself.

Senmet slowly drank from a goblet as his dark eyes followed the pharaoh.

"Daimina-," the pharaoh spoke.

"What happened? What is happening?" she repeated as Aoh followed her, nearly missing the doors closing behind her. Upon seeing the pharaoh, Aoh immediately kissed the floor, almost forgetting to do so and, nearly tripping forward.

"There is nothing to fear, Daimina. We are getting to the bottom of it now," he reassured calmly.

"What was the screaming I heard?"

"My dear, we cannot say what we do not know," Senmet answered calmly, holding the half empty goblet.

"The farms are flooded in the blood of slaughtered animals. The high priest, Kha'y, is going to tell us any moment now why and how this happened."

From the other side of the room, Laggus entered with the queen, leading her in.

"What happen-"

She paused the moment she saw Daimina standing across the room. She bit into her glossed lips and attempted to rush for Daimina when Laggus stepped in front of her quickly, looking down upon her coldly. She shoved herself past him and approached her husband, both angered and horrified at the same time.

"What are you doing waiting in here? You need to tell the people what happened!" she scolded.

"I am not going to insight unnecessary panic," he replied calmly.

"Unnecessary panic?" she asked in disbelief.

"My queen, the people will find out soon enough. At this rate many, if not all, will know and thus the whispers will begin. Spreading faster than a fire through an army. It is best we do not speak about it until we have an answer," Senmet quickly interjected.

The right door slammed opened as a young man rushing forward with a papyrus scroll in his hands. He unrolled it before the pharaoh and announced the status regarding food.

"We have successfully discovered that food supplies are full and should provide enough for the people for at least six months. We have sustained chickpeas, radishes, herbs, lettuces, and olive trees. Our most plentiful wheat crops were partially contaminated. However, if we want to prevent a famine, we'll need to ration the food we have until produce stabilizes. This means ensuring the survival of young."

"When does our next trade arrive to the city?"

The young man looked over to one of the scribes whom stepped forward, and reading directly from the papyrus, answered, "Within the next month. We are expecting pomegranate and fig trees."

"Good. The last rationing has served its purpose," the pharaoh replied as he placed his thumb and index finger to his mouth.

Daimina felt the queen's eyes upon her as she listened, tugging at the ends of her long hair.

"I want the kingdom to begin rationing their food tomorrow," he continued. "See if the farmers can salvage any of the crops. I want a count of what was lost. Once I have numbers, I can begin deciding whether or not to double the trade supplies."

"Yes, my king."

The young man took the scroll and fled from the room, rushing past Daimina and Aoh, nearly bumping into the door before opening it. Once the door came to a solid close, the queen rushed to her husband. Her long train slid behind her.

"My love, for your sake I hope that will not be the case. Now, tell me, what caused this plague?" the queen asked, worriedly.

"That is what I am waiting to find out," the pharaoh replied.

There was a loud commotion from the other side of the doors as they opened and the high priest entered with the rest of his priests behind him, single file. Laggus noticed Aoh shift to the right, attempting to hide behind Daimina.

"My king, I have prayed to the gods for some clarity and they spoke to me. This incident was not the work of the Hyksos as we were meant to believe. My king, the gods were responsible for this travesty."

The room fell into a sigh of relief as everyone released a heavy breath that was weighing on their chests since the morning.

"The gods told me that this supposed evidence of the Hyksos cloth was nothing more than a farce," the high priest continued. "Someone had purposely placed it with the dead cattle to insight a war that will destroy everything Egypt has built. We cannot allow ourselves to be fooled as such."

"And how is it that the gods did not tell you until today?" Senmet asked.

"They told me the reason they ravaged the farms with this spell of death was to prove that, though we are mighty and powerful, we will never outshine the power of the gods. If they had told me beforehand, we would not be learning our lesson. For we will never rule them, it is they who will always rule us," Kha'y explained, on his knees with his arms outward.

"Thank you, Kha'y, and I thank the gods for this message," the pharaoh replied calmly, looking down upon him.

"Make no mistake everyone, as you stand around me today, as you stand at the presence of the pharaoh, the gods have told me this message after prayer and devotion," he explained, turning to look upon every face within the room. "When you look at me, you look at your vessel to the gods. They rule us all, they bless us, they curse us, and they created us. Make no mistake, without them our lives would never be."

He turned to face Aoh, as she kept her head low, focusing on the floor.

"Their words are laws. What they say we must do. They grant us what we want. They will always grant us what we want, as long as we obey them."

28

Farmers worked hard into the night, collecting the bodies of the dead animals, burning them with the dead crops, and sending the horrid smell into the sky with the thick smoke. Every window and door was closed at the palace as several more incense burners were lit, trying to rid the foul smell that made many sick.

The smell was so potent, the pharaoh could hardly eat his dinner, constantly clasping a cloth over his nose and mouth while trying to breathe. Losing his patience, he slammed his goblet down onto the table and shoved his plate forward. He coughed heavily, tossing the cloth onto the floor and grabbed another clean one from the servant's tray next to him – still trying to breathe.

"Once the fires die, the smell will die with it, my king," Senmet reassured, calmly sitting next to him in the dimly lit room, nearly suffocated from both the scent of death and the incense.

The pharaoh groaned, leaning back in his chair. Though, his frustration hardly reflected his solemn expression.

"You need not blame yourself for this," Senmet continued. "It's not your fault this happened. I remember when your father was king and the fields were burned by our enemy. The fields grew back, twice as healthy. Egypt always prevails. History has shown as much. Egypt will always prevail."

The pharaoh didn't respond, taking a quick drink firmly in between his tight lips, barely grasping the goblet with his fingers. He titled the goblet, swirling the wine inside, slowly watching it move in small waves.

"Something else troubles your mind, my pharaoh. What is it?" Senmet asked.

"It's nothing," he replied, standing up.

He walked over to the nearest window, covered with wood and curtains. Looking through the small holes, he could see the pyramids in the dark distance, standing tall in the desert, housing members of his family as their souls crossed into the afterlife. He saw a multitude of boats on the Nile River, carrying crates of fresh grains from storage and fish from the river.

"You will be with them one day, my king," Senmet stated calmly.

Rising from his seat, he stood next to the king, looking out at the pyramids with him, barely keeping the cloth to his mouth, swallowing hard.

"Only yours will be grander. You've done more at your age than your father. While he had his wine, you had your chariot. The people will remember that. You will be celebrated."

The pharaoh nodded, keeping his eyes at the pyramid, remembering his father briefly sitting on the throne and placing him on his knee as a child. His vague memories of him came and went. He would always dress in blue and golden robes, standing at his chariot, yelling out into the air a ferocious roar like a lion.

"But not every king is remembered. That is why," The vizier paused, turned to face the pharaoh, watching him frown deeply. Lowering his voice, he placed a wrinkled hand onto the pharaoh's shoulder, "You need to make sure that every choice you make is the right one. You need to make sure of every decision and not look back once it's made."

"Yes, you are right. Which is why tomorrow I want to call for a meeting. I want you and those closest to me, which means Sefkh and Laggus, present. If the Hyksos had been this quiet, I'd like to know why."

Senmet nodded, placing his hands at his stomach, holding the half empty goblet.

"Would you care for a quick game, my king?" he asked, moving his hand to the right, where a wooden board was positioned between two chairs in the next room. The pharaoh nodded and walked into the other room as Senmet followed close behind, pulling up the silk curtains gently with one hand. After both entered, he lowered the curtain separating the heavy air, containing the scent from the burning carcasses. They took their seats across from each other. The pharaoh sat down, comfortably removing the cloth to inhale the heavy incense several times, feeling his stress levels lower slightly.

He looked down at the white pieces on his side of the board as Senmet took the black pieces into his wrinkled hands.

"Does the pharaoh remember how to play?" Senmet asked.

"Yes, I do," he answered confidently.

The next morning, Laggus came to Daimina's doorway to finding Aoh on her knees scrubbing the bottom of Daimina's feet with freshly scented soaps in a water basin. The gentle sunlight lit the room as the windows were finally opened, allowing fresh air to fill the space. Daimina ran a brush through her long hair slowly with each breath. With a gentle knock of his knuckles against the stone walls of the doorway, Daimina looked up and Aoh stopped momentarily.

"Daimina," he greeted with a bow.

"Yes, Laggus? Something wrong?" she asked.

"The pharaoh has requested you to join him immediately in a most important discussion," he explained sternly.

"Of course," Daimina replied quickly, growing worried.

Aoh took the folded cloth from the floor and hurriedly dried every toe on Daimina's feet before rising to stand like a statue.

"Please, follow me," Laggus instructed.

We followed Laggus down several long hallways to the throne room, surprised to see that the pharaoh was not alone. Standing next to him was his high priest, Kha'y, trusted general Sefkh, his vizier Senmet, his mother, and his queen.

Daimina's face faulted only slightly, making instant eye contact with the queen. She stood towards the back of the room near the pharaoh's mother, dressed almost completely in gold. The moment Daimina entered the room, air itself became thick and heavy, as though an invisible fog surrounded us, the tension smothering any fresh air coming in from the open spaces. As I kissed the floor, my eyes watched Daimina catching the pharaoh's attention. He smiled widely, rubbing his index finger across his mouth. Senmet lowered the opened papyrus he was reading from to look at Daimina and myself with an expression of surprise.

It was obvious the pharaoh withheld telling him we were going to be present.

The queen's knuckles cracked violently as she breathed heavily inward and outward like a panting animal. Her eyes widened, surrounded by exquisitely applied make-up that made her look like a powerful force beyond human nature. The gold and jewels adorned about her slender body reflected every trace of light in the room. Her body chimed upon every slight movement.

"Please, Daimina, come forth," the pharaoh instructed, waving his fingers as he leaned over in his throne.

She hesitated at first, trying to avoid eye contact with the queen who hardly blinked, stepping over animal skin rugs and silk carpets.

"Come, please, sit here with me."

Daimina took her seat to the left of pharaoh, sitting before Senmet whom had a twinkle of confusion in his eyes as he glanced at Kha'y. Smirking from ear to ear, Kha'y rubbed his left hand over to his mouth to prevent himself from laughing, smothering the chuckle with some wine.

The pharaoh turned to look at his queen who was unable to look away from Daimina.

"Please, come," he said to her calmly.

She nodded, walking forward with her head held high, and immediately sat on the left arm of the pharaoh's throne.

Taking the papyrus scroll, Senmet returned his sight to the numbers and names.

"Gentlemen, there is a reason why Egypt has never built walls. We have a large and vast desert separating us from the rest of the world," the pharaoh explained firmly, as he placed his left hand on the middle of his queen's back.

"That didn't stop our enemies from attacking our people several years ago, leaving nothing but ashes," Sefkh commented immediately.

The pharaoh looked at him with cold eyes, and then glanced to his vizier.

"You cannot deny that happened, my king," Senmet noted calmly.

"That was but a small attack by a few, not an army bent on burning the palace to the ground," the pharaoh growled.

"If that was but a few, who knows how many more will attack next time. We could be facing a large army, expanding the length of the desert," Sefkh commented, pointing at the map.

"I appreciate the suggestion, but I don't feel comfortable building walls and hiding behind them. I'd rather set up groups of soldiers at our borders. Have them there day and night keeping constant watch. If need be, we'll send spies into the desert just to make sure there is no imminent threat looming behind the mountains."

"My king…" Senmet spoke lowly, "Whether it's tomorrow, a year from now, or after your death, Egypt will always have threats made against it. The riches we have will be wanted by the rest of the world. The Hyksos lie just beyond the Nile River. That river cannot stop them forever. Look what happened. They came and swept

Egypt from the very hands of its citizens and ruled our land."

"And they brought with them chariots which we now use and weapons we now possess."

"They took our land from us, my king. They took everything until we took it back after years under their rule," Senmet explained desperately, shaking his hands. "Take my words as one who has seen the horrors first hand. I am simply speaking the truth. They are a powerful force, a worthy adversary."

"We were preoccupied with famine, not war then. Not now. We've already established the death of our animals were not by their hands, so what is the rush, gentlemen?" the pharaoh replied, leaning forward. "Why rush and falter? Time will-"

"Time? How much time do you think we have?" Sefkh asked.

The entire room turned their attention onto him.

"And what of their allies? What of ours? What becomes of us, if they bring more than just a few hundred men into our towns, our cities? What happens to us?" he asked, leaning forward, placing his rough hands on the back of Senmet's chair.

"Maybe our lack of allies is because we are attacking harmless armies of nothing more than shepherds and craftsman," Kha'y interjected from behind, with a slight shrug of his bony shoulders. Puckering his lips together, he took slow strides, trailing his cloak behind him. "Perhaps if we left them alone we wouldn't be on the opposite side of someone's favor."

Sefkh turned and frowned deeply at Kha'y from under his thick eyebrows.

"Isn't that something you mentioned, Laggus?" Kha'y asked, turning to him.

"What of the ones who attacked and captured Laggus and those men?" Sefkh asked, looking at Laggus.

"They were not shepherds or craftsmen." Laggus stepped forward, with his arms crossed at his chest. "We were attacked by one enemy whom has been Egypt's foe for hundreds of years. Any chance to attack us, they'll use. However, that does not mean we should engage them first." He lifted his eyes from the map to look at all the eyes of the room. "I agree with the pharaoh," Laggus continued. "We build up our armies and keep watch of the borders. Our only true enemy, is here." He pointed to the location on the map resulting in the group looking over simultaneously. "They have shown us over these past hundred years nothing but patterns. Patterns the Assyrians read well and used against them. They build up their army just enough to attack but not destroy us. They retreat, build up their army just enough, and attack again. They do not have the resources for a full scale war. They hide behind their walls and spend their time plotting, trying to recover. They are unforgiving to anyone who had wronged them."

"And you know all of that how, Laggus?" Senmet asked coldly.

"The guards and I were captured and not fed for days, watching Babylon as we sat in the sun of their compound. The compound was fair enough, but with its equal share of weaknesses. If we hadn't escaped, no doubt we would have been killed as a message to Egypt that there will never be peace between our kingdoms."

Aoh's eyes fell to the floor, feeling as though Laggus wasn't speaking to the rest of the room but speaking directly to her.

"I've seen their soldiers fall. Quite quickly, like sand blown in the wind. It's obvious that their people are weak, having fell to the Assyrians, which means they will need to make an alliance with a kingdom whose men are strong. A kingdom who has experience in fighting back and conquered the one kingdom they have never gotten a chance to. That leaves only one that fits that description," he explained, pointing to it on the map.

I knew exactly whom he was speaking of. It was the same kingdom Queen Huriye had invited into her palace. The same kingdom she wanted to marry into so that she could conquer Egypt.

"The Hyksos," the pharaoh whispered, rubbing his fingers over his chin and mouth.

"That is the same kingdom our king wanted to create an alliance with that, if I'm not mistaken, that all of you disagreed to once he took the crown," Laggus commented firmly, looking at each of them quickly.

"Laggus, we cannot expect to become allies with them after what they did. The people would revolt," Senmet noted. "Their actions speak for themselves."

"The people would be proud, forgiving, and loyal to our king, who has brought them nothing but victory. They are loyal just as they have always been. I've been on those streets since I was a young man. I know these people. If our king wishes it, they will make it so. He is their hero."

"And you think these same people would follow your word when you have seen nothing of the gravity of what they experienced?" Sefkh growled bitterly, rising from his seat. He took slow steps towards Laggus, staring at him, raising his shoulders slightly forward.

"No one had asked for your comment about such an event that was none of your concern," the general spat. "You know nothing... Laggus."

"As an Egyptian, Egypt is, and will always be, my concern."

"Sefkh," Senmet said firmly.

Ignoring the vizier, Sefkh stepped forward, leaning in close to Laggus, breathing into his face.

Laggus didn't flinch nor move. He remained ever still, never faltering to the wrath of weather or time.

"You are not Egyptian," Sefkh boldly claimed.

"Enough," the pharaoh ordered. "Enough arguing. We are all Egyptian here. I would not have brought you all in here if I felt otherwise. General Sefkh, I will make it your responsibility to keep our borders safe at all times. You are to recruit half of your best soldiers to protect the borders, day and night. If there is anything in that desert, I want to hear about it. But by no means are you to engage. We cannot afford to slaughter innocent civilians. And I still want to see our newest additions."

"Does the pharaoh request a new Braves of the King?"

Senmet's left eyebrow raised slightly, impressed with Sefkh's suggestion. His comment grabbed the pharaoh's attention as quickly as Daimina's face.

"Yes, and I am placing them in your hands. I trust you to lead them as you have done many times before."

"Yes, my King," Sefkh agreed with a bow. "I shall not disappoint you."

"Laggus, I want you to accompany me."

"Yes, my king," Laggus nodded.

"The rest of you…go."

The pharaoh rose from his throne as the rest of the room bowed in unison. Laggus waited for him to pass before following behind him, feeling the heat from Sefkh's intense glares. Aoh stepped to the side, allowing them to pass, and bowed. Her eyes watched the pharaoh's feet, and then Laggus' pass her as they exited the room, closing the doors behind him. The moment the solid sound of the doors closed, Senmet cleared his throat.

"Meeting adjourned. Return to your duties and be sure to be diligent. I stand by my statement; actions speak for themselves."

29

"He had the nerve to have her sit in, with me present? It's bad enough we have another servant we have to see every day," the queen spat, as her voice rose and fell upon every other word in between shaking lips. Behind the queen stood her expressionless but loyal servant.

"Daimina is allowed to have a servant," the pharaoh's mother replied.

"Is she? Is she, Aneski?"

Aneski, folding her slightly wrinkled hands, cleared her throat and asked with a hint of rigidity, "What is it exactly that you are asking of me?"

"To put an end to this. I want her gone, and her servant," the queen pleaded with watery eyes. Her servant flinched away from the queen's outburst.

She sniffled, rising her thin hands to catch any tears from slipping down her face.

"Do not cry, your makeup will run down your face. You wouldn't want anyone to see you looking weak," Aneski scolded coldly, swiping the queen's hands away from her eyes. "My queen, you know there is nothing I can do about them."

From the other room, passing a vast array of potted palm trees and rows of displayed fresh fruit, Aoh's steps slowed. As she followed behind Daimina, she could hear the queen trying to lower her voice to an irate whisper.

"What do you mean you cannot do anything? He's your son," the queen asked.

Aneski fell silent.

"And am I not your daughter?"

"You're not," Aneski answered.

"He is your son-"

"Yes, and Pharaoh of Egypt. You, my dear, are his wife. You should talk to him about it. Tell him what you're telling me," she suggested calmly, beginning to walk away. She backtracked and whispered, "A little extra affection couldn't hurt, either. Make it so he will desire no other woman but you."

She stopped when she saw Daimina approaching, lifting up the bottom of her long dress to carefully walk up the steps. Aoh followed behind, nearly stopping in mid-motion, seeing the queen with her servant.

Aneski immediately quickened her steps and said, "Daimina, you shouldn't go any-"

"Is that Daimina's steps I hear?" the queen asked loudly. Her voice echoed off the walls.

"It is," Daimina replied, taking another step forward.

"Come, so that I may see you."

Daimina bravely continued forward with Aoh close by her side, keeping her head slightly downward and her hands folded. She passed the pharaoh's mother who, though aged, looked rather well. Her eyes followed Daimina and Aoh as they approached the queen. Quickly rubbing under her eyes, the queen cleared her throat, revealing a confident smile across her lips. Daimina stopped just before the queen, staring at her in a silence that made the air in the room heavy with tension. The queen placed her hand to her mouth, and released a slight giggle.

"Look at you. Your hair is brushed, your body dressed in silk and linen, the neck covered in, oh, is that perfume I smell?" the queen asked, taking small steps forward. She continued to look at Daimina, flicking a tiny stray piece of a thread from Daimina's shoulder, causing her to flinch slightly in response. "There. That's better, isn't it? Now you are as beautiful as the lowest servant." The queen curled her lower lip and laughed.

Daimina didn't reply, releasing a heavy breath from her chest, keeping her eyes focused at the other end of the room ahead of her. The queen leaned forward slightly, anticipating Daimina to cry. However, she remained as cold as stone.

Without warning, the queen raised her hand and slapped Aoh across the face so hard that she was sent stumbling to the side, nearly colliding into a column. Daimina and Aneski gasped aloud, watching Aoh almost fall over.

The pain was unlike anything I had felt before. The whole left side of my face felt numb and a small trail of blood from my lower lip started to drip down my chin. I felt the deep cut, burning intensely the moment I touched it. The wound was made from the rings the queen wore. I could just barely see a trace of my blood on the gold.

"How could you? You cannot treat my servant like that!" Daimina objected, angered.

"I am the Queen of Egypt. I can do whatever I want to whomever I want. And I want you gone! You will not stay at my palace anymore! You are not welcome here!" she screamed so loud she nearly coughed.

Aneski's look was that of utter astonishment, unable to speak in response to the queen's sudden violence.

I felt as though the room was moving side to side as I tried to stand back up, pressing my fingers against my lip and feeling the rush of blood dripping from the sore wound. Daimina's voice sounded slightly incoherent, as though I was suddenly awaking from a deep sleep. I rolled my tongue slowly across my lip, tasting the bitter blood. As I shifted, nearly falling over, I saw the queen make a sudden movement towards me when Daimina stepped in front of her.

"Get out...of my way," she growled intensely.

"No," Daimina objected.

"You want me to hurt you, too? Because I will."

"Enough of this! Stop it right now before someone sees. You should know better than to hurt her," Aneski scolded, raising her voice. "Do you want him to catch you doing this? Do you?!"

The queen stared at her with widened eyes and a crazed open mouth.

"Don't be stupid!" the pharaoh's mother continued. "You know better than to do this! How can you expect to keep your title if you can't keep your temper? If he-" Aneski lowered her voice, raising a hand to prevent the queen from interrupting her. "If he saw this right now…do you know what comes next? If you continue this behavior, what do you think becomes of you?"

The queen's raging eyes remained fiery and vicious, staring into the old and worn ones before her that had seen things she would take to her tomb. The queen jolted in a fright at the gentle touch of her servant's hand over her shoulder. With a silent nod and look from her weathered eyes, the queen's rage seemed to slip away. The darkness in her pupil's remained, watching Daimina stand firm with her servant.

"Look around you. If he were to see this, what will become of you?" Aneski warned again.

Without uttering a word, the queen tugged her linen dress out of the way and briskly exited the room.

The moment the queen was out of sight, Aneski left through another door nearly hidden behind a large statue of a god, a disappointed disposition upon her face.

Daimina bent downward, trying to hold Aoh. "Come. Come on. Stand up."

Aoh shook her head twice, still stunned. "I'm fine."

"Come, let me help you."

Daimina led Aoh out of the room slowly to where the water met the palace steps. She took a towel from the ones already folded on the steps and dipped it into the water.

"Here," she said, pressing the wet towel onto Aoh's mouth.

Aoh winced at the pain, her left cheek now redder than the peppers eaten at dinner.

"Can you hold it?" she asked.

Aoh nodded, pressing the wet cloth to her mouth and the side of her face, feeling the blood seeping through the sewn threads. Daimina watched, distraught, as she slipped her index finger into her mouth.

A sudden pair of ibis flew from the water and into the air. Aoh lifted her head, watching them fly away together. Lowering her eyes, she saw the ripples they left in the clear, cool water. She could hear the sounds of kites shrieking not far away, along with musical stringed instruments. Aoh blinked heavily, feeling the rush of blood slowly stop.

"She knows she can't hurt me. So, she's hurting you," Daimina said slowly to herself, shaking her head.

Aoh lowered the towel, tainted red, and rubbed her left cheek with the palm of her hand. The numbness was still there no matter how much she massaged it.

"Are you alright?" Daimina asked, worriedly.

I couldn't quite comprehend her question. I was still in shock, but nodded to calm her.

Daimina nodded back and sat on the last step before the waters, pushing the longer ends of her dress underneath her. Aoh came to her side, grabbed the long train and moved it to the right, gently laying it on the steps even though she asked her not to. Daimina stared into her own reflection in the water, able to see herself amongst lily pads, and the pink and purple flowers that bloomed on top of them. Cautiously, she dipped both of her legs into the water, immediately quivering at the sudden cold sensation against her skin. She exhaled slowly, moving her legs to and fro, creating multiple ripples, rocking the lily pads gently.

"I'm sorry," she whispered.

Did she just apologize to me?

"I wouldn't go far into the water if I were you," a voice said behind them.

Turning around, Aneski came forth. I could see the faint wrinkles gently layered around her eyes and mouth. Her eyes were narrow but solid. She was thin, dressed in a linen gown with a few jewels decorating her body. I stood in amazement... I did not know if it was because I was still stunned from the slap, but I didn't realize until that moment...she was the pharaoh's mother. I immediately bowed with my mouth slightly open seeing her there, having not heard a single step approach us. She didn't glance at me once. Her eyes remained focused on Daimina.

Daimina turned around and, upon seeing Aneski, she attempted to stand up only to be received with the former queen's palm.

"No need to stand for me," she said firmly.

Daimina's eyes rattled side to side as though terrified.

"I was only-"

"I'm not the queen of Egypt anymore. Please continue. I am just warning you not to go into the water. The crocodiles have been rather brave as of late. They killed a servant only weeks before you arrived," she explained calmly.

Daimina didn't respond, but stared at the old woman, who wore her experiences all over her face. Aoh remained still, rising from her bow, with her hands at her waist.

As though she could read Daimina's thoughts she spoke, "Please, don't be afraid of me. It's the queen you need to be afraid of."

Her feet remained hidden underneath the long dress that swayed like the fish fins each time she moved – as though walking on the air. Coming to Daimina, she sat on the paws of the nearest lion statue, leaning herself against it. Daimina faced her, staring as though she had never seen such a woman before in her life. She looked to Aoh for just a moment, focusing on her face and noticing the red color.

"There, see. That is what she is capable of," Aneski stated, nodding to Aoh. "I'm not surprised you don't recognize me. I often eat my meals alone. I don't like to be in the company of others in the palace, except for my son. My name is Aneski."

"I am honored to meet you," Daimina replied.

Aneski nodded with a small smile, as she rubbed her hands up and down her thin arms decorated with two golden cuffs trailing a silk cape behind her back. When she opened her arms, the silk cape looked like wings.

"I used to come out here, too, when I was upset. Of course, then there were less flowers and more reeds," she explained, looking at the waters ahead of them.

"How did you-"

"My husband, like all kings before him, had his eyes on another woman right after I gave birth. She was beautiful, too. Quite the competition for his affections. But it was ironic…no matter how many daughters she gave him, she never produced a son. And mine, would be the only child I ever bore."

Daimina attempted to speak but she was stopped.

"I know you're afraid to be here," Aneski continued. "I was afraid when I first came here. I didn't know what he saw in me. Why he chose me to be his queen. But then again…that may have been someone else's doing. I never did ask him. But he loved me. Oh, how he loved me endlessly."

She smiled, as a flare of desire flashed across her eyes like an open flame.

"He used to write these beautiful letters for me to find," she remembered. "Even before I arrived, he'd send me these just beautiful letters that made me so confused and terrified to know someone could love me so much. He loved me, but he loved too much. He wasn't unhappy with me, otherwise I would not be here today. No. I remember the day they found her…"

She paused momentarily, as though she was seeing her memory reoccurring in the reflection of the water, within the ripples from the fish.

"I was never told how she died. She was buried, and her daughters lived in this very palace while my son kept to himself until the day the queen was brought to him. Even as a child, she knew what love was. She loves my son. My son's wife is very afraid of you. You know why, don't you?"

Daimina nodded, silently looking at her hands, slightly worn from years of sewing and carrying heavy pots and vessels. She rubbed her knuckles, feeling the grooves with the tips of her rounded nails.

"Why am I here?" she asked meekly.

"Because my son loves you, more than you realize."

Daimina smiled in response, watching as the ripples in the water from the fish rocked the lily pads closer to her feet.

"I do not know what will become of you here," Aneski declared. "I cannot say what the gods won't tell me. But…I want you to know that it's alright to be happy here. You don't have to be afraid all the time. You don't have to hide from them. Live in the moment. Love and be loved, and do not change. It's when women change that the pharaoh loses all interest in them. For when he was angered with me, he ran to her bed. When he was angered by her, he came to my mine," she warned.

The once Queen of Egypt sympathized with Daimina. Something I didn't believe would happen since even I had noticed that those who are silent speak through their eyes. And their eyes do not want Daimina to stay. Even though Daimina never expressed how afraid she was to me, it was written across her face every day since speaking with Aneski.

Within a matter of days, my wound was healed. My body adjusted to the bed. My hands became worn. My feet tired. As exhausted as I had become, there were nights I could not sleep. As I laid awake, I desperately wanted to climb to the top of the palace and behold the world in darkness like I had done so many times before. To see my friend and listen to the young man playing the flute… But I could not leave Daimina.

I was her very shadow. Everywhere she went I followed, silent, passed by without a second glance by all members of the palace. That was…except for Laggus. When Daimina would walk the gardens, picking flowers that attracted her interest, Laggus would walk by with the pharaoh and, for the slightest of a second, look at me. When Daimina would try to learn how to read Egyptian in the candlelight before the late hours, Laggus would patrol the hallways, pass by the room, and glance at me sitting there in the silence with her. We were both shadows of the day and night, Laggus and I.

30

The sun burned bright and hot as Laggus drove the pharaoh's chariot into the desert, with Senmet following. The pyramid builders followed in separate chariots, driven by servants. The horses ran violently, hurling themselves over the sandy, rocky terrain towards the tall structures made from the hands of dedicated workers.

For hundreds of years, Egypt grew in the rule of their kings. Their lives forever touching the people around them; citizens of the land, prisoners, and enemies alike. Their bodies laid to rest in the peace and quiet of their tombs amongst their riches. Their favorite games buried with their clothing, food, weapons, and pets, to take with them as they moved on into the afterlife to await Anubis and the trials ahead of them.

The walls of the tomb were painted with prayers and spells of protection for safe passage, with images of the gods with them at every moment. These kings and their families were laid to rest together so that, even in death, they would never be apart. They would find each other again, and live in eternal happiness and love.

As the pharaoh's chariot roared to a halt, the horses panted and snarled, chewing on the bars between their mouths. He stepped onto the ground to behold the sight of his own pyramid, which began construction the moment the crown was placed upon his head. Senmet followed, handling several pieces of papyrus as the servants rushed to prepare a small tent of shade for the pharaoh. They carried chairs, a table, food and wine in baskets, and palm tree leaves from the chariots. Within moments, the servants cascaded a tent over wooden poles, tying the ends to the hard ground.

The pharaoh's young eyes studied the construction of his pyramid as hundreds of men worked carrying stones and bricks, grunting with every struggle. Large cattle pulled carts and wooden slabs as the pieces were placed one at a time, rising above the Earth. The workers followed orders, working all hours of the day and some times in darkness building the shafts and tunnels with only torches to light their way. Small displays and models covered tables with specified measurements, constantly adjusting angles.

Water from the nearest wells was carried through several wooden baskets up and down paths across several areas. Mud with straw dried in the sunlight, sweat flowed from the skin of peasants, and prayers were heard like songs sung sweetly through the air.

Senmet's small smile beamed in the glow of the sun as he placed the papyrus scrolls onto the table. The servants waved the palm leaves around the pharaoh as others carried vessels of water and wine to drink.

"Your chamber is here, my king. There is a door adjoining your room with these two here. In order to get to your chamber, one must pass through this one hereafter, of course, passing through the correct tunnel," he explained, pointing to the drawn images on the papyrus scrolls.

"Is that what these tunnels are, here?" he asked, pointing to the several drawn on other pages.

"Yes. We have learned that robbers will always plunder tombs knowing what treasures lay inside. Therefore-" Senmet paused momentarily, noticing Laggus glancing downward at the drawings, gently moving them so he could see them better. "We developed clever traps to trick them so that even if they were to find your tomb, they will not be to find their way back. Once you are buried, we will have established a way to decipher if your tomb has been entered. Needless to say, robbers will think twice before robbing you of your possessions, my pharaoh."

Laggus held the papyrus scrolls, looking at them intently, rubbing the light scruff on his chin.

"Our men are dedicated to their craft. They, and their families, have been building tombs for your ancestors since the beginning. And-" Senmet interrupted himself, gently taking the papyrus scroll from Laggus's hands, "and they know what they're doing." He rolled the scrolls back up, tying them gently and piling them at the end of the table.

"Go up there and fetch me the overseer of my pyramid. I wish to speak with him about a few things," the pharaoh ordered.

"Of course. I shall return momentarily," Senmet replied, bowing and gesturing for several servants to climb the grand structure with him.

Laggus took the papyrus scrolls Senmet tied, unfastening them, transfixed by the detailed images and engineering.

"What do you think?" the pharaoh asked, noticing Laggus' interest in the elaborate drawings.

"Impressive, my king. I've never seen such dedication and work," Laggus replied, amazed.

The pharaoh smiled in response, taking his goblet of wine and walking towards the far left of the tent. He leaned his left arm against the wooden pole, watching his vizier reach the top, standing out amongst all the workers in his white garb.

"One day I'll be buried in there. I'll be placed in a tomb with my organs removed, to await my judgment before Anubis," he explained solemnly.

"One day in the far future, my king. Not in the present," Laggus reassured, towering next to him with his arms crossed against his chest.

"I never dreamed I'd be looking at my own resting place so soon. The last time I remembered seeing such a place was when my father died. The years of my youth flew by me so quickly that I hardly realized the fate I would one day inherit. Do you think it will be glorious? Before you answer me, do not tell me what I want to hear. Tell me the truth."

"A glorious death is a matter of perception, my king. If one was to die in the service of someone more glorious than themselves, if they were to die for a just cause, or die in peace after a long life protecting others than, yes, it will be glorious. Not all deaths are, however, glorious. Not all deaths are remembered, but some haunt those who continue to live."

The pharaoh smirked, looking at the wine in his goblet, staring into the eyes of his reflection.

"You must not blame yourself for his death, Laggus. I know you are one who never needs conviction, but I can tell this weighs heavily on your heart in ways you may not see. But I see it."

Laggus turned his head, looking at the pharaoh, feeling the wind brush by them gently.

"Perhaps it is only the eyes of a brother who can see it."

Laggus silently nodded, watching Senmet speak to several men with the servants following his every step, like small children.

"Daimina…told me that it was my wife who struck Aoh," the pharaoh said calmly, taking a sip of his wine.

Laggus looked at him instantly in response.

"It makes me wonder, am I doing the right thing?"

He looked at Laggus again with worried eyes, and a strong sense of guilt and doubt.

"She's hurting those closest to Daimina because she knows she can…" he continued. "She knows that no one will care if a servant is harmed. But am I doing the right thing?"

"Could you be more specific, my king?" Laggus asked.

"I love Daimina and I love my wife. Could it be possible that a man can love more than one woman?"

"Other kingdoms seem to think so, but we are not like other kingdoms, are we?"

"And yours?"

"Mine is here," Laggus replied.

The pharaoh smirked in response. as Laggus continued, "One must follow their own heart. It must be light, without regrets. Otherwise, how else are we to pass judgment and be happy for eternity?"

"My heart pines for both women. I've known my wife since we were children, yet I feel as though I've known Daimina for over ten lifetimes. Ever since…I saw her in the city that day. It had to be that day. I've been into the city so few times and the one time I'm there, who is caught doing what is right when all those around her only cared about doing wrong? It hurts me to know that my wife did such a thing. I know that if Daimina was my queen she would never do such a thing to another woman's servant. She wouldn't be…so desperate."

"This is a battle for survival, my king. Your wife feels threatened. You said it yourself, you've known her since you were a child. She must have suspected then that one day she'd be sitting beside you on the throne of Egypt. She doesn't want to lose the throne. She doesn't want to lose you."

"Laggus, I want you to make sure that when I pass on from this world both my wife and Daimina are buried with me in my pyramid."

"As you wish."

The sounds of the insects, calling to each other in chirps and buzzes, faded in and out of the cool night as a gentle breeze curled the drapes over the windows. Daimina sighed contently as she rolled from her left side to her right, cradling her hands under her face against the pillows. The light crackle of the burning fire continued, casting its dancing shadow across the room. From her bed, Aoh was able to see Daimina's shadow on the wall, keeping the drapes in her doorway partially open.

That night was the first night I was finally able to sleep soundly until I heard movement outside of the bedroom. I was startled by the sound of something I couldn't quite decipher. Taking the torch from my bedside, I rose to my feet and left my room immediately. Holding the torch near the bed, I could see Daimina was sound asleep. She was wrapped underneath her blankets and pillows, her arms and legs bent inward comfortably, unaware of the sounds that awoke me.

Taking feeble steps towards the doorway, I listened but couldn't hear anything. The silence was far more unsettling than it was before. Even the sounds of the lively insects fell silent. What ungodly being was out there that I couldn't see?

Keeping the torch firmly in her right hand, Aoh backed away and sat down on the golden chair at the end of Daimina's bed staring at the endless darkness at the doorway. She placed her hand against the back of the bed, where she felt an indentation. Through the indentation she felt a dagger. Taking it slowly, she watched the doorway for something to emerge.

She exhaled deeply and slowly. As the blade hovered just over her waist, she heard another noise. It sounded like a very large, heavy door being opened as the long echo of the creak swept through the darkness. Aoh paused, keeping the blade steady as she heard another sound of quick footsteps next to the doorway.

The footsteps sounded familiar to her ears. However, that fact didn't calm her nerves. Glancing quickly at Daimina's shadow on the wall, Aoh noted that she remained undisturbed, still deep into her own fantasy world.

Aoh tightened her hold on the dagger, gripping the detailed handle tightly in her palm, wrapping her fingers completely around it. She remained focused, staring into the darkness, prepared to strike, if necessary. Placing the torch in the holder, she slowly moved to the door.

Taking one last breath, she drew the dagger and, with a fierce swing, lunged at the intruder. She pinned him to the wall, but before she could strike, a strong hand gripped her arm. Startled, she turned to see Laggus. Looking down at her with intense eyes, he spoke.

"No."

Pushing her aside, Laggus stabbed the man, feeling the blade pierce through his flesh. Pulling the knife, the body slid down the wall and onto the floor. Panting heavily, Aoh looked at the dagger dripping with blood as Laggus bent downward to pick up the body.

"Go back inside and don't come out," Laggus ordered.

Aoh nodded, slightly shaking as she put the blade back into the sheath, returning to the seat by the bed.

I was awake for the entirety of the night…just sitting there with the torch in one hand and dagger in the other, waiting for someone to attack. Daimina awoke the next morning with no recollection of what happened the night before, seeing me at the end of her bed. I didn't have the nerve to tell her what happened. I didn't want to worry her more than she was already for her own wellbeing.

Grabbing the heavy tub of water, Aoh poured it evenly over the top of Daimina's face, hearing the loud splash against the small, full bath. Daimina rubbed her face, feeling the cool water wash over her. Her soaked hair laid over both shoulders, and down her back. Taking one of several pieces of soap, Aoh began to scrub Daimina's shoulders and the back of her neck, trying at all costs to not look at her directly.

Exhausted, she slumped forward, nearly missing the back of Daimina's neck, closing her eyes for a moment. Lightly shaking her head, Aoh focused on her scrubbing, filling the basin with water, and then pouring it over the soap remnants. The faint scent from the soap stung her nostrils, causing her to curl her nose like a cat.

31

"Your move, pharaoh," Senmet said calmly, looking down at the board in front of him.

The pharaoh rubbed his index finger over his lips, staring at the board, unsure where to move his next piece as Senmet watched. Lifting one of his white pieces, he placed it onto another square near several of Senmet's black pieces.

The vizier smiled. "Nicely played, my king. However, you've left yourself open."

"Did I, now, Senmet?" he asked, coyly.

Senmet glanced back down at the board, noticing where the pharaoh had left himself open. He, then, glanced at his pieces and made his next move without hesitation, taking one of the pharaoh's pieces with ease. He held it up in between his wrinkled fingers.

"See, there it is," he said.

"Very well."

The pharaoh quickly moved his next piece several times, taking not one but two pieces, clearing a large portion of the board which now only housed his white pieces. Seeing that, Senmet's eyes glistened with a faint reveal of surprise and disbelief.

Holding the two black pieces for Senmet to see, the pharaoh smirked.

"See, there they are. Two ends of the snake after one's sacrifice," he teased.

Senmet smiled warmly and nodded.

"You have gotten better at this game since you first played. I have, too."

"No, do not distract me with-"

"I would never distract the pharaoh. That is beneath me, I assure you. You have gotten better and I believe it comes with practice. You handled yourself very well with that divorced couple and-"

"That was divorce, not diplomacy. I have yet to show a need for it. Not while my palace overlooks my kingdom and the desert remains far."

He looked at the board, and smiled deeply, studying his pieces.

"Now, it seems, I'm getting better than you," the pharaoh replied with a small laugh, placing the black pieces into the tray with the others.

"The day is still young. You have the upper hand for now, but perhaps the game can still be mine. I have been going easy on you."

"Oh, please-"

"No, it's true. I always had," Senmet explained.

"I doubt that as a child you allowed me to win," the pharaoh argued.

"I am your most devoted servant. But now, no more games. I will be making my next move."

As Senmet moved his next piece, the doors were slammed open. Laggus marched inside with several guards behind him trying to restrain a young man. Exhaustion was written all over Laggus's face as he threw the man forward.

Spiting, Laggus panted, "This man was behind last night's attack."

The pharaoh's eyes darkened with hatred.

The wound on Aoh's mouth stung when she curled her lips or opened her mouth too wide. The dried blood faded from sight, and a red line now revealed itself as evidence of the unexpected attack. She gently pushed her hand to her mouth to apply light pressure, wincing slightly at the sting while scrubbing with her other hand.

Finishing Daimina's bath, Aoh looked down at her feet as she held towels for Daimina to dry herself with. She wrapped herself in a linen gown, carefully tying the sides as Aoh began to rub scented oils on her arms, gently flicking some light drops into her hair from the bottles resting on the floor.

The scents brought forth memories of the palace at Babylon. She could visualize the throne room, covered in the potted exotic plants and home to the large luxurious birds. She smiled faintly as she remembered Queen Huriye and the princess sitting across from each other, playing a game while surrounded by servants fanning them slowly. As they raised their eyes to look at Aoh, she suddenly heard a loud smash nearby.

Daimina immediately followed the sound with Aoh close behind, hearing several people shouting over each other and seeing remnants of what shattered on the floor. Several pieces of broken clay bowls scattered, leading down the hallway, as the pharaoh pointed at a man in all white being dragged away.

Holding her arm out gently, Daimina cautioned Aoh to stop, as she looked down and saw an endless trail of broken clay pieces. Ahead of the broken pieces was a fallen row of plants and trees. Stepping around the mess, Aoh saw the pharaoh screaming over the other man whom yelled in pain and objection. Daimina took several steps forward with caution, when the pharaoh saw her.

His eyes were wild and rattled; opened wide and full of rage.

"What is it?" Daimina asked slowly.

"Don't come this way, go around the back. Now!" he screamed.

Startled, Daimina jumped, turning around and nearly stumbling over the broken pieces.

The low and continuous sound of a drum played before a large crowd of people gathered in front of the palace in silence. Men, women, and children watched in the heat of the sun as the pharaoh and his queen sat in their thrones before the large space. The young man stood, arms tied behind his back, in his garb of white. The shine from the sun reflected itself across his bald head. His black makeup was smudged from his salty tears, trailing down the sides of his face.

The lines of guards faced the scene on both sides, silently waiting for the pharaoh's orders. I remained behind Daimina as she stood to the far right side, next to other servants. Laggus remained next to Sefkh and Senmet, standing to the left of Aneski. Her eyes continually fell on her son as she watched the priest stand in the sun, facing the crowd of people.

All of their eyes stared into him as though he were as clear as water. The rich and poor citizens watched with their children at their sides. Abruptly, the pharaoh rose from his seat and approached the young man with Sefkh obediently following. He stared at the young man, circling around him with his arms behind his back. His lips trembling with frustration and impatience.

The long, blue robe dragged across the white floor while the ends of his Nemes headdress draped over his shoulders. A red and white leather crown, symbolizing the unification of lower and upper Egypt, rested upon the Nemes. With one movement of his arm, Sefkh drew his sword from his waist and handed it to the pharaoh.

My heart raced inside my chest as I could feel my throat dry, overcome with a horrible feeling that I knew what was going to happen. I swallowed hard, breathing out through my mouth, watching the pharaoh study the sharp blade. All at once, the crowd of people suddenly erupted into a loud chant. The pharaoh looked at his reflection in the blade, and then lifted his eyes to stare into the priest's. The chanting grew. The rumble of feet stomping the ground intensified.

"You know what you did," he growled lowly, in between his tightened lips and closed teeth.

A powerful hatred filled the pharaoh's heart. He wanted nothing more than to kill the young man at his mercy. The priest didn't speak but lean his head slightly back, tilting his face upward.

"Tell me why and who ordered you to," the pharaoh ordered.

The priest remained silent, glancing to his right, unable to see the queen. She sat on the edge of her throne, grasping both handles tightly.

"Tell me."

"You won't spare me if I do," he replied.

The pharaoh wiped his mouth, feeling an overwhelming wave of emotions drown him.

"Are you at least remorseful for what you attempted to do?" the pharaoh uttered, choking on his words.

The young priest swallowed hard before replying.

"No."

The pharaoh pulled both arms back, gripping the handle of the sword tightly. I couldn't watch. At that last moment, I raised my eyes to look at the blue sky. It was so blue that day. There was nothing but blue in the sky. Nothing but the bright and lively color. But I couldn't stop my imagination from running free upon the sounds of the sword slashing through flesh and bone. The sound of the blood splattering onto the ground, followed by the dying man choking, groaning, and then falling down...empty...soulless...dead. It all made me want to scream.

In an instant, I saw the body of a younger man dressed in tattered clothing, ripped and torn in several places. Once full of life and promise, now left dead, laying in a pool of his own blood, which spurted out from his chest and stomach. His body curled inward as his dried and dirty fingers twitched. I blinked and saw the body of the bald priest again. His white garb was soaked in the red blood. The queen let out a sharp cry, like the shriek of a kite. From out of her tiny chest, she screamed uncontrollably as her older servant rushed to hold her in her seat.

The pharaoh panted, grinding his teeth, shaking violently as the man laid dead before him. The blood was splattered across the pharaoh's chest, staining the golden chest plate encrusted with gemstones. His hands dripped of the man's blood, like a stream flowing from his wrists to his fingertips. He handed Sefkh the sword slowly, nearly dropping it, turning his attention to Kha'y, who stood near the bottom of the stairs.

I couldn't bring myself to lower my eyes, staring endlessly at the dead body. Until…

"My people! Anyone who dares to harm me, harms you! Let this be a reminder! I am your pharaoh! I am your god! Without me, there is no Egypt!"

The people cried his name, wailing and screaming…spitting upon the dead man, cursing his name.

"He has harmed me! He, who now lies dead before you, has harmed me! He has paid for his treachery! As will all who harm me!"

My eyes peeked and I could see the lifeless body of the priest lying on the floor. Pieces of his flesh covered in red scattered about the feet of the pharaoh. I swallowed, struggling to breathe, and glanced at Laggus, whom remained stern, slightly wincing in the sunlight. Nothing fazed him. He caught me looking at him, glancing at me. I could only respond by slowly lowering my eyes from him to the dead body, and then to my feet.

"His name…means nothing to me now," the pharaoh bellowed. "He is nothing to me now! Go my people! Go and remember what you have seen here! Remember what happens when you harm me! Remember! He...is nothing to me now."

The crowd cheered for what seemed like ages, until they finally began to disperse through the large doors. Aoh watched them leave as she waited for Daimina to step ahead of her to return to the palace. She looked sick and disturbed, hearing the pharaoh speaking to several guards and Laggus.

"I want this body taken from my sight. Take it someplace far away and bury it. He will have no peace for what he did," he ordered.

His cold eyes lifted from the dead body to his queen. Straining her voice to cry, she was wrapped in the arms of her servant.

"How? How do you know he was at fault?"

"He was caught."

The queen's tears trailed down her narrow cheeks as her mouth remained stretched, unable to look away from the dead body across the white ground.

"He didn't deserve this. He isn't the one to blame. If he was involved, he was ordered to do so."

The pharaoh approached her coldly, speaking between tight lips, "He deserved what he got."

She shook her head and wept loudly as the servant tried to help her walk back inside the palace, consoling her through soft words and soothing sounds.

Grabbing Senmet, he growled, "Bring me Kha'y."

Aoh lowered her head, swallowing hard again, listening to the small conversations between the people continue. She glanced at the loud crowd of people slowly beginning to return to their lives outside of the pharaoh's realm. As she watched the crowd separate, she noticed a small child looking at her not far from the doors. The girl's arms hung aimlessly about her tiny body, decorated with sand and dirt, as her long, unbrushed hair moved with every breeze. Her eyes remained wide, staring at Aoh quietly.

She could not have been older than ten years. Innocent and curious, gazing upon me with a look of wonder in her brown eyes. She looked upon me and knew... She would never dress like myself. She would never wear thick makeup, a linen gown, nor the sandals on my feet. She would dress in the clothes she made. So would her children. She'd smell of farm animals and the desert. She would never see the lives of kings written across the walls nor hear of their stories.

The child's head turned around, seeing her mother lowering her arm. The girl held her mother's hand, taking small steps towards the rest of the people leaving the realm of the pharaoh. She looked at her mother silently, dragging her feet through the sand.

Aoh's attention was distracted when she noticed Daimina was

already several steps ahead of her. Aoh continually turned around to watch the child leaving with her mother, disappearing behind several others in the crowd, returning to their world in the sun and sand.

32

When we returned, we were immediately restricted from seeing the pharaoh, who had called Kha'y to his throne room.

The rest of the day was ominous and quiet... The red blood was washed away from the white stone, but his face wasn't. In my mind, I kept seeing his face as though he were haunting me...slowly fading away like the sun over the horizon, digging deep to hide so the moon could reveal itself.

That night, I listened to the sounds of the pharaoh and Daimina speaking as they entered his chamber. I watched as their shadows stood against the farthest door before vanishing behind several drapes. I shouldn't have wandered; however, I felt compelled to. I walked down the empty and silent hallways, listening to the sound of my feet against the floor, staring at every image carved and painted onto the walls. I looked at the statues of the gods as I passed them, slowly feeling a deep sense of weakness standing before them. Following the path, passing rooms and chambers, I smelled the remnants of perfumes and food in the air.

I felt the cool wind upon me and, for a moment, I thought of Laggus as I looked upward towards the night sky in the open ceiling. Thinking of him, for the first time since the escape, brought me peace. His presence soothed me in ways that sleep could not. I desired to speak with him again, but as long as I was dressed in servant's clothes, I could not without probable cause.

Passing another statue, Aoh noticed a protrusion against the bottom of the wall. Getting onto her knees, she crawled to the feet of Horus and saw a square outline in the wall. Reaching, she touched the wall with her hand and rubbed the outline, noticing that the texture felt smoother from the rest. She pushed forward slightly and felt the wall gently move. Hearing a noise not far, Aoh got onto her feet, quickly.

She didn't see anyone, but could decipher where the noise came from. Wiping the bottom of her dress, she continued down the hallway, keeping her eyes on the walls to watch for shadows. She felt a deep sense of dread overcome her; as though someone was following her.

Coming near the center of the palace, I saw the flutter of a shadow move across the painted mural of the pharaoh and his queen. They sat together on their thrones as a small group of foreigners came to them with gifts of their crops and wine. I followed the direction I believed I saw the shadow move, when I suddenly heard a shuffle of movement. Quieting my steps, I continued to an open space where the tops of the palm trees still climbed towards the sky.

Standing near the large column, Aoh peered around the side cautiously. Her fingers inched forward, grasping the smooth, thick railing. Down below, she could see the queen speaking to someone she could only view from the waist down. Aoh's hands slid across the railing to the column, moving to the other side, slowly keeping her eyes low as the queen fully came into view – as well as whom she was speaking to.

It was Senmet, the pharaoh's vizier.

Leaning against the column, while keeping both hands against the carved hieroglyphs, Aoh watched, noticing the distraught expression all over the queen's face and the permanent ever calm expression on Senmet's. He hardly spoke, nodding occasionally but keeping his attention on her. His eyes never once strayed from hers as she rolled her lips together, and placed her hands on her stomach. Their voices were not clear.

It was apparent she was still distressed from what happened earlier. She shook her head intermittently and tried to smile. She spoke again, very quickly and intently, as Senmet moved his hands freely. Hearing the heavy slam of a door from the hallway, Aoh quickly moved to the other side, fearing the queen and Senmet would look up and catch her watching them.

She froze, listening to the direction of footsteps. Turning her head, she noticed a small set of stairs nearly hidden in the long hallway. Moving quickly, she headed towards them, climbing the steps, refusing to look behind her, fearing a white robe and dark eyes looking back at her. Following the narrow path all the way to the top…

I was struck with a cold chill of the night air and the sounds of insects chirping. I gasped. Not only was I surrounded by an endless darkness, but I was a guest to the plethora of bright stars. My eyes found them instantly, forcing me to crane my neck upward and behold a sky full of them. I smiled with joy seeing the sea of tiny stars, all sewn together like jewels on a long gown.

The palace walls still rose around her, as she was easily standing at the second highest peak of the entire palace. Walking slowly over to the side, she looked down and saw the palace grounds below, able to see every guard, standing like statues, at their posts in silence.

She trailed the tips of her fingers across the stone railing, walking over to the edge. Looking down, her eyes followed the beginnings of the palm trees deeply rooted in the ground. She traced their tall trunks upward as their thick, green leaves – now appearing almost dark blue in the darkness – reached astounding heights.

Egypt looked so calm at night. It was so quiet. Even the homes were dark. Hardly a candlelight was seen in the darkness. I inhaled the fresh air, feeling uncommonly at ease as thoughts of Laggus raced through my mind like a wild rainstorm. I smiled deeply, unable to prevent my lips from curling, remembering him in the compound and how devoted he was to the pharaoh. But, then, I thought of him unable to see me as I am and the smile ran away from my face.

The next morning, Daimina and Aoh walked together slowly around the gardens, and small ponds of lily pads and flowers. Outside of the palace, they could hear the sounds of music dimly vibrating off the pillars and columns over the outer wall. The wall rose above them, high enough to where they would have had to climb it in order to see over the top.

Across their paths, wild peacocks squawked, walking slowly and pecking at the ground together. Several palace cats hung about lazily while others swatted at the water, tormenting the fish. Watching her reflection in the water, Daimina plucked the lotus flowers from the lily pads, carefully preparing to weave them together using the long stems. Upon seeing more hiding in between the reeds, she smiled, trying to find them like a child trying to find their friend. Her smile was contagious.

Noticing Aoh watching behind her with curiosity, Daimina's tender smile revealed itself. Holding them in her hands, she turned around, gazing at their smooth petals, sprinkled with droplets of water.

"Would you like me to show you how?" she asked brightly.

Aoh stepped forward, watching intently as Daimina's hands moved like calm waves in the Nile. Each long green stem was soft, curling with ease. She would tie them together, and then wrap them under and over each other, so that each flower would rest side by side, slowly curling into the shape of a circle.

"The stems are very soft," she told Aoh, smiling and showing her work. "When you tie them together, they become a beautiful crown. Perhaps the crown Osiris placed on Isis' head."

Something as simple as playing with flowers enlightened me. Perhaps it was the fact it was so simplistic.

Daimina plucked two more flowers and finished the crown.

"There. Now you, too, can be a queen," Daimina smiled, holding the flower crown toward her servant.

Daimina's eyes lifted from the crown, seeing Laggus' reflection in the water passing them. She called to him, gently waving.

Turning around, there he was... He glowed in the sun, the color of his hair matching the leather tightly strapped around his chest. Hints of blue peeked out between the armor, like his eyes hiding behind his thin bangs.

Marching forward, keeping his hand steady on the handle of his sword, he acknowledged them.

"Daimina. Aoh," he greeted, focusing all his attention upon Daimina. "Is there something you needed?"

"No. I wanted to thank you for protecting the pharaoh," she explained firmly.

"It is my duty to protect him every day of his life," Laggus replied.

"Yes, but I know it was you who caught the priest. It was because of you a traitor was caught before it was too late. For that, I wanted to thank you. Truly, thank you," she explained, looking into his eyes.

I was surprised Daimina knew. Two priests plotting to kill her. The man I caught, who Laggus killed was one. The pharaoh killed the other.

Laggus turned towards Aoh briefly, bowed to Daimina and smoothly spoke.

"You are most welcome."

Continuing on his way, Aoh fought to avoid looking at him but couldn't. Her eyes followed him, smiling when suddenly she felt the flower crown placed on her head.

"See? A queen." Daimina's smiled widened seeing the crown.

Aoh touched the flower crown on her head and replied lowly, "Thank you."

Daimina's smile grew as she picked up the bottom of her dress and carefully walked deeper into the water, looking for more lily pads. The water rose to her knees, trailing with light faded scars.

Pulling the lily pads, she plucked the flowers, pushing the thick papyrus reeds, searching for any sight of white in the constant sea of green. She giggled like a child at the touch of fish swimming around her legs.

I had seen that same expression before on Queen Huriye's face. The look of the highest form of joy: complete ecstasy.

"What pleases my lady today?" Aoh asked, her voice soft.

Finding another white lotus flower, Daimina plucked it from the water and replied, "Does there need to be a reason as to why I am happy?"

"This is the first time I have seen you this happy since I became your servant," Aoh admitted.

"Yes, my happiness can be destroyed by the cruelty of others, but…" Pausing, she turned around, cradling the lotus flowers in her arms. "Surely you understand why it is I smile? Why it is I shine?"

Aoh's eyes frowned, lost by Daimina's words.

"You do understand, don't you?" she asked again. "What it is like to be in the arms of a man, to feel his love both physically and spiritually?"

Aoh didn't respond, becoming numb, staring at the white flowers in Daimina's arms. Plucking one more white lotus flower, Daimina walked slowly out of the water and back onto the steps. She squeezed the bottom of her pleated linen dress, releasing water back into the river. She looked at the bundle of white flowers near her feet, noticing she didn't have enough to make another crown.

"I wouldn't have use for a crown. It will never fit upon my head. I will, instead, make a most beautiful bracelet," she explained, looking at the flowers.

"Come, let's go."

She squeezed the ends of her hair, feeling remnants of water slip through her grip. Aoh nodded, taking off the flower crown on her head, and followed Daimina back inside.

33

Daimina's fingers slowly stroked the smooth white petals she wrapped into the bracelet. Aoh struggled brushing her hair, not as soft nor tame as Egyptian hair. The silence unwound her nerves as each stroke rummaged through stubborn knots.

Daimina sat like a figurine, looking at herself in the small reflective mirror, slightly shaking with nervousness. Her cheeks flushed a deep red as she glanced at the necklace around her neck. She gasped, frightened by the sounds of a pair of jackals in the distance. Aoh struggled with a large knot, pulling a little too hard and heard Daimina grunt slightly.

"I'm so sorry, my lady. I didn't mean to harm you," Aoh apologized quickly.

"No need to apologize. I know my hair is different than yours or the queen's," Daimina replied.

"Do you wish me to stop?" Aoh asked.

"No."

Aoh continued, timid with each stroke, using less force while watching the knots untangle. Any moment she reached a knot, she refrained from continuing, lightly tugging at the hair strands until the knot was free. All the slight pain in the world couldn't wipe the smile from Daimina's face. She rubbed her neck with scented oils, returning her attention to the necklace. She turned her head towards the brushstrokes, feeling her tender stomach flip following each breath. Aoh finished her hair by adding more beads.

Aoh used tweezers from the desk and gently tended to Daimina's fingernails first and then her toenails. Each nail was filed smoothly across and when rubbed with oil, shined in the light.

Fixing her dress, running her hands over the pleats, Daimina reached for the bowl and flicked scented oils sporadically. Aoh's eyes avoided the near transparent fabric across Daimina's chest, twirling her fingers through the longer ends of her hair.

Taking the flower bracelet, Aoh wrapped it softly within a white folded sheet and handed it to Daimina. She clasped it against her chest, as her stomach flipped again, staring at it as though she was watching a part of her old self fade away.

In the darkness, I followed Daimina as she walked down a hallway I was not familiar with, carrying the wrapped cloth around her waist. Our shadows moved over epic tales and spells, passing distinct expressions of awe and fear upon the frozen faces. Our steps silently moved as the light from the fires seemed to slowly burn less brightly.

She stopped when she saw the pharaoh several feet away, nervous anticipation breaking through his normal stoicism. He waited in the dim light, standing like a god over men against a wall depicting his throne and subjects serving him. His shadow climbed to the ceiling, lightly moving side to side.

She ran to him, like a child to a friend not seen in years. He embraced her and kissed her passionately as their lips consumed each other's slowly. His hands rubbed the sides of her upper arms tenderly, holding her tightly against him. With each exhale, he grasped her tighter. Their eyes just barely closing as they stood in the dim light of the burning fires.

Together they entered the empty room, slipping behind a variety of silk curtains surrounding the large bed. Silently, they consumed each other in scents. The burning wood shards crackled in the background of their devotion. They rocked to and fro, like water over sand. Their voices called out to each other in between heavy breathing that made my face turn red as I stood by the room, pacing slowly.

From the other side of the door, I saw Laggus appear against the wall in half shadow produced by the large flames. My heart sang seeing him there.

"I wouldn't wander far," Laggus warned firmly.

"I just wanted to give them their privacy," Aoh replied lowly, trying to ignore the passions unfolding from the room.

"When you live in the palace, nothing you do is a private matter."

"Then, I guess, this has proven itself to be a legitimate reason to speak with you."

Laggus looked up and shifted his body to face Aoh, leaning against the wall. She blinked heavily, able to hear the pharaoh and Daimina calling to each other as she walked towards him.

I found myself uncontrollably staring into Laggus' eyes. They were deeper than the center of the hottest flame.

"What happened with the priest?" Aoh asked.

"I thwarted his plot to kill Daimina," Laggus replied bluntly. As though he could read my mind he continued, "Nothing you have to worry about. What's done is done."

"I am worried. Since I am the one protecting her, I would like to know how he was planning to kill her."

Laggus paused for, what seemed like minutes, before answering.

"He was planning to kill her in her sleep after…he killed you."

I could hear the deep hesitation in his voice before his last three words, making my stomach flip.

"Was he alone?"

"No," Laggus replied.

Shaking his head gently to disperse the bangs from covering his eyes, he continued, "The problem is catching the person responsible."

"Who is that?"

Laggus turned and pointed at the image carved before them in the wall. Aoh turned and found the image to be of the queen standing at the presence of the king, as she is crowned by the high priest. Servants surrounded them, carrying baskets of food and linens. Ra was present, with Isis and Nephthys standing beside him with open wings. He watched Aoh stare at the image as a deeper truth revealed itself to her.

"He was the queen's brother."

My eyes instantly fell to the floor as the images of seeing the queen and Senmet speaking uncontrollably returned to me all at once.

"Did you see anything unusual?" Laggus asked immediately.

"I saw the queen and Senmet speaking last night."

Laggus shifted his body weight again, taking a step closer to Aoh as his left eyebrow lifted very slightly in the shadow of his face.

"This was different," she persisted. "I couldn't hear their conversation, but I could feel that something wasn't right."

My concentration was broken when I realized, as we spoke, my own imaginations were taking over me. I covered my mouth noticing how Laggus hardly blinked, remaining composed. Nothing seemed to phase him.

His attention changed as he glanced down the hallway. He looked as though he was listening for something. After a moment, he glanced at the floor.

"They should be finished soon."

I don't know whether it was the way he stood in the light or whether I could read him like papyrus, but I could see in his eyes this sense of fatigue.

"Laggus…you should sleep," Aoh calmly stated, taking small steps towards him.

He looked at her, slightly startled by her statement.

"I will stay here, you go to your bed and sleep. You need it."

Laggus didn't speak but shook his head slightly in response.

"My needs do not matter. Yours does."

He lowered his arm to his side and revealed a blade in a golden cover. The sound of the blade clicked free from his belt.

"After the events that transpired, carry this with you at all times," he instructed her. "Keep the other in her chambers. Our king will be holding a celebration soon and all eyes will be on her. The more time she spends with him, the more powerful she becomes. Claws will be sharpened. Hungers will be unfed. Do you understand me?"

Aoh looked at the knife, suddenly remembering when she killed the men who attempted to kill Princess Mylittia at the well. The sounds of each strike rang inside her head. The feeling of warm blood tingled her hands. She exhaled slowly, taking the knife, staring at the leather cover and light glistening against the golden handle before she tucked it under her the sash tied at her waist, perfectly concealing it.

"I do. Thank you," she replied firmly.

Laggus looked up and could see at the far end of the hallway, Kha'y coming around the corner and then suddenly stop the moment he saw Aoh and Laggus standing there. Aoh read Laggus' frozen expression and refrained from moving.

"Bow to me slowly and then walk back towards the doorway. Stay there and wait for Daimina," Laggus ordered quietly.

I obeyed Laggus' order, bowing to him, lowering my eyes to the floor as I made my way back towards the doorway. I passed the pharaoh and Daimina, as they lay together, wrapped in each other's arms, tangled in each other's clothing and the soft bedding. I could see at the end of the hallway a figure in white, half in the shadow like mist. Immediately, my throat swelled. It looked like the high priest wearing a long, braided wig, cascading over his left shoulder.

I leaned against the wall, wishing Daimina would emerge from the doorway and tell me to leave without her. My skin crawled each second that passed, as though my body was waiting to be attacked. I struggled with each breath to remain calm as a heavy wave of fear crashed over me repeatedly. I couldn't hear their conversation…only mumbles and laughs. She gasped at times as the sounds of him kissing her repeatedly followed. She held him tightly, his arms wrapped about her thin, shapely body as she said his name repeatedly.

It was now clear to me that she was not just a mistress in his eyes. She was his Queen.

Kha'y slowly approached Aoh, keeping to himself down the hallway, thin hands folded at his chest. Just as he passed her, he stopped and declared aloud, "Look at me."

Aoh didn't respond, keeping her head down until she felt his hand touch her chin and lift her face to meet his wicked eyes.

I could see half of his face in the darkness. He didn't smile at first, staring at me as though he were trying to find something in my eyes. I felt my hands rising slowly from my sides to my waist as he took a step forward. I could feel his dress against me, and the faint touch of his long legs. I forced myself to stare at him without so much as a blink. I clenched my mouth shut, and forced my lips to silently lie across my face.

He tilted my head gently higher when I heard Laggus walk towards me. Rubbing his thumb gently across my chin, Kha'y must have found what he was looking for when I saw his lips open slightly, revealing a grin in the corner of his mouth.

"Ah, there you are," he muttered.

Hearing Laggus approach, he released Aoh's chin and spoke with a chill in his voice, "Good evening."

"Evening," Laggus replied.

"I was hoping to speak with the pharaoh. I was told he had come down this way, but I can now see he is preoccupied."

"You wish to speak with him now?" Laggus questioned. "Have you not been sent from his sight until told otherwise?"

"My innocence has been spoken for. It's a very urgent matter, Laggus. I have received a most important message from the gods this evening as I prayed before my meal. Please tell him that I must seek an audience with him tomorrow at the latest. This cannot wait."

"I will," Laggus promised.

Kha'y grinned, nodding forward. "You are his most loyal servant. I do hope he is rewarding you well."

His eyes glanced over to Aoh as he nodded to her momentarily, and then looked at Laggus coldly.

"Good night."

Turning around, he returned to the shadows at the end of the hallway. The long trail of the cheetah skin he wore over his shoulder dragged across the floor. The last thing Aoh saw was the dull eyes of the dead animal in the faint light. The moment he vanished, Laggus grabbed one of Aoh's hands immediately from her waist, raising it upward to her eyes, staring at her with his own. Now, full of darkness with a hue of utter disappointment.

"Not in the palace," he scolded darkly.

Aoh looked at her hand and then down at the other resting at her waist, just over the sash where the knife she received was concealed. Releasing her hand, Aoh kept them at her sides, feeling a flutter of sadness overcome her. Rolling her lips together, she attempted to speak when Daimina's voice hovered at the door. Aoh rubbed her eyes and quickly approached the door, seeing Daimina sweated and smiling. She kissed the pharaoh again.

In between their lips she whispered softly, "Must I go? I want to stay with you."

The pharaoh's expression faded from joy to guilt, as thoughts of his wife rapidly attacked him.

"You must return to your chambers," he told her, with a hint of unexpected severity.

Both Aoh and Laggus glanced at the pharaoh upon hearing his tone, as Daimina's glorious joys were cut short. Regretting his tone, the pharaoh kissed her forehead and then passionately on her lips.

"Sleep well, my love. May the gods grant you endless dreams," he whispered.

34

The next morning, I awoke very tired. I hadn't slept much, and it seemed Daimina hadn't either, considering she was still fast asleep in her bed. I forced myself up to wash her clothing and prepare her something to eat. I could barely keep my eyes open while scrubbing the dress repeatedly, surrounded by other servants I never spoke to.

As I made my way to prepare her some food, amongst the servants doing the same silently working, I passed the throne room finding the pharaoh sitting on his throne, speaking to his subjects. To his left, I saw Laggus listening intently when suddenly a loud sound from outside caught their attention.

I watched them as I carried Daimina's food, hearing the loud shouts of guards calling for the pharaoh, followed by distant trumpets. I rushed back to Daimina's chambers, nearly dropping the tray of food, finding her still sleeping. She hadn't stirred since I left. The smile on her face hadn't faded since the day before. Wrapped in linen's, she curled her hands to her face, caressed in comfort.

"Daimina. Daimina…you need to wake up. You must wake up."

Aoh persisted, as she shook Daimina to and fro repeatedly. The only responses were grunts and objections.

"Someone has arrived to the palace. You must get up. You must get up and get dressed."

Daimina's eyes opened seeing Aoh standing over her.

"Who?" she asked immediately.

Together, Aoh and Daimina quickly walked towards the throne room as it was filling with scribes, servants, and guards. The pharaoh sat on his throne with his queen next to him, fixing the crown snuggly upon his head as the queen's servant brushed her hair. Laggus stood at his usual position, as did Sefkh entering the room behind a rush of guards.

Servants positioned themselves as windows were opened, revealing the sunlight and admitting fresh air, while the floors were quickly swept and furniture moved. Daimina looked for somewhere to stand when Senmet generously guided her near the first of several columns, where she could clearly see what was occurring and not be seen by the visitors.

The pharaoh watched Senmet guide her, rubbing his index and middle fingers against his mouth. Daimina thanked Senmet, moving as Aoh tugged the bottom of her long dress behind her, carefully running her hands across the translucent fabric. Moving to fix her hair, Daimina glanced at the pharaoh, making him smile, flushing red as a result, much to the irritation of his queen.

Senmet nodded to Aoh and took his usual spot, glancing down at the scribe who fixed himself in his chair, prepared with plenty of papyrus paper and ink. The incense burners were lit, filling the room with the new scent, as the horns and other instruments grew louder.

The queen looked to her husband, gently stretching her hand to touch his, grazing her fingers over his skin slowly. He turned to look at her as her eyes, still seemingly wet, surrounded by gorgeous makeup, glowed. Her small smile gleamed with gloss. He couldn't resist, revealing a smile as he held her hand, rubbing his fingers gently over her skin.

Servants waved large palm tree leaves up and down, as others stood with prepared drinks on heavy plates. Aneski was the last to arrive, entering the room slowly, picking up the bottom of her dress and approaching her son. She was wearing a blue and green linen gown with a light array of feathers in her shortened hair. He strained his neck to look at her as she glanced down at him, standing several steps above him. She placed her slightly wrinkled hand onto his shoulder for a moment before clasping her other hand on her waist. The pharaoh let out a heavy breath, feeling nervous as they all waited for the guest to arrive.

Light conversations turned to whispers as men and women guessed whom the guests would be. Egypt's trading was in full bloom; however, they were not expecting another trade for some time.

"It's alright," the queen reassured lowly, squeezing the pharaoh's hand. "You arc a god. You hold all thc power."

He released another heavy breath between his lips as the doors were opened.

Releasing his wife's hand, a multitude of music filled the room. Tyrgnn entered, carrying under his arms several large rolled scrolls. His wool sandals slapped against the solid floor as eight female Egyptian dancers paraded behind him, swinging balls attached to ropes, and twirling long colorful sashes.

His four layers of heavy robes cascaded onto the floor, trailing over the bounty of flower petals tossed into the air, creating a fresh scent across the room. Behind him, a group of men dressed in similar robes followed, older in age, with darkened eyes and black tattoos inked over their hands and up both arms.

Light facial hair touched parts of his face, defining his cheekbones and nose. The moment he stopped in the middle of the room, the music and dancing ended. The room became as a silent as the desert night. Lifting both arms so swiftly the robes spread outward like hawk wings, Tyrgnn bowed, draping his entire body onto the floor before the pharaoh.

"My king, I am honored to be in your kingdom that once housed my ancestors. I am overwhelmed with joy to be in your very presence," he announced.

"You are most welcome, Tyrgnn, ambassador to your King Khian of the Hyksos."

Aoh gasped, staring forward, taking a slight step back and nearly bumping into the guard standing at attention behind her.

"My king has blessed me with the task of offering an eternal friendship to Egypt," Tyrgnn announced. "I have brought with me gifts for you, great pharaoh. Among them, gorgeous beasts of nature. Spotted and diligent. Beautiful wild cats."

From behind him, several of pharaoh's servants pushed and pulled large cages of wild cheetahs and jaguars through the open doors. The room fell silent, amazed by the large beasts. The robed men presented the cages, stopped near Senmet and Sefkh, waving their arms and chanting aloud. The large cats paced in their small space, looking at the room surrounding them, twitching their whiskers and showing their teeth in between small roars and grunts. Their broad shoulders rolled each time they moved their large bodies.

"They are quite tame, when properly trained. We know you will find them to be as loyal as your servants, guards, and soldiers. We also bring fabrics. Textures to keep you cool in the heat of day and warm in the cold of night. Enjoy our food, drink, wines, and breads, and ride our magnificent horses, bred to serve man!"

From the doors, more of the pharaoh's servants entered. They tugged at the reigns of the horses, pulling the black and dark brown steeds into the room. The clasping of their hooves against the floor created a beautiful tune as the room slowly filled with gifts. Fabrics were unrolled, placed on the floor, and the bounty of foods placed on top of them, quickly displayed around cases of gemstones not common to Egypt.

Aoh remembered the intricate patterns of the fabrics as each color brought her back to memories of Babylon. She remembered seeing those very fabrics across Queen Huriye's floor and over her shoulders, as the memory of her face sent chills down her body.

"All of these are yours, great pharaoh, to do with as you seek. Our king only asks for your friendship in return, oh, mighty pharaoh of Egypt. Conquerer. Ruler," Tyrgnn explained, calmly.

"Friendship?" the pharaoh asked in response, causing his wife to look at him.

"Yes. Many years ago, my ancestors and the Egyptians thrived together, sharing the Nile and its blessings. It was apparent we overstayed our welcome, and left without destruction to your city. We have not spoken since and our kingdoms flourished through peace. Please, do not misunderstand. We do not wish to trick or mislead. We only ask for your friendship so that we may never go to war as enemies, but rather allies."

"What war are you referring to?" the pharaoh asked intensely, causing both Senmet and Laggus to turn their attention onto him.

"War. As you have seen, the Mitanni have been moving quite swiftly near your borders. We've caught sight of them, even as we arrived. They are not the only ones."

A cold chill fell over the room as the pharaoh's eyes tightened, resting his index finger against the side of his face. Though his eyes remained still upon Tyrgnn, he was rapidly becoming angered. I glanced to my left and noticed the abrupt change in Sefkh's expression as he stood, listening. Senmet's eyes fell upon him before returning to the pharaoh's, spelling out a faint touch of disappointment and frustration.

"They have not bothered us, for we are not a threat-" Tyrgnn attempted, but was interrupted by the pharaoh.

"Your alliance with Babylon might say otherwise," the pharaoh interrupted.

"Babylon has nothing-"

"Except Assyrians who, also, have their sights on my kingdom."

"They are but a few, great pharaoh. Most have faded away like the temples. Their rule left Babylon nothing-"

"There must be something they left behind, otherwise King Khian would not be married to her."

The pharaoh's swift judgments against the Hyksos did not faze Tyrgnn, as he continued to speak calmly and confidently. He straightened his posture and began to walk to and fro, addressing not just the pharaoh but the entire room.

"I am concerned, Tyrgnn, and I have every right to be. How do I know your king is speaking the truth? How do I know I can trust him?" the pharaoh asked, coldly.

"We come on his behalf with gifts that-"

"That could be luring us into a false sense of security."

"I assure you, King Khian has no such intentions. He is a man of his word. I've known him since we were children. I swear on my very life."

"So, then, all I have is your word, and King Khian's word, of an eternal friendship?"

Tyrgnn frowned suddenly, glancing at the room and noticing how every eye was upon him.

"Yes, only my word, great King of Egypt," he answered lowly.

Tyrgnn pulled one of the scrolls from under his arm and continued, "This letter was written by King Khian himself, explaining everything for our proposal of a peace treaty…if that is, indeed, what Egypt wants."

"What Egypt wants is a truce," the pharaoh said boldly, much to the disappointed facial reactions of several in the room. "Egypt remembers when the Hyksos invaded our lands and ruled our people. We remember how kind and just they were. We remember how they came at a time when we were weak and didn't use such an opportunity against us. We remember taking our kingdom back and pushing them out without spurn nor hatred. Your people have given us gifts, even if they were unintentional, that we cannot live without. We welcome your King Khian, his people, as friends, not foes."

"Please tell your king that we, too, do not want war," the pharaoh progressed, "regardless of what others may say. The shadows whisper at all hours of the day and night, but they do not rule this kingdom. We want peace. An eternity of peace, so that even after we fade and new kings rule our people, we will always be there as allies. Like a bridge over the Nile River. We will read the proposal, but, for certain, we want to avoid war."

Tyrgnn smiled, bowing deeply. To Aoh, however, the smile seemed disingenuous, disbelieving. It never quite reached his eyes.

"These words comfort not only myself but the kingdom I represent. You are truly a great pharaoh. Much beloved."

"We will read this proposal and pray for guidance in this matter. We will respond quickly, rest assured all of what is said is true and not false. We will trust you and King Khian. Thank you for coming, Tyrgnn. The journey must have been quite tiring."

"I am honored to have done so. I shall return and tell my king what you have told me, and that your official response will be delivered soon. I wish for you a long and bountiful reign."

The pharaoh nodded as Tyrgnn bowed once more, draping his entire body over the floor.

As he rose, the pharaoh spoke. "Please, take some provisions with you for your journey back. We do not wish all of you to return to the desert empty handed."

He waved over several servants who carried with them sacks full of water and food. Tyrgnn smiled, taking them into his arms, smelling the exotic scents. He turned to the older gentlemen behind him who nodded in agreement, stone-faced, expressionless. His eyes narrowed in a way that, in Aoh's view, cast doubt upon his sincerity.

"Thank you. You are generous and kind. I look forward to meeting with you again on matters of peace in the coming days."

With one final bow, the cold chill in the room faded, slipping behind the doors as they closed behind the group.

The moment the room dispersed, the pharaoh called for Daimina, Senmet, Laggus, and several others to meet with him. Taking the only opportunity I had, I fled as fast as I could to return to my room. I removed my makeup, retrieving my bow and arrows, and a cloth to wrap myself in.

Rushing to the stables, I looked around. A heavy scent of grains and oils ensnared my nostrils, itching the skin upon my nose. Ten horses remained, standing at attention, intrigued by my presence. I quickly tucked the bow over my shoulder and slipped the quiver around the saddle of a horse I knew the pharaoh did not use.

The horse remained calm, watching me slide my hands across it's back. The horse grunted in response, taking two steps forward and back.

The hot breath blew over my hand as I slowly tried to obtain some sense of emotion coming from the trained animal. Quickly untying the long rope from the reigns of the horse, I heard the back door open. Turning around, I saw Laggus. His eyes hardened, confused, slowly closing the door behind him.

"What are you doing?" he asked immediately.

"I'm going to follow Tyrgnn before he returns to Babylon," Aoh replied, unraveling the heavy rope and quickly pulling herself onto the saddle.

"No, you cannot-"

"Laggus, you have to let me go. I knew Tyrgnn, and I can prevent Egypt from going to war with Babylon," Aoh spewed so quickly Laggus could barely understand her.

Promptly standing in front of the horse, he asked, brow furrowed.

"What are you talking about?"

"Tyrgnn is King Khian's ambassador. If I can assure him the pharaoh doesn't want war, he will tell his king and listen to him. He just left. I can still catch up. He will listen to me."

Laggus refrained from moving, firmly stretching both of his arms over the wooden door, staring at me with this intense refusal to allow me to pass.

"Laggus, you have to trust me."

"You can't go. You're not going out there on your own to speak with a man who might be feeding the king ambitions of war! You saw his face! I will speak to the king about this-"

"There's no time! I have to go!"

"Aoh!"

"Laggus, I didn't ask for this! I didn't! I didn't ask for this, any of it!" she screamed surprising him. "I have to do this. You have to let me go!"

Grunting, Laggus removed himself from the post as it opened and the horse began to grow anxious.

"Protect Daimina until I return."

"And what of the palace? They will know you're missing."

"You will think of something."

35

The horse screeched wildly, kicking its feet repeatedly. Running out of the stable and into the sunlight, Aoh rode as fast as she could through the city, dodging citizens. Rushing through the city and into the town, the wind whipped at her face, spraying sand across her skin.

Her body rattled to and fro, constantly snapping the reigns, wrapping them around her hands several times. Crossing the Nile River, startling the fish in the calming waters, the horse screeched. Her eyes followed the path to the desert burning in the wind.

The more the stallion fussed, the slower it moved through the cool water. Aoh constantly smacked her feet against the saddle, ordering it to keep moving, clicking her teeth and tongue together. Once across the other side, hurdling through the thick papyrus reeds, Aoh could see the burning sun beginning to fade away, touching the mountain tops, turning the sky into an array of wild colors.

The harsh heat faded into a cooling breeze. Each heavy breath from her horse sounded like roaring grunts, panting as foam dripped around its lips and nose. Her body rose and fell, her hands and legs cramping. A light trail of smoke faded high into the sky, coming from the distance.

Aoh ground her teeth, able to see the tiny speck ahead of her moving at an alarming speed. Kicking her feet against the sides of the horse aggressively, Aoh shouted. She roared, ordering the horse to run faster and faster as the small speck soon grew in size. Pulling the horse to the side, she called out, straining her voice.

"Tyrgnn!" Aoh shouted.

His head didn't turn as he continued to ride.

"TYRGNN!"

He turned around, seeing me, and instantly released his tightened grip on the reigns as his horse nearly lost control. Trying to steady his horse, Tyrgnn grunted, pulling back roughly, nearly falling off and into the sand.

Aoh screamed, leaning forward and coming to the front of his horse. Panting slightly, Tyrgnn looked upon Aoh with confusion, rolling his hands to and fro as his horse breathed heavily. His face was hidden underneath a wool hat and shoulder length black hair. The youth in his eyes darkened like the tattoos on his knuckles.

"Aoh? Is that you?" he asked, unsure.

"Yes," Aoh nodded, slightly out of breath, feeling the hood flutter against her face in the brief wind.

"What…what are you doing out here? Were you following me?"

"Yes. Yes…to speak with you about something very important."

"I cannot stall…King Khian is awaiting my return," Tyrgnn insisted.

He pulled the reigns back, attempting to pass Aoh when she viciously pulled her horse in front of his, stopping him.

"Aoh-"

"Tell your king that no matter what the pharaoh says, to not declare war," Aoh ordered firmly.

"Excuse me?" Tyrgnn asked, wincing.

"The pharaoh doesn't want to go to war. He has no interest in expanding his territory. His generals and inner circle will say otherwise. They will try to convince him the Hyksos are a threat."

"That is not my decision-"

"You have to beg him not to go to war. Tell him the truth, he will listen to you."

"Egypt wants to be allies, not enemies? My king wants nothing more than peace, but the fact that your king shows little expression for such a truth-"

"Don't...do this. King Khian doesn't want to go to war either. He wants peace. You told me that yourself, so don't lie. It's Queen Huriye who wants to. It's all her, it's always her," Aoh explained breathlessly.

Tyrgnn's eyes narrowed as he angrily forced his horse forward and into Aoh's horse. She pulled back as he drew his sword, only for Aoh to respond by drawing her bow. In a quick motion, she had her bow and arrow aligned. Hiding within the dark fabrics, she stared down her arrow, calmly releasing breaths from her lips.

"You dare draw your bow at the king's ambassador?" he asked bitterly.

"Not you. Turn around," Aoh warned.

Doing as she said, he spotted six men on horseback approached them, covered in black robes. They rode as a group, near invisible in the growing darkness. Their wolf-like eyes revealed them. Aoh remained positioned to fire her arrow as Tyrgnn turned his horse around to face the cloaked men, all equal in beastly size.

Simultaneously pulling their horses to a halt, the air changed. It felt colder... From the shadows cast upon their faces, dark scars trailed across their skin. They stood in silence, staring at Aoh and Tyrgnn, expressionless.

"Give us everything you have and you live," the first in the row of six ordered with a heavy accent that Aoh could barely understand.

Tyrgnn slowly lowered his sword, keeping both hands steady around the handle, watching the gang of men. Both Aoh and Tyrgnn refused to answer, feeling a sense of dread brewing. Impatient, the first rider approached them slowly, stopping mere feet from them, lowering the cloth from his mouth and revealing several deep scars running up and down both sides of his even darker skinned face.

"I will not repeat myself again," he proclaimed.

"We have nothing worth taking," Tyrgnn replied coldly, moving his horse in front of Aoh's.

"Your weapons will do. A curved sword crafted by Hyksos. A bow with plenty of arrows. No doubt you are carrying daggers under your garments."

"This is all we have. If you take it we will not survive the desert," Tyrgnn explained. "Perhaps we can provide a more useful exchange for…riders such as yourselves?"

Tugging his horse forward another step, he stared into Aoh's eyes as she remained focused upon him like a hunter stalking prey. Her hands remained tightly grasped on the bow and arrow, aimed directly at him with no signs of intending to miss.

The fear began to take ahold of me, as my breathing hastened between my teeth.

"You dare threaten to strike me?" the cloaked man growled.

Aoh drawing the string further answered his question. With one swift movement he drew his sword, clashing against Tyrgnn's. Aoh released her arrow, striking him in the chest, and attempted to shoot another arrow when suddenly she was thrown from her horse. Both she and her horse were knocked over and onto the ground, as the beastly horses circled around them kicking their feet in the air.

Freeing her left foot from under her horse, Aoh struggled across the sand, trying to find her bow and arrows, when two men came charging towards her, screaming at the top of their lungs.

Tyrgnn swung at the nearest rider's leg, and then jabbed the blade into his chest. The horse collapsed, roaring loudly, kicking up the sand into the air as Aoh dodged them, rolling across the ground. Getting onto her feet, she ran towards Tyrgnn, who pulled his sword from the dead body forcefully, spraying blood into the air. He swung, missing the rider near him before tossing the sword to Aoh. Almost dropping it, unprepared for the heavy weight, she rose it above her head as both swords swooped downward.

Grabbing his bag, Tyrgnn found his dagger just as Aoh ducked underneath the two blades and rolled forward. She swung her sword, cutting off the man's arm as Tyrgnn threw his dagger at the other, killing him instantly. Aoh stumbled, running with no time towards the man she wounded, taking the sword and slashing his chest.

The last man rushed to her in a wild rage, swinging two swords, spit slipping down his hairy chin. Aoh froze instantly. She witnessed him be beheaded by Tyrgnn's blade. With a flash, she heard the sound of ripping and slurping of decapitation.

All six men lay dead on the ground.

Tyrgnn rolled their cold, dismembered bodies into one pile as Aoh waited, staring at the trails of blood across the sand. She wrapped her arms around her chest, unable to feel anything.

"Aoh," Tyrgnn said, coming to her out of breath.

Remaining unresponsive, Aoh stared at the blood until Tyrgnn lifted her chin with his hand.

Turning her head to look for wounds, he asked, "You alright?"

Aoh nodded in response.

Tyrgnn sat in front of the small fire he made using stone and wooden tools, digging through the belongings of the six men he and Aoh killed. Aoh dropped two pieces of wood onto the fire, listening to the loud crackles and snaps, glancing at the pile of dead bodies not far from them.

The six horses remained tied together to the side of the large tent as Aoh and Tyrgnn's belongings remained together on the other side of the tent.

Out of the corner of her eyes, Aoh noticed Tyrgnn rummaging through the bags and said, "We shouldn't keep any of this."

"Why? No one will remember them," he replied, pulling out a heavy, leather- bound composition of texts written in another language.

"I don't carry anything with me that's not mine," she explained.

"Don't want to remember, do you?" he sighed, looking at the

foreign script in the light of the fire.

Aoh didn't answer, sitting near the six horses, feeling the warmth of the fire against her chilled body. She rubbed her hands together repeatedly in between wrapping her cloak tighter around herself.

She coughed loudly, feeling remnants of sand in her throat. She reached for water, noticing the pile of belongings Tyrgnn collected from the dead riders. She barely drank, unable to ignore what occurred, trying to put it past her.

"That bow you use…did Queen Huriye give that to you?" he asked, looking at her bow near her feet.

"No. This one I made. I left hers behind when I left," she replied, wiping her mouth.

He nodded, pulling out several blankets made from sheep's wool. He smiled widely when he found two curved blades wrapped within the blankets. Aoh watched him pull them out with haste, studying their craftsmanship in the fire light. Almost every second his mouth opened and closed, his eyes widening, amazed by the details in the weapons. He rubbed his fingers down the sharp end of the blade, slowly.

"Stunning," Tyrgnn commented.

"There is nothing stunning about weapons," Aoh replied, harshly.

"Yes, there is. Without your bow, my blade, they would have killed you."

"If you hadn't let your company go ahead of you, we wouldn't have needed to kill those men," she snapped in response.

"You regret killing them?"

"Yes, I do," she declared with finality.

Aoh wrapped her arms across her knees, resting her head against her arms, looking at the fire. Tyrgnn wrapped the blades back in the sheep's wool, putting them near the other items he collected.

"Why?"

"I-" Aoh's voice trailed.

As Tyrgnn rolled up his sleeves, Aoh's eyes followed the tattoos running up both arms.

"Is Egypt where you live now?" he asked calmly, looking at her.

"I do," she replied, gently pushing the nearest piece of wood closer with her foot to the colorful flames.

"Do you want to know how Queen Huriye is doing?"

Aoh didn't respond, watching the colors of the flames dance and shake over the charring wood.

"The alliance was made after you left," he informed her. "She married the prince, now King Khian, much to her daughter's dismay. She was married to one of the other princes in case…you were concerned about her. I couldn't stop thinking about you since I last saw you."

Aoh's fingers gripped the fabrics over her arms tightly, unable to stop the nervousness inside of her from growing, boiling, flooding her body.

"You were everywhere I went, Aoh," he continued, pouring his heart out – his pain dripping from every word he uttered. "In every tree, rock, flower that bloomed. And then, when they married, I didn't see you there. I panicked. My mind raced with all these horrible thoughts. I couldn't understand why you weren't there. So…I…asked for you."

Aoh turned her head and looked at him.

"Queen Huriye wouldn't say where you were," he announced, disappointment and sorrow clouding his tone. "The way she was so abrupt made me believe she killed you… But Princess Mylittia told me what really happened."

Tyrgnn stopped and slowly faced Aoh, falling into the color of her eyes, reflecting the dancing flames as a bitterness grew.

"Now…I see why you spoke to me that night," he reminisced. "You didn't care for me, you only cared for Egypt. That was all you ever cared about."

"Tyrgnn, that isn't-"

"You could have had a throne and ruled a nation. You were like a daughter to her. Mylittia trusted you to protect her. Why did you give it up?" he asked, with a faint smile of disbelief in her actions while shaking his head.

"I wasn't lying when I said that I trusted you. I meant every word, and I told you then that the gods had other plans for me," she replied firmly.

"Really? The gods? Which gods? Yours? The ones who plague Egypt time and time again?"

"You wouldn't understand," she whispered, frustrated.

"Help me to," he urged.

Aoh shook her head and replied, "I have to go back at sunrise."

"For who? Your husband?" he asked bitterly.

Annoyed by his tone, Aoh stood up.

"You didn't answer my question, Aoh. You could still be my wife."

"Your wife?" Aoh asked breathlessly.

Tyrgnn looked at her as he rummaged through the bags again with anger. The bitterness grew.

"I wasn't lying when I said you're beautiful. You still are and always will be to me."

His face distorted as his eyes narrowed.

"Do you know how many nights I lost sleep before I found out what happened to you?" he fumed. "I wrote to you several times and never heard back. Not once! You owed me that at least, for what I confessed to you. Did you wear that necklace I sent you? At least once? Did you feel anything after reading my poems? Anything at all?"

"Tyrgnn-"

"Oh, wait, you already said you didn't keep anything that wasn't yours."

He released an aggravated sigh, throwing a bag full of objects down near Aoh's feet. The sounds of metal and bronze clanked against each other.

"My duty is to my homeland, Tyrgnn. You should understand that."

"I do understand. And I understand that my life will always be someone else's. My life will be lived by rules, orders, and duties. But that does not mean I can forget you. I cannot. I want to marry you,

Aoh."

"When I marry, it will be to someone of my homeland," she defended firmly.

"He will never love you as much as I."

I wouldn't let myself believe that. I couldn't.

"Tyrgnn..."

"It's the truth."

"Tyrgnn-"

"Why won't you see me as I see you? Why?"

"Take these horses and all of their belongings back to your King Khian and Queen Huriye as gifts from Egypt," Aoh interrupted.

"What?" he asked baffled.

"Tell them that these are gifts from the pharaoh as a promise that he does not want to go to war. They are gifts of friendship."

"You're not coming back with me?"

"If I go back, she will know these aren't gifts. She spared me once, but won't make that mistake again. She'll kill me to set an example," she replied, untying the rope from the horse saddle.

"I won't let her," Tyrgnn objected, standing up.

"Then she'll kill you, too."

Aoh got onto her horse, tugging at the cloak, trying to wrap herself within the warmth of the heavy fabric. The horse jolted for a moment, feeling her legs rest against the leather saddle.

"Hurry back before she bends his mind to her will," Aoh begged.

"Why should I do what you asked? Why should I trust that Egypt will keep their word?"

"Because if you love me, you'll do this for me."

"What if I come across murdering thieves?" Tyrgnn asked.

"I have faith in you," Aoh replied.

Pulling on the reigns, she moved to his side, preparing her feet, facing the direction of her homeland.

"Wait," he paused. "Let this be a promise to you. This is the last you will see of my kindness."

Riding all the way back without rest through the hours of the night and into the morning, Aoh felt tired and weak. The remainder of the path to the stables her horse trotted, breathing heavily, twitching its soft ears, wanting to rest.

Bringing the horse back to the stables, I quickly tied the rope around the post and prepared it some food and water. I slid my hands against the back of the neck and to the top of the its nose, feeling the heavy breath against my skin. I stumbled to the other side of the room, drawing fresh water, and gathered hay from the overflowing pile.

As I watched him drink, I was startled by the sound of the stable doors closing quickly behind me. I screamed and turned, seeing Laggus there. I raised my hands to my chest, panting, feeling my arms and legs twitch.

"Laggus, you terrified me," Aoh said quickly.

"What happened? Did you find him?" he asked.

"Yes. He will tell King Khian that Egypt agrees to the alliance."

"And you believe him?" Laggus asked with suspicion.

"I do. It's not King Khian who wants war," Aoh replied bitterly, walking past him.

"Then, who does?"

"Who do you think?"

"Have I offended you for some reason? Because, as I recall, I am the only one you have to trust in this palace," Laggus replied, hearing the bitterness in her voice.

"No, no, you didn't… I've just…you, you're -- never mind," Aoh stammered as her eyelids became heavy.

"War has been averted between Egypt and the Hyksos as long as the pharaoh writes back accepting with warmth the agreement to a friendship. This will unite us with the other most powerful kingdom in the world. Egypt will become a greater force to reckon with, keeping the Mitanni and other kingdoms away."

She wrapped her bow and quiver of arrows around the inside of the cloak, hiding every inch, tucking it under her arm. Laggus listened intently as she approached the stable doors weakly, desperate for a bed to collapse onto. Stopping at the doors, she noticed Laggus hadn't left, watching her.

"Is there anything you'd like to speak to me about before I leave?

Anything that I should be aware of?" she asked, placing her hands on the doors.

Laggus shook his head in response. Aoh nodded and proceeded to push the doors open. Entering the light, she winced closing the doors behind her. Once she closed them, she felt an overwhelming sense of sadness as her heart began to cry.

I don't know why I was so sad, but my heart kept crying. My heart had cried several times in my life, but this time it was different. I couldn't understand it.

That night I couldn't sleep. I was worried that my judgment may have been wrong. Did Tyrgnn do as I had asked? Or did he do the exact opposite to spite me?

The pharaoh leaned over, reading the letter he had Senmet and his scribes compose as a response to King Khian's alliance. Senmet waited patiently, observing Laggus standing next to the pharaoh's throne. Feeling Senmet's eyes on him, Laggus glanced at him. Senmet nodded, exposing a small smile across his old face with a hint of excitement. A yawning jackal strolled towards the pharaoh, rubbing against the throne, moving its head under his right arm, then leaning on the armrest.

The pharaoh rubbed the jackal's smooth head, concentrating on the letter. His mouth moved slightly, reading every word carefully. His eyes shifted from the inked wording towards the nearest wall, depicting his father with his mother sitting behind him. Senmet sighed heavily, waiting, having read every word in its entirety multiple times.

Those questions raced through my mind for weeks until, finally, pharaoh received a response from King Khian after sending his acceptance of an alliance.

36

"It is with great honor and pleasure that I inform you a friendship, an alliance, has been met between our kingdoms. I believe with all of the life left in me that this will bring both of our kingdoms together. We are both powerful in our own right, and we thrive on knowing our neighbors. Let this not be mistaken for anything more than the truth. My father may have wished me to go to war, so would his father before him. However, I believe enough blood has been spilled over petty things, and the only blood that should be spilled would come from the real enemies that lurk in the shadows of our borders. I look forward to sharing more letters with you and wish you and your queen the best, now and forever."

Putting the papyrus onto his lap, the pharaoh's lips parted as a smile spread from ear to ear. He let out a sigh of relief, and then a groan as he felt the pressure on his shoulders drop in between Daimina's hands while she rolled them gently up and down like soothing waves. He leaned into the pressure, feeling the intense tightness soften and disappear between her fingers. Her smooth arms cascaded around his neck as her hands dropped over his chest to his waist.

"Our children will see many great things because of this alliance,

Daimina," he smiled looking at her.

"Yes, they will. Hopefully, one day…soon."

He smiled and leaned his head, straining his neck to kiss her.

"You are so beautiful."

"My king should know better. Flattery will get you everywhere," she smiled in response.

He kissed her again and again, moving his kisses from her mouth to her cheeks and then her neck. She refrained slightly, lowering herself to her knees, seeing the bracelet of white lilies around his left golden wrist cuff.

"Tell me, how many children do you wish for?" she asked, wrapping her arms around his chest.

"As many as you wish for," he replied with a smile.

"All sons?"

"Some daughters would be nice, but I do not mind as long they grow with Egypt's bright future."

Holding him closer, Daimina's smile deepened as she responded, "Sometimes I wish it was just us in this palace. No one else."

"It would certainly help stop the lies and deceit," he agreed with a sigh of frustration. "Sefkh is one of my best generals. He has won many battles and trained me well. I just worry he's becoming lazy when it comes to protecting my people. And Kha'y will not drop this request he received from the gods. He's become obsessive…"

"I'm sure Senmet can be trusted."

"Oh, yes, he is trusted. He hasn't steered me wrong and would only act for this kingdom. He reminds me of my father sometimes," he continued, leaning back in his seat as Daimina's hand returned to his shoulders, rolling her palms to and fro.

His eyes narrowed as he glanced out the nearest window, noticing the location of the sun in the sky.

"If you do not trust Sefkh to do as you ask, assign the task to another."

"Trouble is…I already have." Frowning slightly, he studied the white lilies wrapped around his wrist. Turning his wrist to the side, he asked, "Are these truly my color?"

Daimina released a low but hearty chuckle, unable to control a bright smile from emerging between her glossed lips.

"What?" he questioned. " I want to know. No one has ever given me lilies like this before."

"You are quite an oddity, pharaoh of Egypt," Daimina whispered, kissing the side of his neck slowly.

"Odd? How so? I do have my grandfather's increasingly weak back, which-" He paused, craning his neck, stretching his shoulders, "Lion hunting hasn't improved the matter."

Releasing the stretch, he felt his muscles loosen as Daimina's hands slowly caressed the skin across his broad shoulders.

"I feel older than the statues that stand day and night over this kingdom," he commented. "It's as though my father never left."

Daimina stopped massaging him and leaned her face over his neck slowly.

"He won't ever know a thing as long as you keep the curtains closed," she breathed.

The pharaoh's heart raced like a horse drawing a chariot as he turned around to kiss her passionately.

Aoh entered the shadows, barely able to see much in front of her, returning from Daimina's bedroom where she had all of the bedding freshly cleaned. Her clothing washed and folded. Her jewelry and makeup organized. Windows opened widely, enabling the wind from the desert to enter, and even made sure that the tiniest piece of sand was removed from the floors.

She stopped, standing against the wall across from one of many rooms of well-kept records placed into small shelves on the walls. They were often occupied by scribes and priests. She glanced at the open doorway when she felt something against the other side of the stone wall.

"Laggus," she whispered to the wall.

"You could tell it was me by my footsteps?" he asked, baffled from the other side of the wall.

Aoh didn't respond, turning slightly, hearing the sounds of his breathing against the tight armor.

"I wanted to let you know that the pharaoh received the letter of agreement to the alliance. Egypt will not be going to war," he explained.

The relief I felt could not have been described in words even if I had a thousand years' time to write them down.

Aoh sighed heavily with relief, resting herself against the wall, feeling the coolness against her skin.

"Thank you, Laggus. Thank you for telling me."

"You were right. I should be the one thanking you for doing what you did. Egypt owes you its gratitude."

"I don't want anyone to know what I did. Let it remain a secret," she insisted.

Laggus paused for a long second before replying.

"Alright," he agreed.

There was another long pause before Aoh spoke up.

"Laggus? Are you there?"

"I am."

Aoh slowly moved herself against the wall, dragging her hand downward to the corner, and then just barely feeling the rough skin around his knuckles.

I wanted to say something else, but suddenly couldn't. My mind went blank…I couldn't understand it.

"Aoh?" he asked, concerned.

"It was nothing. Thank you for telling me. Good night."

As Aoh left from the end of the long hallway, she suddenly sensed someone there. She smelled a familiar scent that terrified her. She looked behind her, but saw no one in the long hallway. Continuing forward, she felt as though someone was watching her from the heavy shadows.

Remaining as silent as the dead in tombs, *he* watched her intently, with a strong desire to claim her.

In the following days, when Aoh found herself able to move freely without Daimina, she stood by, what became known as, her favorite balcony. As Daimina entertained the pharaoh, often leaving the palace with him to retreat to the desert or ride down the Nile River, Aoh made it a point to enjoy her solitude. The balcony was made and designed like the other balconies, in the shade of the palace overlooking from a minor height.

Feeling the heat warm her skin the moment she stepped into the sunlight, she stretched her long arms and curled her toes. Picking up the bottom of her dress, she tenderly sat on the thick ledge. She leaned her back against the wall, falling away into the shade, noticing not far from her sight Laggus sparring with a soldier in the training pit below. The entire area was covered in sand, surrounded by remnants of fallen columns and obelisks.

For the past several days, Aoh watched Laggus practice his fighting skills, using a multitude of weapons and maneuvers, training with the same soldier.

I was mesmerized by him. By his every breath. I've seen many men, but none quite like him. His strength was insurmountable. Each strike, swing, and blow was like watching a dance. He was brutal, vicious, and beyond any force of men.

Laggus and the soldier of the same age grunted and growled, swinging wooden swords, clashing their wooden shields, jumping, dodging, and rolling across the sand. The two of them battled without holding back, using all of their strength. The sound of a loud crack startled the soldier slightly as Laggus let out one more shout, dodging the sword and taking his shield, hitting the soldier across the chest, and sending him rolling across the ground roughly.

Tiny pieces of stone and marble indented his skin as the world around him spun wildly. Laggus stood over the soldier laying in the sand, coughing loudly, feeling his breath snatched from his chest every time he inhaled.

He glanced upward, laying in the shadow of Laggus who blocked out the sun. Bending down, Laggus held out his light, muscular arm, covered in sweat and beads of blood. The soldier took it with a grin, feeling his chest ache as his breaths slowly returned.

Sweat soaked Laggus' hair, dripping down his neck and arms, slipping behind his tightened armor as he groaned, feeling his left leg throb. The soldier picked up Laggus' wooden sword, noticing the deep cracks spread throughout the entirety of the blade.

"Fighting with force today?" he asked Laggus calmly.

Walking over to the basin full of water, Laggus cupped his rough hands, filling them with water, and drank it quickly. Cupping his hands again, he washed his face, spitting the excess water onto the ground. He let out a loud, exhausted sigh, feeling the water cool him, washing away the layers of dirt and sand across his body. His soaked, short hair slicked back. Strands of hair separating like splitting ends of papyrus reeds.

"I haven't seen you fight like this in some time," the soldier commented. "Full of fire. I'm beginning to wonder where you're finding all of this rage."

He chuckled, walking over to another water basin, dipping a goblet from the tray in the silent servant's hand, and drank quickly. Trails of water ran down both sides of his small face, evaporating near his neck. Swallowing, he released a hearty scream.

"Have you thought about challenging Sefkh again? You may become a soldier by the end of the week," the soldier asked, walking over to Laggus, slowly rubbing water up and down his short arms.

Laggus didn't answer him, but continue to splash water onto his face and rub the back of his neck.

"In my eyes, based on today's performance, you will beat him. That is…if he doesn't cheat."

Laggus placed both of his hands against the water basin, leaning forward, staring into the water as though he were in an intense trance. Tiny droplets slipped down his bangs, dropping into the basin.

"That is what you want, right? To be a soldier in pharaoh's army? To ride into battle for his name and kingdom, prevent enemies from breeching our realm and protecting the people? That is…what you want, right?"

Laggus turned around and saw the soldier handing him his wooden sword. He took the sword and looked at the deep cracks that ran deep into the wood. If he used it once more, the entire blade would snap. The soldier spit onto the ground, feeling a slight chill.

"From what I heard, the way things are going, the pharaoh is going to want to take action soon. Too many foreigners have been crossing our borders unchecked. They've been seen in our city and even the towns."

Laggus looked at him intensely, finally responding, "Who have they seen?"

"Rumors of Mitanni…Hittite," the soldier answered.

There was a solid pause as the information sunk into his head, unable to fully grasp the idea of such enemies returning.

"When the time comes, we could use a man like you in our army. You'll be fighting for the cause. Inspire the other soldiers and you could become a general."

"Let's not put the chariot in front of the horse yet," Laggus replied.

"I'm not lying to you, Laggus. You've improved greatly. And I'm not the only who notices."

Taking another drink of water, the soldier roared loudly, spitting into the air.

"Even the servants know the pharaoh trusts you," he continued. "I don't see why you think it's impossible. You're ready. If anything, I should be the one training under you. I could learn a thing or two."

Laggus answered by spitting water from his chapped lips again, running a hand through his wet fine hair.

"The army needs a man like you," the soldier continued.

"Right now the pharaoh needs me," Laggus answered.

He glanced at his reflection in the water, and then the dim reflection of the palace above him. Glancing upward at the palace from the water, he observed it in all its glory, standing tall like a tower to the sky. Aoh's warm smile widened seeing him glancing at the palace.

I was tempted to call out to him…biting my tongue and my own desires, I remained silent, almost invisible in comparison to the magnificence of the palace.

"Aoh."

Aoh turned, hearing her name called not far from where she laid. Rising to her feet, she followed the voice that called out to her, entering a nearby room she had not seen before. Inside the mostly blue and ivory colored room, she found Aneski sitting with two cats on her lap by the windows that provided a beautiful view of the Nile River. She stroked them gently while a servant played a harp in the background, picking at the strings, concentrating on the tune.

Aoh immediately bowed at her presence, a little taken aback by her linen pleated dress covered in shades of blue and green and gems. She appeared stunning. Like a goddess.

"I called you forward because I need you to send a message for me," she explained calmly, plucking several discolored hairs from the back of the cat's ears.

She leaned over and reached for the sealed scroll on the small table next to her cushioned chair. The char was made out of gold, designed to look like she was sitting on the back of a lion.

Aoh questioned her immediately, "Does the pharaoh approve?"

"He is not to know about this. Or anyone for that matter," she snapped wickedly in response.

Aoh didn't move, staring at the scroll in the woman's wrinkled hand, baffled as to why the previous queen of Egypt called for her in particular.

Once again reading her expression, Aneski continued, "Do not give me that look. You are not with Daimina now. My son is keeping her occupied, I'm sure. She can manage a simple hour or two without you aiding her every command."

Aoh remained still, and immediately hid her expression behind cold and hard eyes, straightening her back, releasing her tense shoulders. She refused to move, keeping her feet straight.

"My arm is getting tired," Aneski snapped, holding out the scroll.

Giving in, Aoh leaned forward and hesitated once more before taking the scroll. Upon taking it, a deep sense of regret overcame her.

"Listen to me very…carefully…" the pharaoh's mother instructed. "Wait until it gets dark…there will be few guards standing watch. In the city, there is a place with dark red drapes and two statues outside. Go inside and find a young man dressed with a dark blue robe and two rings on each hand. He will be drinking alone in the furthest corner. Hand him this message and leave. He will know whom it's from. Do not open it. Do not speak to anyone else in there. You are to go there and come back to the palace. Nowhere else. Understand me?"

"Yes," Aoh replied quietly.

She stared at the scroll, turning it to observe the detailed seal.

"Oh, for goodness sake, stop worrying. The pharaoh won't kill you if you leave."

Aoh lowered her head, focusing her attention to the scroll as her curiosity to what was written inside began to grow.

"If you are fearful going alone, I will have Laggus go with you."

Aoh's eyes immediately lifted to meet Aneski's in surprise. She lengthened the strokes through the thick cat fur, tilting her head slightly, hiding a wide grin underneath her cold demeanor.

My heart sank… Did she know?

"Is that what you want? I can have him assist you," Aneski asked.

"That…will not be necessary-"

"Then…go."

37

The city at night was a different world than during the day. It seemed the moment the sun set, every desire and pleasure would emerge from the streets. Men and women alike sought entertainment: drinking, eating, dancing, and gambling.

Guards walked in groups, staring at anything that moved. Aoh tugged the hood closer to her face, keeping her movement consistent, avoiding eye contact. Two statues stood before red drapes, nearly hidden behind rows of lodges; bars where prostitution ran rampant.

Keeping her eyes forward, ignoring any looks she received, Aoh remained calm, hurrying her feet through the red silk and almost colliding into a soldier leaving. He watched Aoh as she moved past him, remaining close to the wall near a row of burning pits, unable to hear herself think due to the several loud conversations taking place.

The room had an aurora of exuberance. Men gambled, played board games in corners, laughing about the events that unfolded throughout the day. Others sat alone with their drink, trying to recover from a day of hard work.

Scanning the debauchery around her, Aoh caught sight of Sefkh with a group of soldiers drinking together as a group of women slid their way to them, barely wearing any clothing. Unable to look away, she watched as the women draped themselves around the men, finishing drink after drink, oblivious to the group of untrustworthy men sitting to the far right in all black, and to the young men about to fight from within a back room half covered in a red drape.

I forced my fear back down my throat, keeping my hands firm, looking at anything I could use as a weapon if I needed to. Without my bow and arrows, I felt like a helpless peasant at the mercy of unchecked violence.

Aoh slide between tables, behind occupied seats, grabbing the attention of several jackals lying about the feet of thieves. Moving in between people standing about the room, she dodged the soldiers, continuing to the back of the room.

She didn't need to search for long, finding the young man almost instantly sitting all alone, enjoying a small cup of liquor. Taking calm strides towards him, Aoh stopped at the end of the table, drawn to the rings on his hands, gleaming in the flames. Without raising his gaze to look at her, Aoh revealed the scroll from under the thin cloak.

From two tables away, a man lunged, slitting the young man's throat with a long blade, splattering his blood all over the table, floor, and wall. The red color flashed before Aoh's eyes, stunning her as the man clasped both hands over his throat in shock. His wide eyes were about to burst from his skull.

She stumbled over a chair and fell when the table was thrown, clutching the scroll tightly in her hand. The man threw himself on top of her, as Aoh kicked him several times, grunting. Reaching for the blood soaked knife on the floor, she struggled to grasp it due to the slick red liquid across her fingers.

Rolling to her left, she slammed the knife through his hand and into the thick carpet. She felt heat from the nearby floor ablaze from a candle that had fallen with the table. He bellowed loudly when suddenly soldiers tackled him to the floor, knocking over burning wood. Aoh crawled under chairs and tables towards the nearest window, fleeing, running all the way back to the palace.

Upon entering, Aoh nearly collapsed against the large doors, as the blood on her hands began to dry and flake. She gasped aloud, trying to keep her stomach from spewing out of her mouth. Seeing Aneski's shadow emerge from the corner, moving across the decorated columns, she forced herself to her feet.

Noticing Aoh standing there with slashes of blood across her cloak, her face faulted immediately. Aneski's eyes fell to Aoh's left hand…

I nearly forgot the scroll was still clutched in my blood- dried hand, slightly wrinkled and sprayed with streams of red. The sound of the doors opening behind me were enough to harden Aneski's terrified expression. I didn't need to turn around…I knew he stood right behind me.

Glaring at his mother intensely, the pharaoh ordered immediately, "Leave us."

Aoh quickly picked up the bottom of her dress, passing Laggus as he waited by the large doors, having followed the pharaoh. The pharaoh closed the doors tightly as the solid thud echoed in the empty room.

From the inside of Aoh's long cloak, she pulled out the scroll, staring at the remnants. She coughed several times from the smoke inhalation, feeling her neck. She winced knowing bruises were going to form.

"Mother, why was Aoh with you?" the pharaoh asked, keeping his arms behind his back.

"She was passing through-"

"Oh. Yes, I'm sure she was," he interrupted coldly.

He paced in front of her, shaking his head, rubbing his mouth repeatedly.

"Mother, what did you do now?"

"I didn't do anything that I haven't done before," she replied calmly.

"That's precious, real precious, because the last time something like this happened, everyone knew but me. Everyone… I was the last one to hear all of it. And by then, it was too late to act."

"Then, perhaps you should reevaluate the company you keep," she answered, holding her ground.

Rolling his lips several times over, she continued, "I know you want to make your own decisions and you don't want to hear what I think, but-"

"I'm the pharaoh, not you."

"I'm your mother. I will always be your mother. No amount of prayers to the gods will change that. I've raised you since birth, and my love for you will outlast any pyramid built, obelisk, statue on this land," she shrieked.

She rubbed her glossy lips as a flicker of a tear shined in her right eye.

"How can you ignore my willingness to help and see it as your own destruction?" she continued to cry.

"Mother, please spare me. Just tell me what is going on," he demanded.

Taking a quick breath, Aneski bit into her lower lip and explained, "For the past several years I've been in contact with your uncle."

"What? Why? Why would you do that?" the pharaoh asked rapidly.

"Because the men you keep in this palace do not tell you everything. He is on the outside. He sees and knows things you will never know as long as those same men are in here, wrapped in your crown."

The pharaoh shook his head in response, sneering slightly, taking steps away from her.

Losing her patience at his antics, she yelled to him.

"Listen to me!" she bellowed. "Stop it and listen right now! As much as you think you know you need to broaden yourself beyond the walls."

Seeing her son continually shake his head, baffled, she stormed away from him towards the back of the room. Rushing over to the table, she swiped her long arms across it, knocking over several empty wine vessels as they smashed onto the floor. She shattered a mirror resting over a tray, revealing a small piece of papyrus hiding underneath it.

Storming over to her son she spat, "This is the last message I received from him. I received this three…days…ago."

Taking the papyrus, he read it thoroughly with his dark eyes, as each word seemed to lift his eyebrows higher and higher. His grip on the message tightened and his eyes narrowed intensely.

"I heard it myself when the Hyksos ambassador arrived, the entire room heard it! Egypt is getting breeched all around you! Mitanni, Hittites, and the Hyksos themselves."

Lowering the papyrus, the pharaoh cupped his mouth with his left hand immediately. His dark eyes shaking to and fro.

"It is for reasons like this I have kept in touch with him," she insisted. "He is your most loyal servant."

"Was my most loyal servant," he stated, slightly weeping.

Seeing his tears, she trembled. Her hands running cold, her head feeling faint.

"He was killed tonight."

Her mouth opened as she stumbled backwards to the nearest chair, falling into it, slamming her back against it and nearly hitting her head on the frame. Her eyes glistened with small tears staring at her son, silently.

"He…was…killed?" she choked, shaking her head.

He nodded in response, rubbing his hand over his mouth as the tears in his eyes slipped down his cheeks. He collapsed into a nearby chair, sinking into the soft cushions as the papyrus in his hand slipped, floating in the air before landing on the floor.

Seeing the scroll, Laggus focused his attention on it.

"What is that?" he asked suddenly.

"Nothing," Aoh lied, immediately rubbing her hands against the cloak.

"Is that blood?" he asked, grabbing both of her hands, rubbing the dried red flakes from her fingers.

His intense eyes tightened. "Who attacked you?"

Before Aoh could answer, they saw guards rushing down the stairs as a loud ruckus below was growing in strength and magnitude. Seeing the madness unfold, he left Aoh to follow them.

She watched him rush down the hallway, remaining against the door, feeling herself losing control of her emotions that began to overflow from her heart.

Trampling carpets and nearly knocking over incense burners, Laggus entered the loud room, finding several soldiers and guards screaming at each other wildly. In the midst of the madness, one man was forcefully held down onto the floor with two others to the side, as they all tried to escape from the tied ropes around their arms and legs.

"My uncle…" the pharaoh gasped, rubbing his face slowly, purposely feeling the indentations in his cheeks.

"Oh, my son. My son," Aneski gasped, getting up and coming to him, holding out her thin arms.

She fell to her knees, holding his face with her delicate hands, rubbing her fingers near his eyes. She turned his face from the floor to look at her.

"My son. He loved you like his own. It's not your fault," she explained calmly.

He nodded silently.

"He died for you, for Egypt. He knew the risk. We all do…"

"We will give him a proper burial and give his family our utmost condolences for this tragedy. We shall provide for them."

"Alright. He would appreciate that very much. Your father, too."

Wiping the tears from her eyes, she rose to her feet as the pharaoh rubbed his face, collapsing into the comfort of the chair.

"I'm going to get some air. I won't be long, alright? Stay here," Aneski instructed, moving towards the door.

Opening the door, she pulled her dress to her left side and found Aoh sitting on the floor, her legs drawn to her chest, leaning against a thick pillar. Aneski's face hardened, as the remnants of her sadness flickered in her eyes. Glancing in both directions first, she tugged her dress again as it caught on her foot again.

"Have you been waiting all this time?" she asked.

Aoh nodded with half open eyes.

"The letter," she ordered, holding out her hand

Aoh stood up and revealed the scroll from underneath her arm. Keeping her eyes focused on the floor, Aoh approached her slowly, handing her the scroll. Aneski immediately inspected the scroll, checking that the seal was still intact.

"Who killed him?" she asked firmly.

"Soldiers…" Aoh replied with a slight quiver.

I heard her breath suddenly fade from her chest as her mouth opened in astonishment.

"Did they see you?" the pharaoh's mother asked.

Aoh shook her head in response, wiping her eyes with the very end of her sleeve.

"Clean yourself up before someone sees you," she scolded.

Looking at the scroll, Aneski sniffled for a brief moment, trying to contain her sadness. Glancing to her right, she saw a fire pit and immediately walked over to it. Looking at the scroll once more, she lowered it to the flames. Exhaling heavily, she dropped it into the open fire.

Aneski sat in front of the flames watching the papyrus turn to nothing but small ashes underneath the vibrant, hot colors. She watched intently, refusing to remove her eyes from the flames until she felt satisfied that every last remnant of the papyrus was gone.

Noticing a goblet of water, she poured it over the flames as a cloud of smoke filled the air, causing a displeasing scent to burst into the atmosphere.

38

The pharaoh watched Daimina from the balcony as she walked the gardens, with Aoh following behind her. She smelled the flowers, rubbing the petals between her fingers. The glow upon her face in the sunlight ensnared his heart as he cupped his mouth, still mourning the death of his uncle whom was buried in a side chamber of his father's tomb. He was buried with everything he had used in his lifetime, able to take them with him to the next life where he would be reunited with his brother, and the two could begin a new life.

Brief and faded memories of his uncle, a once prince of Egypt, haunted him as his mind wandered. His eyes remained transfixed upon Daimina…his breath slowed, his hands running cold. He remembered his uncle's face, a small smile across his lips as he rubbed the top of his nephew's head to and fro. He remembered embracing his legs, too small to reach his waist. Too young to even understand the life he would one day live, only knowing what he saw before him.

Hearing the sound of Laggus calling his name, the pharaoh rubbed his eyes and mouth, rejoining the world around him. As Daimina walked carelessly, taking slow strides near the peacocks and ibises, he uncontrollably smiled, desiring to hold her and kiss her. The peacocks squawked, barely acknowledging her walking by to peck at the ground.

"My king?" Laggus asked, approaching with heavy concern.

"Yes. Thank you for coming," the pharaoh replied, trying to recover from his daze.

Leaning over, Laggus tilted his head, trying to look at the pharaoh's face that continually shifted between bewilderment and distress.

"Are you alright?"

"Yes. Are you?"

Laggus hesitated from answering, standing next to the pharaoh and looking downward, seeing Daimina walking with Aoh following her every step like a musical rhythm.

"I feel responsible," Laggus admitted, causing the pharaoh to instantly look at him with a deep frown.

"Responsible for what?"

"None of this would have happened if I had been there. I failed you," Laggus explained, leaning himself forward, to rest his thick arms on the railing.

"You haven't failed me, Laggus."

"This city is getting worse every night and there is nothing I can do to stop it."

"You mean, while you're in here you cannot do anything to stop it," the pharaoh interjected.

Laggus' facial expressions tightened as the pharaoh leaned forward slightly and asked, "Would you have rather I send you back to guarding the streets?"

"With all due respect, my place is here in the palace," Laggus answered. "You asked me to reside in the palace for a reason."

The pharaoh nodded, clearing his throat several times.

"I'm worried that Sefkh isn't reporting the several cases that come into my hands on a daily basis," he confessed. "I'm worried that he's not the general he used to be. The latest of which has kept me from sleeping since... What do you think?"

"Sefkh is one of your best generals. Your army will follow him no matter the cause. He's helped lead Egypt to victory for both you and your father."

"Do you trust him?"

"No, my king. I don't," Laggus replied.

"I'll send Senmet to pull the records, see what else he is hiding. But this…I cannot delay any longer."

The pharaoh pulled the message from inside his robe, still rolled together, nibbled around the edges and slightly crinkled. Laggus looked at the papyrus and then the pharaoh's face.

"I cannot put my people at risk. I need to know if this is true," he growled, gripping the balcony tightly in between his hands. "It's time I learn who I can trust."

He shoved himself away from the balcony and stared in Laggus' eyes, rolling his lips together.

"I want you to take Aoh into the city, under the cover of dark and follow this map to where these supposed Hyksos soldiers are hiding," the pharaoh ordered. "I will be keeping both my wife and Daimina occupied tonight. No one will notice she's gone."

Laggus glanced at the papyrus.

"Can you do this for me?"

"Yes, my king."

39

Senmet opened the wooden chest clad in gold. He stared into the darkness of the deep chest, hovering both wrinkled hands over the edges. Slowly reaching inside he gently pulled out a wilted lily crown. Each branch hardened, cracking in their weaved pattern as dead flower petals dropped from the bud into the chest. Turning the crown, his eyes followed each lily, feeling his stomach turn hard like a rock.

Reaching into the deep chest a second time, he removed a wooden toy alligator. Seeing the sight of the toy he shuttered, clasping his hand over his mouth, feeling his eyes begin to swell. Turning the alligator, the wooden movable pieces put together with links clicked and groaned. Moving the thick tail, the jaw opened and closed revealing jagged wooden teeth. Faded remnants of black ink detailing every scale, claw, and tooth covered the entire piece. With one last heavy, shaken breath, Senmet quickly dropped both objects into the wooden chest. His hands clasped over his face, as his lips quivered in between a gentle moan of grief.

Swallowing his sadness, he cleared his throat, glaring at the crown and the toy, laying at the bottom of the chest. Rolling his tongue over his teeth, he slammed the chest closed, locking it.

Draping both of his arms over the rounded cover, he leaned forward, distracted by the hieroglyphics on the wall to his left depicting the pharaoh as a child sitting with his father and mother.

Returning to Daimina's chambers, Aoh knelt down to look under the end of the bed, making sure the blade still resided there untouched. She coughed. Her throat remained sore. While she searched, she saw in the warped reflection of the gold embellishments her tiny room, noticing her bow was missing. Freezing at the light sound in the doorway, she turned and saw her bow in Laggus' hand.

"You need to come with me," he stated firmly.

Taking her bow, Aoh quickly drew the curtain over the door and followed Laggus as he handed her long robes.

"Wear these," he insisted, handing a few folded garments to her.

Aoh took the robes and placed them over herself as she followed him. Tucking her hair underneath the hood, she took her bow and placed it over her shoulder as he handed her the quiver full of newly made arrows.

Laggus tugged his armor slightly to the right, feeling it fit snuggly over his chest. He quickly unrolled the cloak from under his arm and tugged it over his head as it draped over him, just barely covering his upper body.

Aoh followed him down several steps hidden in the shadows as Laggus kept constant watch around every corner, ensuring no one was present before moving further. He paused next to a statue, leaning against it as Aoh moved against the wall. Laggus' eyes peeked through the small gaps between the arms of the statue, seeing two guards conversing freely while keeping one hand on their sword handles positioned at their sides.

"Where are we going?" Aoh whispered, moving slightly.

"Into the city to find this location."

Laggus retrieved a piece of papyrus from under his armor and unrolled it, revealing a map and a second piece behind it with a note.

The map wasn't very legible. The outline of the city was accurate; however, there were several noted locations I wasn't aware existed. I could barely see the note, written neatly with, what I could assume, the most expensive and fine ink.

Hearing the sound of a solid door opening, Laggus gently leaned forward, rolling the scroll tightly closed. Aoh mirrored his action, watching the two guards speak to another guard and following him away. Laggus waited until the last sound of their harsh steps faded away before motioning Aoh forward with him.

Together they moved quickly across the floors, watching for every shadow and flicker of flames. Exiting the palace, the darkness of night overcame them, leaving through a secret door to enter the loud city. The sounds of laughter and conversation hung over every corner as men and women took to the streets in search of good wine, tasty beer, and pleasurable entertainment.

Aoh glanced behind her momentarily, seeing the palace a glow in the shade of night.

It looked glorious...like a palace of starlight. It was a beacon over the city of white and gold.

Fixing the hood over her head, she remained by Laggus' side, following his firm strides and feeling less afraid with him present. Along every street, the heat of burning fires attracted wondering eyes. Guards in groups of no more than four moved in and out of bars and shops, silently like spirits.

Laggus and Aoh watched every movement, often approached by drunks wandering the streets looking for trouble. From doorways, they spotted soldiers drinking and conversing with each other while playing games. Pulling the map from underneath his chest armor, Laggus unraveled it slowly, trying to read the note and frowning deeply.

Wiping his dry mouth with his left hand, he listened to the chatter of several men dressed in dark robes, spitting onto the ground and making comments to foreigners who passed. Walls covered in sloppy graffiti with crude depictions of men and phrases like "Hittites not far" caught his attention. Keeping his hand nearly against Aoh's back, he turned around to look at the graffiti again before losing sight of it.

Turning at the next corner, Laggus protectively moved in front of Aoh, blocking her from incoming drunken men stumbling through.

"You wish to know why I don't sleep?" he asked her.

Aoh hesitated before answering. "A story would be nice, considering I never had one as a child."

"Story is, Gavril died because I fell asleep on watch. I was tired and no matter what I did I couldn't stay awake. As my life was about to be ended by a man and a blade, Gavril stepped in front…"

"I'm sorry, Laggus."

Knowing he didn't hear her, Aoh stopped walking momentarily, forcing him to turn back and look at her.

"I didn't say it before and I should have. I'm sorry," she insisted.

Laggus nodded.

"May I please see the map again?" she asked, clearing her throat.

Laggus sighed heavily, handing her the map slowly, making sure no one was watching. Looking at the map with one hand and holding the letter with the other, Aoh frowned as she mouthed the words to herself while Laggus kept constant watch.

"If this is true, they must have kept soldiers here during their unannounced visit for peace," he snapped.

"Strange," she said aloud, stopping just ahead of the busy brewery.

"What is?" Laggus asked, standing next to her.

"Why would Hyksos soldiers write this letter in both their language and Egyptian?"

"How is it that you can read it?" Laggus asked firmly.

Aoh didn't reply, tugging the brim of the hood lower to hide her face deeper in the shadow. They entered the busiest area, where men drank excessively and the women either served them their drinks or sat on their laps. They hesitated before entering the loud establishment, finding no difference in what occurred indoors and out. From the women serving drinks to the men gambling their savings, the environment bustled in the Egyptian language.

"There," Laggus said boldly, nodding forward.

"Alright," Aoh agreed lowly with a hint of uncertainty.

They made their way to the very back of the large space, passing several tables filled with wine and beer. There they encountered two men gambling who immediately rose to their feet, blocking the wooden door behind them.

"Step aside, we are here upon orders of the pharaoh to check this vicinity," Aoh explained firmly.

"Palace rats are not welcome here," the man on the left snapped between his cracked teeth.

"Do as she says," Laggus interjected.

"No..." the man to the left responded again, folding his thick arms over his chest and leaning back.

The other man repeated the gesture, proving themselves to be taller and thicker than Laggus. In an instance, Laggus killed the man to the left as Aoh stabbed the man to the right with an arrow from her quiver. With both dead, Aoh prepared her bow, drawing an arrow back as she and Laggus approached the closed door.

Keeping both swords ready in his rough hands, Laggus hunched over, moving towards the left and nodded to Aoh to stay to the right. She nodded in return, feeling a rush of anxiety. Her eyes fell on the man she just killed without a second thought.

Coming to the door, Laggus noticed it was not closed. Looking, he saw light on the other side of the door and shadows slowly moving. He paused, nodding to Aoh one last time as she prepared herself, taking aim. Her fingers tightly wrapped around the bow, shifting her weight slightly to enable better reach of the arrows in the quiver against her back. She swallowed hard, feeling the anxiety grow, glancing at Laggus.

His eyes were empty of fear. I saw self-discipline, concentration. Every move and decision he made was without hesitation.

Taking one last breath, Laggus kicked the door open and retreated to the left side while Aoh remained on the right. Arrows soared from the other side of the door and into the open space behind them, rapidly striking the wall on the other side causing a loud panic to erupt.

The moment the arrows stopped, they charged inside with fury. Aoh struck the first man furthest from the group of five and struck another over the head with her wooden bow. Laggus killed the third and fourth with ease, blocking a blow from the fifth man. Aoh fired an arrow into the second man's chest, and quickly drew another arrow as Laggus grappled with the fifth man across the room.

Aoh prepared her bow, watching Laggus wrestle with the man over tables and chairs. The man screamed, grappling Laggus against the wall, nearly breaking his left arm as his sword dropped to the floor. Turning the man around, Laggus used his arms to bind him, keeping his blade near his throat. The man's lower forearm armor was the only thing keeping the blade from killing him.

As Laggus struggled to keep the man still, Aoh put her arrow back into her quiver and began to assess the men they killed across the room. Each man wore Hyksos armor from head to toe. She rubbed her hands over each piece across their chests and backs, trying to see their faces hidden behind hair and fresh blood.

She gently moved her hand over the armor as she noticed the darker skin tone. Grabbing the dead man's arm, Aoh pulled it roughly towards the candlelight, noticed the tone was a different shade than those of Hyksos heritage. Removing her hand from his thick arm, she noticed a black residue across her fingertips. Raising her hand, she found blackened images across the arm, smudged, leaving the black ink across the palm of her hand. The ink felt fresh…

At that moment, I came to a horrific realization.

"Laggus…" Aoh said, shaking her arm slightly.

She held out her hand covered in the black ink as the shadow of her arm stood against the stone wall. Seeing the black ink, Laggus understood immediately as a rage from within him erupted.

"Who are these people? Huh? Who are they and why are they dressed in Hyksos uniforms?" he growled to the man, tightening his grip.

The man grunted from the pain but didn't answer him.

"Did someone tell you to do this? Did someone pay all of you to do this? Who was it?"

The man looked away from Laggus, rolling his tongue from within his mouth, attempting to spit in his face.

Laggus shook him violently and screamed, "Tell me, who did this?! Answer me!"

The man stopped resisting and lowered his arms, enabling the blade to slip and strike his throat and upper chest. He grunted one last time, collapsing onto the floor amongst the other dead men as blood flowed from his body.

Aoh stared at the black ink across her palm, seeping into the tiny lines across her skin, unable to stop shaking. Seeing the red blood slowly creeping towards her, she moved, nearly falling over the dead man towards Laggus.

"Why would he kill himself instead of telling us?" she asked Laggus, worried.

"Because the person he's protecting is bigger than ourselves," he answered.

Taking his blades, Laggus swiped the blood onto the clothing of the dead quickly.

"We must go back before someone sees us," he ordered.

Aoh didn't answer him, trying to reach the door, attempting to comprehend what had happened.

"Hey…you alright?" he asked, noticing her strange behavior.

Aoh nodded, slipping her fingers to pull the hood over her head. Together they quickly rushed back to the palace without running. Putting himself before Aoh, Laggus watched every corner, feeling as though someone was following them when he saw another graffiti covered wall with the same message he saw before.

"Someone told the Egyptian guards to dress in Hyksos armor," Laggus explained quietly with anger. "Whoever did this wants the pharaoh to go to war with them. It's out for all the world to see now."

"We need to find him first before whoever is behind this changes his mind," Aoh added worriedly.

40

The sun leaked light through the open windows as the sounds of the wild cats groaned and yawned in their cages, about to be fed their breakfast by humbled servants. Flowers were tended to. Papyrus reeds were collected to be made into paper. Fish salted, grains spread, and wines poured as the scent of several dishes were cooked over an open fire.

The faint scents of perfumes were sprinkled about several rooms from the servant's fingertips. Fresh bathes were drawn with clean robes and linen gowns. Newly-built golden furniture with animal features were carried in, replacing older pieces. Newly-woven carpets were quickly removed and replaced with the ones gifted from the Hyksos.

The pharaoh's hand, covered in a multitude of golden, gemmed rings, grasped the linen fabric from the ground and quickly uncovered the dead body hiding beneath it. Tossing the fabric onto the floor, Sefkh stared at the dead body in silence. Laggus and Senmet directed their attention to his reaction. Placing both hands against his waist, covered in blue and white linen robes, the pharaoh's eyes tightly glared upon his general. Silence hung over the room…

"What is this?" he asked.

Sefkh refrained from answering, keeping his straight posture. His dark eyes rattled side to side, lifting from the dead body to glance at Laggus. His teeth slowly grinding to the point he gasped aloud.

"My king…"

"Don't," the pharaoh interrupted coldly.

"My king, I must," Sefkh defended.

The pharaoh raised his eyes in response.

"This is precisely why any sort of alliance with the Hyksos is a farce."

"A farce?!" the pharaoh screamed. "A farce? Do you know what a farce is a farce?"

The pharaoh grasped the dead man's arm tightly. Upon removing it, he revealed the black ink across the palm of his hand. Storming to Sefkh, he shoved his ink-covered hand near his face.

"THIS IS THE FARCE, SEFKH!" he screamed. "These are not Hyksos men invading our borders but Egyptian men dressed as Hyksos! Tell me how this is so! Tell me why this happened! TELL ME!"

Fear struck Sefkh cold, as his eyes continued to rattle and now his hands began to violently shake.

"My king…I do not know," he admitted calmly.

"You don't know?" the pharaoh repeated confused.

"That is correct. I was not aware…that Egyptians were posing as Hyksos soldiers. However, it is clear that whoever is responsible has all intentions of making sure an alliance with them will never be."

"Well, well, what a calculated response."

"It is the truth, my king."

"The TRUTH? IS IT THE TRUTH?" he bellowed.

"It is, my king," Sefkh defended. "I have been leading Egypt's army to victory all my life. I have bled for Egypt. I have killed for Egypt. I have been there for your father. I have been there for you. A mere teenager taking on a force bent on your destruction. Would I be so careless as to create such chaos?"

"No one is immune to carelessness, Sefkh. The TRUTH is that someone is trying to destroy this kingdom from the inside and I want to know who it is. I want every single guard, soldier, and servant questioned. I want more guards on the streets. AND if anything else emerges without my knowing I will be holding you personally responsible," the pharaoh threatened.

"Understood."

"But first, present the new soldiers to me. NOW!"

"Yes, my king," Sefkh agreed.

Daimina constantly folded and unfolded her hands; her eyes were focused on the floor as she paced in her room to and fro. Her long linen gown, threaded with tiny pieces of golden kites and falcons, chimed with each swift movement. Her smile continually changed to a frown as her thoughts kept colliding from happiness to fear and worry. Aoh glanced outside at the sun's position, immediately growing tense herself.

I knew the pharaoh was calling his realm to the attention of last night's events, worried what the outcome was going to be. I couldn't understand who would be responsible and why they were determined to ensure that Egypt remained enemies with their neighbors across the Nile and into the desert. I could think of several minds capable of such actions; however, I had no proof of it.

As Daimina paced across the soft carpets, Aoh prepared the jewelry for her to wear, as well as a golden hair piece from a large variety of pieces gifted from the pharaoh when she arrived. Aoh watched her from the corner of her eyes.

She seemed somewhere else. Her eyes twitched nervously. Her fingers wouldn't stop bending. Each time she paced, her dress would lightly drag across the smooth carpet to the floor. She didn't speak nor sigh. She just paced…over and over. She was tense, as though the slightest sound would suddenly scare her to the point of shrieking.

After clasping two large earrings over Daimina's un-pierced lobes, Aoh reached for two golden cuffs, shaped like the crescent moon with a prayer of protection carved across them. Daimina held out her arms as Aoh clasped them snuggly over her wrists.

Aoh grabbed two more cuffs as Daimina stretched out both arms. The cuffs clasped snuggly just above her elbows. Aoh then placed the golden hair piece to the middle of the back of her head. The ends of the golden hair piece laid like rivers of gold in her dark, thick hair. Fixing the ends of her hair, and then the thin sleeves of the dress over her shoulders, Aoh felt Daimina tremble.

"Something wrong?" Aoh asked calmly.

Daimina's mouth opened but no words came out. She hesitated from speaking.

Opening her mouth a second time she whispered to her servant, "I need to speak to the pharaoh."

Together Aoh and Daimina left, in search of where the pharaoh might be. Aoh could barely keep up as Daimina looked in nearly every room, frustrated and sighing each time he wasn't there.

The longer it was taking for her to find him, the more panicked she was becoming. I refused to lead her to the throne room for fear he may still be in there and acting unlike himself, which would only upset her more than she already appeared to be.

Daimina passed several rooms and upon seeing Senmet, she made eye contact for only a second as he sat reading several pieces of papyrus intently. Senmet didn't speak upon seeing her. His expressionless eyes turned to Aoh, grabbing his attention.

The moment the two left his sight, he called out calmly, "The pharaoh is not here, my lady."

Finally, Daimina spotted Aneski standing in front of one of three cheetahs in cages alone in the exotic room. Daimina was taken aback by the extraordinary display of wild animals and foreign plants housing several breeds of birds. The room was full of green and a variety of blue, pink, yellow, and red flowers speckled about the large columns.

A calming essence in the room soothed her temporarily. Draped in sheer linen and silk, Aneski gently touched the frizzy, smooth fur across the legs and back of the wild cats with her fingers through the spaces of the cage. She stroked them, unafraid, taming the wild animal who willingly sat down, hunching its back to the side, leaning into her soft fingers.

Cautiously following the brief steps into the room, Daimina looked at every creature and beast she passed with wonder. Each wild cat followed her movements, sitting or lying in their cages, soaking in the cool breezes from the large open spaces between the white and rustic red granite columns.

"Your majesty," Daimina said, bowing. Aoh repeated the action behind her.

Aneski turned to reveal a warm smile as she twirled her fingers around the black spots in the sandy colored fur.

"Do you know where I can find the pharaoh?"

"My son should be finally checking on his new soldiers in training," she answered.

"Thank goodness," Daimina sighed in relief.

"I certainly hope the soldiers are as good as I've been hearing. Not all of them can be as strong as Laggus."

I could feel Aneski's eyes fall on me as I kept my mine down at the floor and my hands at my waist. The comment, however, seemed to fly over Daimina's head who simply thanked her.

As Daimina began to walk away, Aneski added a last comment.

"Oh, I must warn you, I would drink some water, if I were you, before going out there," the pharaoh's mother stated.

Daimina frowned slightly, turning around, confused.

She continued, "You need to stay hydrated so that you won't get sick. You're not the only one that needs protecting now."

"Thank you," Daimina replied appreciatively.

"You are most welcome. Oh, and do tell my son that his vizier is reading letters without his permission again. I caught him last night while the queen occupied his time. I'm growing quite fed up with him, actually. Isn't it tragic?"

Trying to keep a solid face without tearing, Daimina answered, "I will." She only moved several a few steps before the woman spoke again.

"It's about time," Aneski commented causing Daimina to stop.

"For Sefkh to present the new soldiers? The pharaoh had been waiting some time to see them," Daimina replied slowly with confusion.

"Oh, yes…that, too," she replied smiling.

Daimina nodded, leaving the large space, unable to prevent herself from looking behind her and at the last queen, who simply admired the wild animals without fear.

Daimina and Aoh followed the paths around the outside of the palace, finding the pharaoh watching two soldiers wrestling each other in the sand and then four others grappling with the generals, watching closely to determine a winner. Earlier, the men had been running as evidence pointed to their heavy breathing and sweated bodies.

Several men cheered on their wrestling comrades as they shoved each other into the dirt, growling, and biting. The pharaoh watched intently, troubled. He placed his thumb under his chin, staring at the wrestling duos, focusing on them and ignoring the rest of the world around him.

Every soldier ranged in size and weight. Most were married men with families they needed to support. A smaller portion were young men with desires of fighting for the kingdom and bringing home riches from conquered enemies. The promise to be in an unknown place was inviting. Who knew what lied beyond the desert?

Approaching the pharaoh, Daimina's breathing became heavier as she constantly played with her fingers.

"My king," Daimina spoke carefully next to him.

He turned and, upon seeing her, faked a small smile. He leaned over and kissed her forehead, inhaling the scent of her washed hair.

"Daimina, how did you find me?" he asked.

"Your mother told me you were here."

"I'm observing our new recruits. All of them here wish to be soldiers in my army. They are very young in the ways of war and have a long way to go in such a short amount of time. What takes years for my soldiers to perfect, they will need to learn in weeks," he explained, worried.

Able to sense his tenseness she asked concerned, "What's wrong?"

"I don't know what to think anymore, Daimina. I-"

His voice trailed off, shaking his head gently, gripping the stone railing tightly in his hands. Daimina rubbed her hand over his shoulder slowly as her soft eyes devoted themselves to his youthful, torn face.

"The revelation that it was Egyptian men, my guards dressed in Hyksos uniforms..." he continued, voice wavering. " How do I know if there are Hyksos soldiers here or not? I should trust King Khian's word. He hasn't shown otherwise, but...how do I know that my own palace isn't working against me?"

He watched the fighting reach its peak as both men seemed equally tied.

"My mother hasn't been quiet about her feelings towards... several men in my company," he mused. "There are too many variables. I feel as though..."

He stopped talking, sighing heavily and placing a hand to his head. Daimina's fingers gently rubbed his arm, moving up to his shoulder, as she rested her chin on her hand. He rubbed the smooth skin on her arm twice and inhaled the scent from her hair again.

"My king, there is something I need to tell you," she said lowly.

At that moment, one of the matches finished as the group of soldiers in training roared with applause to the winner of the epic battle that lasted the longest.

"Ah, see there, Daimina," the pharaoh commented, gesturing his hand forward to the winner of the match. He was a man near thirty, strongly built, with a rather youthful face conquering a man equal in size.

"He has won the past three matches, but the others seem equally matched..." Rolling his tongue with intensity the pharaoh continued speaking his thoughts. "General Sefkh isn't doing enough. Those men posing as Hyksos soldiers went unnoticed. The supposed Mitanni as well. Who else? I need to find out why. They need to work harder. They need to. They have to. We don't have enough time and…"

He glanced to Daimina, able to read the woe painted on her face.

"My love…what is wrong?"

"Nothing… Your mother wanted me to tell you that your vizier is reading your letters again without your permission," she replied.

"Again and again, Senmet. I know he means well. He was more of a father to me than my own… Alright. I will speak with him about it," he promised her.

Daimina nodded, wrapping her arms around him.

The pharaoh kissed her forehead and reassured her, "We'll be alright, Daimina. Egypt will be alright. It has to. I promise."

Feeling her squeeze him slightly upon those words, he frowned. He could sense something wasn't right. There was more than just the issue of Senmet taking on more responsibilities than he previously had. There was more than just the concern of secrets being kept.

"Something is still bothering you isn't there, Daimina? You are not alright, are you? Your eyes are full of… Are you drinking enough?" he asked.

"I could use some water."

"Fear not, I will fetch some for you," Aoh interrupted immediately.

Walking over to retrieve Daimina water from the large basin, I was able to see the match more clearly. Each young man couldn't have been much older than myself. Some around Laggus' age. Most of them were very skinny, attempting to build some kind of muscle. They were loyal men.

As they all shouted to each other, watching their comrades wrestle, I could see in between them Sefkh speaking with another general with tight lips and angered expressions as though he was struggling to contain all of his rage. I couldn't hear them but I could see them very clearly, wearing their uniforms, carrying their weapons, drinking from their goblets.

As Sefkh continued to speak, I tried to decipher the words. Most of it seemed to have been growls and irritated chattering until I realized whom he was talking about. It wasn't a secret whom he was talking about. I was sure he knew how Sefkh felt about him. He knew.

41

"Pharaoh! My King!"

Kha'y raised his hands, chasing after the king pharaoh and Laggus as they walked down the hallway together ignoring his loud pleas. They stopped when the high priest threw himself onto the ground, bowing deeply with loud cries, nearly ripping the bottom of the pharaoh's robe with his long fingers.

"My king, I beg of you to, please, listen to my words!" he cried.

"For the final time, no, she will not be aiding you," the pharaoh denied harshly.

"But, my king, the gods! The gods, they asked of her…they promised her-"

"My answer is no. Find yourself another wife to have a family with. She is to remain in my palace where her services are required."

"The gods made a promise to me…they made a promise and you are disobeying them."

"I am sorry, Kha'y, but she will remain in my palace. This is her destiny."

He continued with Laggus down the hallway as Kha'y watched, saddened by the pharaoh's final answer. Turning the corner, passing several craftsman preparing a new obelisk to be placed in the center of the city, the pharaoh glanced behind him. Several servants rushed past him carrying large baskets full of food and wine. The sounds of instruments being fine-tuned and fixed echoed off the walls every now and again.

"Laggus," the pharaoh ordered firmly, overlooking the creation of the new obelisk.

"My king?" Laggus asked.

"I want someone I can trust with me when I speak to my vizier tonight. But it cannot be you."

"Send Aoh," Laggus answered without hesitation.

The pharaoh paused for only a second.

"Bring her to me."

The room was covered in endless silks in several colors, filled with soothing music and a fresh aroma of wine. I rested on my knees beside a column laden with several jars of wine as several women, all dressed the same, entered. The linen dresses hardly covered their bodies, as parts of their chest were revealed behind near transparent pieces of silk. Their long legs moved like snakes answering to the spell of a charmer. The bangles on their ankles musically rang with each movement. Their youthful faces faded in and out of the silk curtains.

Their decorated eyes followed every movement, entrancing anyone who looked into them. I watched the women as I waited in silence, still obligated to wear servant's clothes, feeling envious of their beauty. All of them were slender to the point of snapping in half if they were not careful how they moved. The golden glow of the room reflected from their cheeks and lips. They naturally smelt of roses and irises.

Dipping their smooth hands and arms into large bowls with a faint odor of olive, they began to slowly massage the pharaoh's and Senmet's shoulders. They sat diagonally from each other in stone seats with several cushions and animal skins laid across them, rocking their heads gently to the soothing touch of the servant's hands.

Senmet sat back, with a calm smile on his face, glancing around him as he grabbed the goblet of wine to his left and drank it slowly. The pharaoh did the same, leaning forward slightly, enjoying the massage, yet keeping a hint of seriousness across his face. With each sip he took of the wine, he rubbed his lips tightly together.

It must have been nearly an hour of silence between the two of them rolling with the waves of such pleasing sensations. Neither of them spoke. They sat there, getting their shoulders, arms, legs, and feet massaged slowly by the soft hands of the servant women while they drank and listened to the sweet music and the dim sounds of night insects chirping.

"My king…" Senmet finally spoke.

The pharaoh glanced his way and replied,"Yes?"

"I am somewhat confused as to why you called me here tonight. We've done this many times before but I have a suspicion that this time you have something to tell me. Something you don't want anyone else to hear."

The pharaoh didn't respond but finished his goblet of wine with one last large swallow, rolling his tongue over his lips, capturing the last residue of the pleasing refreshment. Glancing over at the jar already empty, he raised his goblet to Aoh. In response, she rose to her feet and immediately poured more wine into the jar and then filled the goblet with the golden and stone vessel. She bowed when finished, and returned to her place to sit on her knees in silence, keeping her eyes on the pharaoh.

"Have I done something to upset the pharaoh?" the vizier inquired. "Have my actions bothered you in a way I'm not aware of?"

"Well…you are half right, my friend," the pharaoh answered. "I did want to speak to you in private. This conversation is not to be repeated. This is between you and I. Disobey me…and you disobey the gods and everything Egypt stands for. I only want your insight. You did not upset me."

Senmet tilted his head slightly, changing his seated position to focus all of his attention on the pharaoh.

"Can I trust General Sefkh?" the pharaoh confided.

"Strange question. Do you not trust him?" Senmet asked.

"I didn't say that. I'm only asking…can I?" the pharaoh answered.

"Of course you can, my king. He's a leader among men. Intelligent, somewhat foolish when it comes to his appetites, but we shouldn't fault him for them. He's loyal to you unlike…his equal."

"Laggus," the pharaoh said bitterly.

Aoh's eyes gently shifted towards Senmet.

"He's loyal and equal to General Sefkh, but he has yet to become a soldier. I find it rather odd the amount of trust you bestow upon a man who has spent most of his life in the city. By all accounts, for that matter, he is not born of Egypt. One day you just decide to bring an outsider in and he's been attached to your hip ever since."

"He…saved my life "

"Ah, yes, the lion attack in the desert," Senmet replied, unimpressed.

"He saved me out of bravery and kindness. He was unaware who I really was."

"So he says."

"It's the truth," the pharaoh interjected, with a harsh tone.

"The truth?"

Senmet stopped himself, glancing at Aoh unexpectedly. Aoh's eyes remained planted to the floor, as she realized how reflective the surface was. Perhaps the floors would tell her more about the palace than the walls.

"The truth is, my pharaoh, you may think I'm surprised he's not present with us tonight but I assure I am not," Senmet admitted. "You must have your doubts about him and General Sefkh if you are to ask of them to me. Truth is, I've spent the most amount of time with Sefkh. He's been present at every gathering, battle, meeting, party. Laggus has not, and it's no secret that he hasn't made any attempts to truly be around anyone within the palace. He's very reclusive, even among the guards."

The pharaoh didn't respond but listened intently. Senmet leaned forward, slightly hunched, as his folded hands rested near his chest.

The servants repositioned themselves to massage his back, dipping their hands and arms back into the basins and crawled their fingers down his back to his sides.

"I…am troubled by what Laggus had found that night in the city," Senmet continued. "The fact that our own men disguised themselves as Hyksos soldiers and would rather die than reveal as to whom ordered them to do so troubles me. The soldiers are very loyal to Sefkh. They would follow him to the end of their lives, whereas they do not share the same enthusiasm for Laggus. They, like you, see a man who is nothing near their level of skill and power. The results of what occurred in Babylon proves as much, wouldn't you agree? Do you think its possible Sefkh had told them to do it?"

The pharaoh didn't respond.

"What do you want me to say?" Senmet asked.

He glanced at Aoh as she turned her eyes away from him and focused them on the wall across the room, hidden behind silk curtains. The pharaoh's head rolled back again, feeling the hands make their way to his sides and chest.

"If General Sefkh didn't order the guards, then who did?" the pharaoh asked.

"I do not know. I have the records of the men already questioned, and thus far they are unaware of who is at fault. Truth is, all of them were unaware of such an event until Laggus brought it to your attention."

"So it seems."

"In the end, you are the pharaoh. You make the final decision. I cannot. I can only advise you, as I've always done. Sometimes I may do things you do not approve of, but I always do them out of love for you and Egypt. I've stood by many times, when your father was pharaoh, when I shouldn't have. Now that I've grown old in this palace, I've come to learn from those missed opportunities. I do believe if you trust yourself and your instincts, you will make the right choice," Senmet smiled.

"Such as your choice in wines for the Festival of Nephthys." The pharaoh smirked for a moment, glancing at his goblet.

Taking another sip, Senmet gasped, "It is quite delicious."

"I'm glad you think so. Will they please our guests' tomorrow?"

"They most certainly will. Nephthys will gladly shine upon you and Egypt. Your family will grow in her protection for eternity."

42

There was a moment when I couldn't recognize whom I was looking at in the mirror. I touched my eyes, and the reflection repeated my action. I turned my head to look at the dazzling golden strands in my hair, and the reflection did the same gentle movement. I looked down upon both arms seeing golden cuffs clasped at my elbows and wrists, holding a thin white fabric from under my arms, laying across my back.

The linen dress was sheer, yet did not reveal every part of my body as I feared it would. Unlike the dresses the women around me were donned in, as they wrapped themselves around men. The glorious statue of Nephthys was carried in by servants as lines of priests followed, praying loudly for her. The release of flower petals fell from the ceiling like silent rain.

My hands trailed the thick stone railing down the steps, following Daimina as she carried herself like a queen with a sickened countenance on her face. Our shadows followed us on the walls. She smelled like a freshly, planted garden. When she entered the room, all eyes fell on her immediately. She was a glistening jewel, shinning like the brightest star, bringing all those towards her.

The crowds dispersed to allow the pharaoh to meet her at the bottom of the stairs, where she gladly accepted his hand. Helping her down the last step, he stared into her warm eyes. Her hands traced up both of his arms, grazing every muscle as his hands massaged her slowly. With calming breaths, he dipped his face towards her, rubbing his forehead against hers and, with one breath, fell into a dreamlike trance. He whispered her name, drowning in her essence.

Watching the pharaoh and Daimina filled me with joy and contentment. They joined the festival, receiving bows and words of praise by everyone in the room. A look of overwhelming distress danced upon her face, but her smile beamed. She wrapped her arm with his, passing many faces she never saw before.

Remaining on the stairs, I craned my neck searching for Laggus, anxious to see him…but he was not there. I found it alarming to not see him present at the festival. He was the pharaoh's shadow, and yet nowhere to be seen.

Of course, he could have been in the shadows observing from a distance but…I couldn't find him.

The high pitched instruments surrounded the atmosphere, covered in hanging drapes and silks… It was as though I somehow entered another world. Every face I saw was gazing into another's passionately. Arms were intertwined with drinks and food. The smooth sounds of horns protruded into the air as women massaged their men repeatedly and fed them slowly. Everyone was dancing. The more faces I saw that were not Laggus', the more my heart longed to see him.

Now in the arms of the pharaoh, I did not have to follow Daimina. I was free to wander. Tracing my fingers across the silk curtains and grasping the soft threads, I imagined seeing Laggus on the other side.

I held my breath, desiring to be in his arms, to feel his heartbeat against mine… I felt lost in a place I knew. Walking outside, the celebration faded away and I was met with the moon, half covered in thin clouds spread across the sky. It was quiet.

Turning around, I thought I heard the sound of someone there only to find it was a cat, passing by without acknowledging me. Was I being foolish to be thinking of him? I waited in silence when, suddenly, I heard distinct footsteps coming from behind me. A wave of scents flew around me from the opening in the silk curtains as the footsteps came to my side.

The horse came to a violent halt, kicking up sand, casting it aside and over the high edge of the plateau. Tightening his grip on the leather reigns of the horse, his narrow eyes looked down and saw an onslaught unlike any he had seen before. The rising flames burned repeatedly, casting a shadow of smoke into the atmosphere. The grey and black smoke suffocated the cool air.

Clasping his hand against the sash over his mouth, he watched the unexpected attacks burn several towns, taking several as prisoners. Their hands and legs were bound together as their terrified shrieks pierced the sounds of the last breaths of many soldiers and servants.

The fierce army moved like a swarm of insects, eating away at the town piece by piece, leaving nothing but remnants in flames. The town guards rushed into the slaughter, unprepared and outnumbered, as the beastly horses trampled over women and children alike. The roar of satisfaction spewed from the soldiers' mouths, becoming hungrier for more despair.

His horse wouldn't stop fidgeting, becoming frightened by the ungodly sight unfolding before them. It was as though the god Set had begun to play a game with the lives of other nations who neglected to worship him. Pulling the reigns to the side, he called the horse's name quickly, turning him it around, unable to wash the reflection of the flames from his eyes.

Aoh turned her head ever so slightly to find Senmet approaching her. Returning her gaze to the desert, as she slipped one hand to the sash around her waist, feeling the top of the handle. She heard the footsteps growing louder as Senmet stood next to her, looking out at the desert in silence. He inhaled the fresh air, observing the multitude of statues and obelisks, when the sudden screech of a kite startled them.

"I've come up here many a night to listen to the silence and sometimes the haunting calls of a falcon," the vizier commented. "I've heard the shrieks, the cries, like a weeping widow who has... just lost everything."

Aoh's eyes flickered towards Senmet from underneath the heavy bangs and glistening makeup.

"I feel the gods send us signs and messages every day," he continued. "I've tried to read them. I've tried, but failed. Perhaps that is why I am not a priest."

He looked at her with his painted eyes surrounded in wrinkles, trying to study her hidden expression.

"You do not look overjoyed," he announced.

Aoh didn't answer him, but keep her eyes focused at the sights ahead, while still keeping close attention to his words.

"Celebrations do not please you? I suppose you feel lonely. Why celebrate when you have no one to celebrate with?"

Aoh shook her head in response, growing increasingly worried being alone with him and away from the festival.

"Were you born here?" he asked.

"Not in the palace, no," Aoh responded.

"Oh, that I know. I would have known of you if you were. But you are Egyptian, yes?"

Aoh didn't reply, growing suddenly tense by his presence.

Lowering his head slightly towards her, Senmet asked her another question. "Tell me, Aoh, where do you see Egypt in the next thousand years?"

"I do not know," she answered.

"Exactly. We will never know, because one day we will be gone. It is our responsibility to do what we can to keep it as glorious as it is now. As someone who has had the liberty and blessing of the gods of advising and guiding the pharaoh these many years, I know to stay on this path. To not diverge."

Aoh listened as she carefully glanced at the celebration continuing from the corner of her eyes. She felt someone nearby watching. That someone remained eerily still and silent, absorbing every word that flew from their mouths, like blood on linen.

"Because of my focus, I can tell you feel very lonely and secluded here," the vizier advised. "You have but one you trust, and yet cannot be with, yes?"

I didn't understand where this was coming from. And the longer this conversation was becoming, the more unsettled I was. I was beginning to feel as though Senmet wanted me to reveal something. I received the impression he knew more than previously told and wanted some form of conviction.

Aoh didn't speak, but cleared her throat, prepared to draw the knife if need be, readily accepting the fact she'd be disobeying Laggus' orders.

"Do I make you feel uncomfortable?" Senmet asked, calmly.

"No," Aoh replied.

"You're probably wondering why I'm speaking so bluntly to you. Truth is, I do not need to give you a reason why. Though, I'm sure you have your suspicions. Daimina is a lovely woman. She exudes warmth. But…we are all in our place for a reason. It is best to accept our fate, because we cannot change it, no matter how much we want to."

Aoh's fingers twirled around the knife handle as she held her breath.

"You do understand what it is I'm telling you, don't you Aoh?" he asked lowly.

"I'm afraid I do not," Aoh lied, facing him.

I stared into his eyes, unmoved and unchallenged. I was not going to allow myself to be frightened by a man who had everything handed to him since birth. I did not care what he said next. I was not going to let him break me.

"Then, what do you understand?"

"That I am Daimina's servant, as ordered by the pharaoh of Egypt. I shall obey him and serve her," Aoh replied.

"Yes, a servant who came from where?" Senmet released a slight chuckle. "If one is to be a servant, let it be a loyal servant. So, that even in the afterlife, you are rewarded greatly for your service."

Aoh watched Senmet leave to join the festival as she remained alone, to watch the night.

"Truth is, we are all servants," he informed her. "We are. All of us. It's important to remember who we serve and why."

The loud gurgling sounds of a foul, watery mixture emptying repeatedly into a basin. Remnants of the previous night spewed from her mouth as she coughed heavily, trying to breath. Hovering her head over the basin, she paused, coughing, feeling the pain in her stomach continue. She panted, taking the cloth Aoh handed her and wiping her mouth clean, feeling her throat swell. Light sweat dazzled her forehead and under her eyelids.

Leaning back, Aoh tried to give her small amounts of water. The water refused to enter her mouth as Daimina leaned over and began to profusely vomit again. Aoh tried to hold her hair back while rubbing her back gently with the palm of her hand. Spitting fluid into the basin, Daimina leaned back, breathing heavily.

Aoh cleaned her mouth again and quickly poured light streams of water between her dried lips. Daimina swallowed with a slight struggle, feeling the cool liquid drop down her throat. She tenderly wiped away light trails of the water spilled around her neck. Aoh glanced out the door, beginning to grow impatient, worried as to why it was taking the servant so long to return with the pharaoh.

Keeping Daimina's hair in her hand, Aoh rubbed her shoulders with her other hand, trying her best to keep her calm. Daimina sighed heavily, trying to laugh, rubbing her shaking hands over her stomach. From the hallway outside the door, she heard the loud sounds of armor clattering with each movement.

"What is happening?!" the pharaoh asked, rushing towards them with wide eyes as Senmet remained in the doorway.

Aoh sighed heavily with relief.

"What happened? What's wrong with her?" he asked, panicked.

He picked Daimina up with ease in his arms as she began to sweat profusely. He watched her hands slightly twitch, listening to her heavy breathing escaping her partially opened mouth. The large basin caught the pharaoh's attention as his voice crackled with a heavy panic.

"Guards! Guards, help me, please!" he screamed.

Senmet remained stunned in the doorway, taking him a moment to turn around and call for the guards repeatedly. The loud marching grew as they rushed forward, lifting Daimina into their arms. Distraught was carved all over the pharaoh's face.

Aoh followed them, ignoring Senmet, hearing the pharaoh's weeps of worry, watching Daimina's limp body remain weightless in the strong guard's arms. As they carried her into her chambers, the pharaoh stopped them harshly, wanting to lay Daimina on her bed. He carefully took her into his arms, unable to stop weeping, trying to lay her down carefully. He kissed her forehead, feeling the sweat on her body. Her slightly pale complexion haunted him.

"It will be alright. It will be alright, Daimina. I promise it will be alright," he repeated to her constantly, holding her hands tightly, kissing them repeatedly.

Aoh entered the room, immediately preparing water just as the physician rushed inside, nearly colliding into her. The group of guards stood in a line near the bed, looking down at Daimina in silent confusion, growing increasingly concerned at the sight of their panicked king.

"Where is the physician?!" he screamed.

The man came to the bedside, out of breath, and immediately asked for water as Senmet followed slowly, peering from the doorway. Aoh carried the large basin of water to him with linen rags.

"She needs air," the physician instructed.

"Everyone out! Everyone! OUT! NOW!" the pharaoh screamed.

The guards left, immediately passing Senmet, preparing to follow behind them with Aoh.

"Not you, Aoh. Stay here," the pharaoh spat quickly.

Senmet looked at her as a trace of disbelief washed over his face. Startled by the pharaoh's tone, Aoh came to his side and bowed quickly.

"She's burning up. I'll need my things. Keep her cool," the physician explained, and sprinted out of the room like a jackal in the desert.

Aoh remained bowing, watching as the pharaoh caressed the side of Daimina's face with the back of his hand. They locked fingers with each other's hands. He wiped the sweat slowly from her face, listening to her heavy breathing and coughing.

"What happened to her?" he asked wickedly.

"My king," Aoh spoke, choking slightly on her words, "I believe Daimina is with child."

"What?" he asked breathlessly, looking at her.

"My king!" Laggus shouted, running into the room.

"Laggus, stand guard at the door. I do not want anyone but the physician coming in or out, do you understand me?!" the pharaoh commanded quickly.

Slightly panting, he answered with a solid, "Yes."

Laggus glanced at me only for a second before standing at the doorway, facing the hallway. My heart danced seeing him again.

"With child?" the pharaoh gasped in disbelief. He stared upon Daimina in shock, swallowing hard and trembling. He whispered to himself as he pressed the water soaked linens across Daimina's face, gently. "This means both she and my queen are carrying my child."

"The queen is with child too?" Aoh asked aloud, causing Laggus to suddenly turn towards them.

"Coming through!" the physician shouted, unwilling to wait for Laggus to move, nearly tripping over his large feet. Running to the bed, he quickly served a drink for Daimina, stirring it continually with a thin stick.

"Please, prop her head," he instructed the pharaoh.

Lifting Daimina's head, the physician opened her mouth gently, lightly pouring the liquid. Daimina responded with several coughs and choking sounds.

"Yes, yes, drink it all. Yes, there you go," he reassured calmly, slowly pouring the entire goblet.

"My king, I will be needing all the space I can obtain. We may need to call a priest for good measure."

"The rest of you leave us now," the pharaoh ordered, turning around and looking at Aoh and Laggus.

Laggus pulled the curtains closed over the doorway the moment Aoh passed them and seized her arm tightly.

Feeling the grip on her arm, Aoh turned around.

"I need to speak with you," Laggus said firmly.

Pulling her arm, he looked around for the nearest empty room and led her inside, unaware that a pair of dark eyes watched them from down the hallway, lurking in the shadows. Several startled cats fled as they entered the room. Laggus pulled the silk drapes closed, standing in near darkness. Aoh stood in the faint light of the burning fires, staring at him silently. Laggus panted facing the curtains. Wiping his mouth before turning around to look at Aoh.

"The Hyksos are making camps just beyond the Nile River," he confessed.

A poisonous combination of horror and turmoil struck Aoh like a blade through her chest.

"I saw it myself."

"W-w-why?" Aoh muttered, growing angry.

"I do not know. I couldn't engage them as per the pharaoh's orders. But I saw them."

"They could just be more Egyptian guards in their uniforms."

Laggus shook his head in disagreement.

"We don't know how far this goes?" she queried. "There could be hundreds of guards under orders. We can't-"

"They were not Egyptians, Aoh."

"This doesn't make sense," Aoh cried.

"The pharaoh is going to want to engage…it's apparent King Khian's alliance was a lie. His ambassador lied to you that night," Laggus added.

Aoh shook her head repeatedly, feeling the anger within her rise and tears swell in her eyes.

"No…no, Tyrgnn promised me-"

"He lied to you."

Aoh's eyes narrowed deeply, unable to accept that Tyrgnn's promise was a lie just to spite her.

"I have to tell him," Laggus insisted. "You cannot ask me not to. We can't afford to lose more innocent lives."

"Wait!" Aoh bellowed, stopping Laggus in mid motion, lifting the first silk curtain.

He looked at her as she raised her eyes, wet with small tears.

"You can't tell him now. Daimina is with child and so is the queen."

Laggus nodded, dropping the silk curtain behind him as he reentered the room.

"Are you certain?" he asked.

"As certain as I'll ever be. You can't leave the palace now. Once everyone finds out they will all be coming for her."

"I will leave the palace if the pharaoh orders it so," Laggus corrected firmly. "You are her protector. That is why you were brought here."

43

"How many?" the pharaoh asked.

"At least fifty, my king," Laggus answered, standing with his arms folded behind his back.

The pharaoh's tongue turned to stone, unable to speak. He sat still in his golden chair, listening to the calm water roll on the sides of his boat as it floated down the Nile River slowly. The servant's steady hands pushed the long poles into the water. The boat glided forward, dodging sunbathing crocodiles and curious hippopotamuses.

Senmet glanced to the king from the left, feeling the tickle of the breeze around his ears, waiting for him to speak. The pharaoh's eyes lifted from the wooden floor to the feet of the chair as, behind it, the delicate silk curtains swayed to and fro. Next to the chair, a large limestone bust made of his father's face remained silent, watching over the conversation.

Laggus remained before the king, inhaling the scent of the water and the fresh soil at the banks. Farmers dug into the ground, tossing seeds from baskets, as oxen ploughed the land slowly and forcefully. Reeds were cut with fatal swoops, bundled and carried to be made into papyrus paper and wrappings for mummification.

The pharaoh covered his goblet as the nearest servant attempted to pour him more wine from a lion shaped vessel. Glancing at the bust of his father's face, the pharaoh lifted his heavy eyes, glancing beyond Laggus, seeing in the distance a statue of his father at the entrance of a grand temple miles away. Exhaling heavily, he tapped his fingers against his face. He looked at Laggus, feeling Senmet's eyes on his shoulders.

"Did they see you?" the pharaoh finally asked, avoiding the obvious question.

"No, my king."

"This cannot wait, can it?" he asked wearily, dropping his hand to tap his fingers against the armrest.

Laggus glanced at Senmet who glanced back at him in return.

"My king, there is more you need to know," Laggus explained with a heavy feeling of regret.

"Yes?" the pharaoh asked.

"Upon my observations of the Hyksos at our borders, the Hittites are not far."

Senmet glanced to the king, as a slight trace of shock glossed over his eyes before quickly vanishing behind the dark color.

"They were destroying a town. I could not tell whom the unfortunate people were; however, that is the closest I've seen them to Egypt."

"Hittites? Egypt's very few enemies seem to be coming out of the ground like snakes all at once," Senmet commented, concerned.

"The Hyksos will be our first priority. They are nearly at our doorstep," the pharaoh commanded, standing up. "If the Hyksos are plotting a betrayal, we'll need to take care of it before dealing with another enemy. If the treaty was true and they are now our ally, we can then prepare for what will be a necessary action against the Hittites."

"Agreed, great pharaoh. We mustn't act too irrationally. Shall I order the servants to make haste back to the palace and call forth General Sefkh-"

"No," the pharaoh interrupted. "I want you to look into his

records. Myself, Laggus, and a group of our best soldiers will get to the bottom of this tonight. If General Sefkh cannot be trusted, he cannot come. I will hold you personally accountable with this task."

Senmet bowed, "Yes, my king. It would be my greatest honor. I want no stone unturned."

Senmet dipped his head into the large bathroom, complete with a bathing pool, flowing fountains, and several female servants waiting patiently for further instructions. The painted walls looked fresh, detailed in sensual imagery with hints of golden clad over several objects, including a couch on the farthest side of the room.

Taking it all in, turning around, he caught Sefkh entering the room. He walked down several steps, halting at the sight of the bald and determined vizier adorned in his finest linen dress with several rolled pieces of papyrus under his left arm.

Sefkh sighed heavily, walking to the nearest display of several wines, beer, and bowls full of imported dates. He quickly ate a few, watching Senmet lurk in the doorway of the bathroom before finally deciding to approach, taking slow, calculated steps.

"Has all of this been taken into account?" Senmet asked, looking around the room, gazing at every column, drape, statue, and servant.

"Yes," Sefkh replied dully in between eating dates.

Walking to the other side of the lavished golden and limestone table, Senmet inquired, "What of all this beer and wine?"

"Yes," Sefkh replied with a hint of annoyance.

"And the furniture? The…unusually amount of servants for just one…general? Especially…an unmarried one."

"Yes, Senmet. All of it has been taken into account. May I ask why you're here?"

"The pharaoh has given me direct orders to view your records," Senmet explained, looking about the room, picking up the vessels full of wine and beer. His darkly outlined eyes studied the design and weight of each vessel and then rolled his lips at the sight of the imported dates.

"Why would he ask for those?" Sefkh asked, rotating the handle of his sword at his waist slowly with the palm of his hand.

"That statement doesn't make you sound very convincing."

"Convincing of what?"

"That you're not hiding something."

Sefkh glanced at his sword and smirked with a hint of disbelief in his voice. "How much do you want?"

"I don't want anything," Senmet replied, standing before another long table made of limestone and marble near the back entrance of the home, purposely placed on a slight hill where Sefkh could overlook the Nile River. Everything was made by the most gifted craftsmen, using the finest materials.

"Why?"

"I can't have anything trace itself back to me. Unlike you, I actually want to keep my position in the palace."

"Then, what do I have to do to keep you from talking?" Sefkh asked, taking steps towards the table.

"You can aid me in getting rid of the pharaoh's mistress, her servant, and all loyal to her tonight while the pharaoh is away. It must be done before the sun rises. It must be quick."

"Why the sudden urgency?"

"This may be the only chance where he will be away from the palace long enough. As you assume, I have made proper preparations. I obtained a piece of fabric from the Hyksos when they visited our kingdom. When the pharaoh returns to find both women killed outside the walls with this fabric, there will be no need to convince him any further that war must be declared against the Hyksos."

"And why do you want her killed?" Sefkh asked slickly.

"Because she is carrying the pharaoh's child. Whether boy or girl, that child is now an heir to the throne."

Sefkh's eyebrows raised slightly and asked curiously, "So, the pharaoh discovers her dead…then what?"

"The pharaoh returns to correct matters at the borders. Keep those uncivilized barbarians in their place. Assembles an army with you as its leader to destroy those horrid men…whether they be Hyksos, Hittites, or anyone that dares to get in the way. He and the queen will raise their children, their future heirs to the throne. And in the end…Egypt prevails, as it always has and always will."

"You thought of all of this yourself?" Sefkh smirked, shaking his head.

"Whom else would be so wise as myself to prevent Egypt from destroying itself?" Senmet asked. "Egypt is becoming a fading jewel, mixed with other gemstones unworthy of its presence. Of those fading Egypt's glory are people like Daimina. Her unborn child, no doubt a son, will destroy everything."

Sefkh listened, unswayed by Senmet's strict words. He tilted his head slightly as though trying to find a hidden message within Senmet's outlined eyes.

"It matters not to me who rules this kingdom," Sefkh proclaimed, turning around to look out the nearest open window at his own small kingdom of servants growing flowers, working in the gardens, fishing by the Nile, and taking care of his horses.

"It should. If you wish to keep this lavished lifestyle, you must be in the king's favor everyday of your life. The moment you slip from his sights…the decline begins."

Senmet rubbed his fingers over the table, tugging the right side of his robe away from his feet.

"The pharaoh doesn't trust you or your pretty words," Senmet announced. "He believes you were behind the plot of having his guards posing as those Hyksos soldiers to implement the need for war. He doesn't suspect you of anything else."

Sefkh turned around heavily. Shaking his head in response he replied lowly, "No."

"I will make it worth your while."

"How? Why should I take any part in this? Why should I give the pharaoh reason to distrust me? Why take the risk?" Sefkh asked.

"Because if you agree, when Laggus returns to the palace, which undoubtedly he will before pharaoh, you have my permission to kill him."

Sefkh's eyes glowed for a moment, as the blade handle he had been incessantly rotating in his hand stopped. A small grin appeared, partially revealing his teeth, lifting his rough cheeks.

"I'm not forcing your hand, only providing you a way to rise without climbing. It's all a matter of perception, really. Is Daimina's life worth more than yours? Because you know what the pharaoh will do to you, if he finds out about all of this," Senmet explained, pacing across from Sefkh, raising his eyes about the room, opening his long arms.

Sefkh didn't answer as the small grin vanished behind a firm grimace.

"As I thought," Senmet teased. "Then, I shall expect you an hour after the sun sets in the palace with your friends. If any of them refuse to do as your order...dispose of them. We cannot afford any liabilities. Oh, and I want the guards whom were captured with Laggus in Babylon to come with you."

"Why?" Sefkh coldly asked.

"I believe there is a reason why they escaped. Would the lives of a few guards sway you?" Senmet questioned.

"They matter not to me, they are not my soldiers."

Senmet nodded, pleased with the response. Pulling the ends of his robe slightly, Senmet passed Sefkh, moving towards the entrance of the magnificent home. Sefkh's eyes following Senmet, glowing like lightning.

Senmet paused and said, "Oh, and if you're thinking of rewriting all those records in time to get out of this...how adorable."

The high priest rolled his head around repeatedly while the strong burning incense surrounded him in white smoke, curling and shifting from the small hanging trays. He hummed and mumbled words, standing before several statues of the gods within the temple.

His voice boomed loudly, his lanky reflection in the water basins where he washed his hands before prayer vibrating. His eyelids trembled slightly, over his eyes as he hummed, hunching, twisting his shoulders.

He drank tainted wine, throwing spices over the flames in small spurts, rubbing his fingers above the peaks of the dancing fire. His hands rummaged over scrolls and across the stone prayers, throwing himself over them repeatedly, begging to be heard. His eyes tightened as images flashed in the darkness. He saw flickers of faces and the pyramids as the sun rose and set rapidly, signifying the passing of days. Finishing his prayers, he opened his eyes, beholding the statues of the gods standing before him.

He smiled deeply, waving his hands over the incense trays, watching as the light of the fire faded into heavy amounts of white smoke. The black ashes of what remained released a deathly scent. He craned his hands, bending his fingers around the smoke, watching it soar into the air and vanish. He looked at the statues again and bowed, lowering his entire body onto the marble floor.

Rising, he dipped his hands into the tainted wine and then the water basin, stopping when he heard the sound of sandals walking onto the shiny floor at the temple entrance behind him.

"Yes, what is it?" Kha'y asked aloud, facing the statues.

"It's the king's vizier, Senmet. He wishes to speak with you alone," the priest explained, holding a faience against his thin chest.

Turning around, Kha'y saw Senmet waiting patiently for him outside the temple in the burning sunlight.

"Send him to my chambers," Kha'y ordered.

Slinking into a cushioned chair, Kha'y stared at Senmet standing above him with a mix of irritability and intrigue, waiting for the sound of his doors to close. Senmet remained standing before him, concentrating his expressionless eyes on the corrupted and depraved high priest. As the doors closed tightly, Kha'y released a breath, crossing his long legs.

"You've been planning this since the moment the pharaoh first uttered her name. This is not some scheme that dawned upon you in a dream," Kha'y spoke with a sneer.

The heavy groan of wind against drapes and window shutters filled the room as the two looked into each other intensely.

"You've been waiting for this," the high priest continued. "Waiting for such an opportunity. What makes you think I want to take part in this?" he asked coldly, sitting comfortably in his seat of white marble draped with animal skins.

"You have yet to say otherwise," Senmet answered with a smug smile. Swiping his hands across the sides of the seat next to him, he sat down, feeling the smooth cut of sublime stone against the palms of his wrinkled hands. The arms and legs carved into the paws of a mighty lion.

Touching the stone, rubbing the tips of his fingers together, he continued, "Your tastes do not attach themselves to gold and silver like your priests do. You do not thirst for more land, more power, or anything tangible really. You thirst for what you feel you are owed. Yes?"

Kha'y leaned forward, lowering his head like a snake when observing what lies before it.

"I want Aoh. I thirst for the servant girl."

"If she lives, she will be yours," Senmet promised calmly.

"No. She must live or it is you who will be dead, and I won't be there to pray for your safe passage to the afterlife," Kha'y threatened, rising from his seat. "And that I would gladly see that happen to you, snake of the palace."

Senmet remained unmoved by Kha'y's thrash of spite. He watched Kha'y take slick steps towards him with a distorted face.

"You seize this opportunity to ensure others perish in your place. Make no mistake, I am doing this for the gods, not you."

"The gods?" Senmet asked flatly.

"The gods had sent me visions of her before she arrived. They told me she was to be mine. They brought her to the palace so that I could claim her as I rightfully am owed for my dedication and practice. For my works and…lack of rewards. I asked several times for her and the pharaoh denies me. He denies the gods! He denies them time and time again! His kingdom will suffer due to his arrogance and neglect! A man like myself cannot rule anything in this world, but I will rule her. She is mine, Senmet, and I will do anything to obey the gods."

"Looking to start a family, are you?" he asked sarcastically.

Kha'y didn't answer as he caressed his face and bald head, closing his eyes and falling into a trance, swaying his thin body to and fro. Unfazed, Senmet approached the closed doors covered in spells and incantations of protection and livelihood. He read the spells, listening to Kha'y mumble a variety of words, humming and rubbing his tongue across his lips. His arms and legs swaying like the breeze.

"I shall take your silence as your agreement," the vizier commented.

"Only…if she lives," Kha'y reminded, opening his eyes slowly.

Turning to the side, hunched over, his bold eyes widened as his fingers stretched. A sudden sprout of a breeze from the balcony smothered the burning flames as an eerie shadow swallowed the room.

"If she doesn't live…neither…will…you."

"Be at the palace an hour after sunset," Senmet responded, unmoved by Kha'y supposed threat.

44

Aoh carried newly-made linen pleated dresses, embroidered with beads and silk, down the illuminated hallway towards Daimina's chambers when she heard the sounds of horses screeching. She slowed her steps, listening, followed by the shouts of men trying to tame them. Quickening her steps again, she continued to the chambers, about to enter the room, when she heard Aneski's voice.

"Is this why you called me? Is this why you have asked for my presence? To sadden a loving mother, and once proud and beloved queen of Egypt? You know my son doesn't need to go. Neither does Laggus, or anyone from his army," Aneski explained firmly, keeping her folded hands against her waist, just underneath her layers of golden necklaces.

I took slow steps backwards, slipping my feet against the floor, keeping my back against the wall. Inching closer with each step.

"As his vizier, do you not have anything to say?" she asked firmly.

"As the king's vizier and most loyal servant, I have spoken and he has decided to go himself," Senmet replied.

Tucking the linen dresses closer to my chest, I felt my breath diminish to a faint wheeze.

"If you question his decision, than go to him. I believe he will be safe as long as he has Laggus and his soldiers with him."

Aneski released a grunt in suspicion.

"The lies have been mounting and are about to reach a peak in this palace," Senmet continued. "You know I'm telling the truth. You've noticed the shadows revealing themselves ever since Daimina arrived," Senmet continued calmly.

"She has nothing to do with this conversation," Aneski scolded.

Senmet's voice vanished faster than wine from a drunken man's goblet. What followed was the sound of Aneski's dazzled sandals leaving in the opposite direction of Senmet. I waited against the wall for Senmet to do something, however…he remained as silent as nights in the desert when, suddenly, a horrible thought dwelled upon my mind, nearly causing me to drop the linen dresses.

I felt my heart ache and breath escape my body as though I was being choked. I rushed into Daimina's chambers, quickly placing her dresses onto her bed and left.

Rushing down the narrow hallway, with panic and fear overtaking her, Aoh saw a natural fading light coming from the room ahead and the sounds of movement. Stopping at the corner, Aoh peeked inside.

"Are you leaving?" Aoh asked from the wooden doorway, rubbing both of her arms.

Laggus paused momentarily. He picked up his blade, which had been recently sharpened, from the table. Holding it in his hand, he looked at the shine and precision that went into its creation, remembering the first time he received it. The memory remained as clear as his morals drawn in the sand. Gently running his fingertips across its smooth sides, he could feel it prick the very texture of his rough skin. Tear sized drops of blood formed where the skin was pierced, like a thin red thread across linen.

"We can't be seen talking too much," he replied without looking at her.

"I don't care."

Laggus immediately turned and looked upon hearing Aoh's

defiance.

His eyes struck me, sending an untraceable heat through my body. I felt my lips tremble, ignoring my commands to remain expressionless. A rush of overwhelming sensations made me fall deeper into his eyes. He knew something was troubling me. I could tell. It must have been why pharaoh trusted him so much, above all others in his palace. He saw people for who they were. He saw me…

"The pharaoh wants to get a closer look at the borders. Make sure everything is as it should be," he replied vaguely, sitting on the edge of the wooden table with a hint of frustration.

"That could be at least a week's time," Aoh commented in between her thin lips.

Laggus nodded, placing his sword into the sheath at his side. He picked up another sword underneath a stack of spears from the table and placed it into the leather sheath, strapping it to his defined back.

"I'll leave you a signal if anything should happen," Aoh explained, unable to look away, beguiled by him more and more every day.

Laggus didn't reply, fiddling with more tools and weapons on the table. A guard came into the room to quickly take a weapon from the table and left without acknowledging Aoh, but nodding to Laggus firmly between his narrowed eyes. He strapped a leather belt to his waist, tugging at the uncomfortable leather armor across his chest.

"The pharaoh is counting on me to keep, not only him safe, but his soldiers, his people…and Egypt."

Planting his hands firmly onto the table, he whispered, "I am not just a guard anymore. I am now a leader among men."

"He has every right to rely on you, because you saved his life. He trusts you…you never lived in a palace before, so you are the only one who can best see what he cannot. That's why General Sefkh hates you…"

One truth had been haunting me since I first arrived at the palace that I couldn't keep silent anymore. One truth that I knew. Not a hallucination, nor spell. Not a dream nor nightmare. Only one truth...

Aoh blinked heavily, inhaled and then said, "Laggus, I...don't feel safe being here when you're not nearby."

"Why?" he asked, baffled.

From behind me, I heard someone approaching from the dark hallway. I recognized the sounds of those sandals anywhere. They were smooth, yet slick. Quick, yet slow...slipping and crawling simultaneously. Fear rose from my stomach, chilling my body. I felt my face falter...my eyes rattle uncontrollably.

"Take off your right sandal now and hand it to me," Aoh said quickly, hearing the steps drawer nearer.

Laggus lifted his head, staring at the doorway behind Aoh as he quickly removed his sandal and tossed it onto the floor, mere inches from her. Getting onto her knees, she quickly took the sandal, pulling and tugging the straps, frantically ripping the leather, hurting her fingers. Just as the steps stopped at the doorway, Aoh rose to her feet, hunching slightly, trying to hide her fearful face behind her hair.

"The tear doesn't seem too horrible. I may be able to salvage it," Aoh explained lowly, looking at the sandal.

"Why repair what you can replace?" Kha'y asked, approaching from behind her slowly.

The smooth silk from his robes swayed around Aoh's shoulders and the right side of her body. A strong odor consumed her like smoke. Her eyes turned towards the open small window in the mud-brick wall, fixated by the fading sunlight.

"They are quite valuable to me," Laggus explained, pointing to the sandal in Aoh's hands.

"Why waste a servant's time with your sandals when she could be keeping the pharaoh comfortable before his journey?" he asked with confusion, looking at Aoh with a trace of drool hanging from the right corner of his thin lips.

"He should have a taste of something now that both his wife and mistress are with child."

Aoh slowly tucked the sandal in the sash against her waist,

feeling the knife underneath the smooth folds, tempted to draw it.

"I've come to ask what your offering will be to the temple before you leave. The last offering proved to have been inefficient since you and your company were captured and nearly killed."

"We will offer what the pharaoh tells us to, high priest," Laggus answered.

"Nothing short of generous, I hope. Our king, as wise as he is... seems to offend the gods often and thinks...nothing of it. I've been praying for them to show him guidance. They are trying to help, they speak to me and do not like to be disobeyed."

"One can never pray too much. Sandals can be replaced, high priest, kings cannot," Laggus added.

"How very true, Laggus; perhaps becoming a priest is your calling. Trying to be someone you are not does not become you," the priest commented. He rolled his lips together, glancing at the array of weapons behind Laggus.

"Well, I'll be paying our king a visit. I am eager to begin praying for their protection. We do not know what awaits him in the desert. We must be diligent and trust that, whatever the outcome tonight, that it is the gods' will. We must accept that..." Kha'y proclaimed.

Looking down at Aoh, he released a soft gasp of awe, moving his hand near her braided hair, trailing his fingers through the loose hairs towards her cheek.

"Such a loyal servant, unlike the rest. So obedient. Do you mind if I take Aoh with me? I could use her help in preparing the gifts," Kha'y asked.

"Aoh is not my servant but Daimina's. You will need to ask her for permission," Laggus replied.

"Oh, I'm sorry, how foolish of me to have mistaken her for someone else's servant. After all, this is your sandal she will fix, isn't it? Not Daimina's? How foolish of me."

Kha'y's horrid smile, between two wrinkled lips, remained plastered as he turned to leave, but not before grazing Aoh again with his silk robes. His lowered hand brushed Aoh's cheek. She turned her head, rejecting his touch, trying not to reveal her disgust no matter how sick she was becoming.

His touch was like poison against my skin.

"Coming, Aoh?" he asked, noticing she remained still.

Clearing her throat, Aoh replied, "I shall return on my own momentarily, high priest Kha'y."

Kha'y grinned, enthralled by the sound of her voice. "Then, I shall let her know you are on your way. May the gods bless you with your safe return, Laggus."

The palace in Egypt was not like Queen Huriye's in Babylon. I was never this well-read before. And no matter how hard I tried to be brave, Kha'y's presence terrified me to no end. He sent me into a world of terror that I would never wish upon the cruelest of enemies.

Aoh and Laggus remained still, listening intently to Kha'y's steps fading away, reverberating off the narrow hallway. Upon the second silence overcame them, Laggus swiped his hand across the table with an intense grunt, knocking over tools and weapons. Aoh flinched at the loud sounds of the weapons banging into each other onto the floor. Breathing heavily, Laggus caught the table, firmly clasping both of his scrapped and battered hands against the snapping wood.

The sandal lie wasn't enough to fool a high priest who, for reasons I didn't understand, craved me like a sweet wine. He wanted to pour me from a golden spout onto himself underneath peacock feathers and white silk curtains, surrounded by foreign delicacies and wild scents. Uncaring who watched…ravaging me like an immortal city from a dream, far, far away.

I expected Laggus to say something to my defense, but he remained silent. He didn't move, clenching his hands around the table so tightly I could see traces of his veins in his arms. I felt embarrassed at myself… embarrassed once again for believing Laggus could have seen something more in me than just this servant… I was bitter…

"Don't get yourself killed. Come back alive, or don't come back at all," Aoh snapped firmly, tossing the sandal onto the floor, leaving.

I watched as Kha'y, and the other lesser priests whom blindly followed him, blessed the pharaoh and his soldiers with scents and exotic leaves from the balcony. He prayed aloud, waving thin smoke about them as the guards, servants, scribes, Senmet, and the queen looked on behind him, watching silently.

The queen's eyes were clear of any tears or rage. Her countenance exuded strength and passion, looking onto her husband with love and bravery.

The wind blew softly, waving the hairs in her beautiful wig, pulling at the bottom of her linen dress, catching the casted flower petals from the floor. She listened to the prayers, slowly moving her hands over her stomach.

Senmet hardly blinked, keeping his arms tucked behind his back. He glanced to Sefkh on the other side of the pharaoh, watching in silence and standing among the two generals. Daimina remained behind me, trembling as she looked over the vast height to see the man she loved more than anything in the world about to leave for, what could become, weeks before returning.

Her lips quivered as her rounded eyes swelled. She didn't cry, but the look of worry was painted across her face in thick strokes. Her heavy breathing presented itself, tugging at her chest, rising and falling deeply. I've seen her look like this before. She wouldn't speak to me about it. She wouldn't speak at all, in fact, that entire day. She was as silent as a secret she didn't want the gods to hear. It was as though she lost her voice entirely. She barely ate. When she slept, I noticed her holding a pillow close to her chest, wrapping it tenderly as though wishing she were holding another person.

One by one, the priests blessed the horses and chariots, feeding the powerful animals with hay and fruits. Each soldier dressed in new armor, strapped and belted across their chests, arms, and legs, mentally preparing themselves for the worst. They winced briefly as the hot sun burned over them. I could hear every word Kha'y said, pronouncing every syllable with flavor, covering every spell fluidly. Once he finished blessing them, the small palace audience repeated the pharaoh's name in a rhythmic, powerful chant.

There wasn't a hint of fear in the pharaoh's young eyes. He was determined and strong. Brave. Dressed in full armor, standing in his chariot proudly…Nephthys wings draped over his chest, snuggly. Each feather defined in metal armor, pieces sewn onto the leather. His crown, towering over his head, emphasizing his power.

He could have easily been riding to a trap, ending his life all too soon, and yet he wasn't going to turn back. He was willing to risk his life for his kingdom. When the pharaoh looked upward at us, I heard Daimina's voice let out a breath. It sounded like she was about to say his name but stopped herself. Not because the queen noticed him looking at the palace… No. It was because Daimina knew he had to go. He had to go.

I watched Daimina and caught sight of a single tear leaving her right eye, rolling over her lower eyelid, and down her cheek. His eyes remained on her, concentrating all of his love for her through them, nearly stopping time.

I do not recall how long they stared at each other before he broke contact, but it occurred to me then that what she was feeling had overcome myself the moment Laggus looked up at me: standing next to the pharaoh's chariot, donned in full armor, prepared to lead his king. He winced, turning boldly to look up at me. He didn't blink, nor falter as light bangs brandished his forehead. He just…looked at me the same way he did after he and the Egyptian soldiers escaped that night in Babylon…

I couldn't explain what it was that I saw in his eyes… All I knew was, at that very moment, I felt terrified. Not the terror Kha'y casted upon me with his existence. A fear similar to what I felt when I questioned my family's survival. I felt it crawl over my body, choking me, rubbing my eyes, and pulling at the roots of my hair. Pulling on my heart, grasping me tightly…his eyes… I feared I'd never see him again.

The pharaoh's voice boomed loudly, raising his sickle sword into the air proudly, distracting Laggus from my gaze. The roar of the soldiers followed, as they raised their spears and swords from on top of their horses. Taking a step back, Laggus climbed into the chariot, taking the reins into his hands, swathing them twice. He shouted loudly as the horses took charge, pounding the ground. Pointing his sickle sword forward, the pharaoh roared once more as one by one the chariots rushed into the light, onto the path, heading towards the desert, like a raging sea of wind and sand.

I watched them go, not once taking my eyes off Laggus, as I slowly moved towards Daimina. Her lips continued to tremble, unwilling to go inside no matter how many times I told her to. She wanted to stay. To watch him until he became a speck in the sunlight. She loved the pharaoh. She was in love.

I thought of Laggus, remembering Tyrgnn's words. I didn't want to believe him, but now…I couldn't let myself think of such things. Not when I had Daimina to protect. With the pharaoh gone, Laggus gone…I was alone in a realm, with many enthusiastically awaiting Daimina's sudden demise.

As the remaining hours of daylight faded behind the pyramids and statues across the kingdom, the quieting sounds of the palace followed. Aoh gently brushed Daimina's hair in light strokes as the delicate scent of lavender filled the room, smoking over a small glass vase near an open window. Daimina stared at her reflection in the mirror, muting the light chirping of insects and barking of jackals in the desert. The night had come. It was colder than any night before.

Running her fingers between the knots, gently tugging them, Aoh's fear of Laggus turned to determination. Mentally recounting the knife and her bow and arrows in her chambers under her bed… Feeling the knot tug free, she ran the hairbrush through it like a boat through water.

"I think it's best you do not wander about the palace until the pharaoh returns," Aoh suggested lowly.

Daimina nodded.

"I will go and bring anything you need, whenever you request it. But you…should remain here."

Daimina dropped her gaze to her stomach, beginning to show from the linen dress like a sunrise on a desert horizon.

"Aoh…"

Senmet closed the door behind him as the Egyptian guards remained standing silently at attention facing General Sefkh. Cuffing his hands behind his back, Senmet stepped before them, looking at each of them.

"Noble guards of the palace, I ask you to speak the truth. Not what you may think I want to hear," Senmet spoke as General Sefkh's eyes followed his movements.

"How did you escape the Babylonian compound?"

The guards glanced at each other slightly, quickly shifting their eyes, remaining still.

"Laggus found a way to break open the gate. We managed to avoid the guards and fled in the early hours of the morning," one of the guards explained firmly.

Senmet looked at each of them patiently in response, trying to read their silent expressions. The longer Senmet spent looking at the them, the more intense he became.

"Laggus was the mind behind your escape?" Senmet finally asked.

"Yes," the guard replied.

Sefkh let out a grunt in disbelief, keeping his arms crossed at his chest.

"I must agree with General Sefkh. That is simply not true, is it? No, you had help, didn't you?"

The guards glanced at each other again. Many looked to the guard who spoke up, expecting him to speak again.

"I want the truth," the vizier demanded.

“That is the truth,” the guard responded with a hint of anger.

Senmet took several steps towards him, raising his head to look at him. His lips formed a small smile.

“No, it isn’t. And if you do not tell me the truth, it will be seen as treason towards the pharaoh. You all know what happens to traitors.”

“She helped us,” a guard at the other end of the line sputtered.

The first guard who spoke closed his eyes tightly as Senmet walked past the guards to the one at the far end. The second guard twitched nervously, trying to remained calm under the pressure of Senmet’s presence.

“Who?” he demanded, a devilish smile never fading from his greasy lips.

“Daimina’s servant.”

Senmet’s smile widened as his suspicions were validated.

“There, was that so difficult, gentlemen?” he asked, opening his arms. “So, she’s not Egyptian but a Babylonian.”

“She told us she was an Egyptian peasant,” the guard added, looking at the floor.

Sefkh frowned and asked in response, “Why was she in Bablylon?”

“We do not know.”

Sefkh turned to Senmet, who nodded. Rubbing his mouth and chin, Senmet paced but once in front of them before stopping.

“The pharaoh owes you a great deal of gratitude. He will remember you for your service to this kingdom.”

With one swoop, Sefkh removed his sword from his belt and slashed the throat of the guard. Before the others could react, he killed them one by one, striking the last as he attempted to flee, only to find the doors were locked. Their bloodied bodies covered the length of the long carpet, drowning the dark blue color with red.

“I knew it,” Senmet whispered, rubbing his chin.

“Knew what?” Sefkh asked, flicking his sword to swipe the blood off.

“That she wasn’t who she was pretending to be…”

Senmet's feet slipped across the floor as the blood stopped flowing.... He listened to the sounds of soldiers gathering outside and the nighttime squawks of the peacocks.

"Get rid of their bodies, wrap them in the carpet," the vizier ordered. "Lock the queen and Aneski into their chambers. Send word to your men, Daimina and her servant will be killed."

Aoh stopped brushing Daimina's hair, momentarily alarmed by her low tone.

"I never did ask you, where are you from?"

"I am from Egypt," Aoh replied proudly, with a small smile.

"Where is your family? Surely, they must miss you."

"Not sure. I don't know if they're alive or dead."

"How awful..." Daimina whispered.

"The last time I saw them I was ten years old," Aoh replied, looking at her reflection in the mirror next to Daimina.

"What happened?"

"We were attacked. My brother told me to run, so I did. It happened so fast that when I stopped running, I realized I had crossed the Nile and made my way into the desert. I was alone, and saw nothing but smoke and flames rising from the homes."

"That's horrible. Who attacked?" Daimina asked, turning around with softened eyes.

"I've heard rumors as to whom was responsible, but..."

Aoh's voice trailed off as Tyrgnn's face haunted her mind. She visualized him upon his horse the last time she saw him: riding into the desert in the night, carrying the belongings of the dead thieves, back towards his homeland.

"All I know is that the gods must have had a plan for me to have escaped and lived on after their deaths..." she finished.

"I'm sorry..." Daimina whispered nearly crying, turning back around and, dipping her head.

"I am not angry that you asked of them," Aoh comforted. "The truth is…my life would have been very different if the town was not attacked… I would not be here, in the pharaoh's palace, where so many kings had lived."

Daimina listened. Her soft eyes were unable to pry away from the deep sadness building from her heart. She closed her eyes, pleased with the touch of the brush through her hair. Upon the last stroke, Aoh ran her hand over Daimina's hair, believing it to be as smooth as possible. Taking several strands of hair on both sides of Daimina's head, Aoh carefully began to twist and twirl them, one at a time, between her fingers.

"Does your family know you're here?" Aoh asked, focused on braiding Daimina's hair.

"They do," Daimina replied, surprising Aoh.

"And?"

"And what?"

"Are they…happy for you?"

"I'm not sure anymore. I haven't spoken to them since I arrived," Daimina answered, sighing heavily.

"Have you thought about seeing them?"

"Somewhat. But my place is here. With him…" Daimina added as she felt the clasp of her hair against the back of her head.

The beaded clip sparkled like stars, shinning in the flames. Aoh looked at her reflection in the clip, unable to recognize herself again. The makeup hid her face. The linen gown hid her body.

If the town was never attacked, I would not be in the palace because I would have never been found by Queen Huriye… I would have never met her. Never learned how to use a bow and arrow. I would have never saved the Egyptians and met-

"The pharaoh had sent a letter to my family informing them of my new residence in his palace. He gave them gifts and expressed how much he loved me," Daimina explained, as Aoh chose a necklace for her to wear the next day from the array of choices.

"He understood that, as much as they loved him, they loved me more. They…wanted me to be married with children of my own…

not as a pharaoh's mistress. I do hope they will meet my child when he is born."

"How do you know it is a boy?" Aoh asked, gently placing the necklace around Daimina's neck, making sure it would not choke her, tugging the long golden chain in the back.

Daimina rubbed her stomach and answered with a confident smile, "I just do."

Hearing the solid clasp of the chain, Aoh released the necklace, letting it rest against Daimina's collarbone.

"Wow…" Aoh gasped aloud.

I would have had the same reaction if my mind wasn't preoccupied. However, seeing the golden platted necklace encrusted with several stones and beads upon Daimina immediately made me mistake her for the very Queen of Egypt. When all was placed upon her, she looked like a queen. No doubt she'd be dressed similarly if she were crowned. I had learned much since my first day in the palace. It seemed even queens were replaceable in Egypt…not just soldiers, guards, servants…

"When the pharaoh returns, I want him to see me as I am, not as they want me to be," Daimina declared, moving her hands behind her neck to unclasp the necklace.

Removing it, she put it down on the dresser and ran her hands under her hair.

"I want him, not the crown."

"What do you think you will name your son?" Aoh asked, trying to distract her.

"He will have a grand name that will be remembered for thousands of years to come. The people will call his name in joy. It will be written on every monument and column. He will be a warrior. A deliverer of promise," Daimina explained with a smile.

Aoh couldn't resist a smile in response, walking to Daimina's bed and pulling back the sheets slowly, fixing the pillows and closing the windows on both sides. Daimina rose from her chair but stumbled back, feeling suddenly lightheaded.

"Daimina?" Aoh asked, rushing to her side.

"Oh…just the baby, I'm sure. He's growing strongly," Daimina replied, with a nod.

Aoh helped Daimina into her bed, tucking her in carefully, keeping water close to the bedside. Tugging at the sheets, Aoh's hands slipped in between the smoothness, unable to avoid finding the textures relaxing and pleasurable to touch.

"If you knew your family was still alive, would you leave the palace and go to them?" Daimina whispered, closing her eyes.

Aoh smiled in response, pulling the sheets over Daimina, gently moving her hair to the left side of her face. Placing her hand to Daimina's head, she waited, feeling no warmth. As she moved the sandals away from the side of the bed, Aoh paused, realizing she had not pondered if her family had survived. She came to assume they were long gone… She suddenly wondered if they were thinking of her…

And then…I thought to myself, would I leave the palace for my family?

The shadow crawled up the closed doors slowly, increasing in size and height. Stopping, the shadow laid over the painted hieroglyphics and images. The shadow reached as two thick, muscular hands pushed both doors to ensure a solid close. Moving to the right, a thick handle was pulled downward from the center of the door. A thick, deep thud sound locked both doors. Reaching for another handle, turning in the opposite direction, it was placed horizontally across both doors. The process was repeated once more, moving swiftly and silently…

45

The sounds of the silent palace were disturbed when a pair of doors were opened with a concrete shove. Aoh's head tilted from the side of the couch at the end of Daimina's bed, opening her eyes slowly, seeing nothing but the shadows from the light of fire pits against the wall. Dragging the light sheet over her, she looked out the bedroom doorway and into the darkness, hearing the sounds of doors opening and closing.

Leaning forward, Aoh focused on the darkness, listening for another sound but heard nothing. Glancing behind her, Daimina remained fast asleep, curling a pillow in between her arms and legs, breathing heavily between light groans. The dim light down distant hallways provided a faint glow, attracting Aoh's attention as she watched for shadows.

Slowly getting up, she glanced at Daimina once more before leaving the room. Entering the dark hallway, she followed the faint light, able to see that nearly every object and wall were cast in darker shadows as the sounds creak and thud of doors opening and closing followed, startling her.

I was tense and alarmed at sounds I had heard a multitude of times before. But with the pharaoh and Laggus gone...I became fearful and worried something was coming that I could not see.

Continuing down the hallway, Aoh listened and watched, expecting to see the cause of the sounds. Guards were known to pace down the halls, ensuring the safety of those who slept. However, they never seemed to come as far as Daimina's chambers.

Turning down a hallway, Aoh saw rows of fire pits aglow, burning fiercely, when the sounds of the fires suddenly extinguished behind her, sending chills down her back, striking the tips of her fingers and toes.

I listened, quieting my breath, hearing nothing but eerie silence unlike any I had ever heard before. I took one step forward and heard the grinding sound of something bronze against stone. I peered over my shoulder, terrified to see someone standing behind me. However, nothing revealed itself. Facing forward, the grinding sound repeated…

From down the hall, two guards made their approach calmly, marching towards her. Aoh turned around and immediately drew her dagger from under her sash as light panic began.

Withdrawing the dagger, she walked firmly towards them, hearing their firm steps. In an instant, a guard rushed from the right side from behind a column, startling her. Aoh swung her arm, slashing the guard in the face and then stabbing him in the neck just above his armor, splattering his blood onto her face and arms. Removing the blade, blood spewed onto the walls.

The two guards threw their spears simultaneously, as she ducked them without having time to think. Holding the blade, she killed them both with such ferocity that their blood spilled across the floor and onto the statues in waves, striking the painted depictions of the pharaoh conquering his enemies with his chariots.

My chest rose and fell heavily as drops of their blood, fell from the tip of my nose and ends of my hair as I looked down at the dead guards. I swiped them of their weapons, and ran for Daimina's chambers as fast as I could, terrified I would find her massacred beyond recognition. A light red trail followed me, falling from my body like raindrops. Reaching her room, I found that she was sitting on her bed. She looked pale, holding her stomach, and was hunched over the side about to vomit.

Daimina rose upward, trying to get out of the bed, discovering Aoh covered in blood.

"What happened?" she asked, terrified.

"The guards are going to kill you, they are going to kill me, and won't stop until they do. I need to send a signal to the pharaoh, and you need to survive until he arrives."

Daimina nodded, trembling wildly. She cringed at the clash of the weapons thrown to the floor, quivering at the sensation of foreign blood on her skin.

Aoh quickly splashed water across her face, trying to wash away the red color, now tainting the clear water in the basin. Rushing to her small room, she grabbed her bow and quiver full of arrows, tugging them over her shoulder. Daimina's pale complexion glistened in sweat as she watched Aoh, trying to keep her balance, wrapping her arms around the nearest chair.

Removing the blade from under her sash, Aoh handed it to Daimina who stared at it as though she had never seen a weapon before. Blowing out the fires, Aoh grabbed a full vessel of cool water. She lead Daimina down the hallway, hearing nothing but eerie silence again, knowing that at any moment the guards would be rushing to kill them like wild animals.

Daimina could barely walk, let alone run, still feeling sick, looking as though at any moment she would faint. I had to keep her in my sight as well as the darkness of the palace that seemed to grow thicker the deeper we moved into the long hallways. Wandering for, what felt like an eternity, watching every corner, every wall, I found the statue.

Daimina slouched over, watching me shove the statue, struggling to move it without making a sound. I grunted, feeling sweat slide down the sides of my face as the statue slid slowly, dragging across the smooth floor and revealing the small outline in the wall. Running my sweated hands over the rough texture, I pushed slightly, crawling my fingers around the thin sides and removed the thick piece of stone. Daimina nearly collapsed onto her knees, fitting into the small space in the wall. I helped tuck her head and arms inside as she blinked heavily, dread and fear covering her rounded face as she looked at me weakly.

I'd be lying if I said I wasn't afraid...

Handing Daimina the vessel of water, Aoh instructed her, "Do not leave, no matter what you hear. You must stay hidden. They cannot find you. Do you understand me?"

Daimina nodded slowly, drinking the water, barely able to wrap her shaking hands around the curved handle. Swallowing slowly, she groaned, resting her head against the rough wall.

"If any guard finds you, kill them. You cannot trust anyone... Do you understand?"

Daimina nodded again, feeling slightly dizzy, constantly opening and closing her tired eyes.

Moving her bow across her back, Aoh forced herself into the statue, struggling to shove it back in place. She grunted loudly, growing aggravated, feeling the bottom slide slowly, creating a loud echo of unsettling noise.

Now that Daimina was concealed, my adrenaline was rushing through my veins like a running horse. I couldn't protect Daimina alone. I knew of only one place to go, to send a signal to the pharaoh and Laggus.

Remaining tight to the shadows, Aoh tip-toed down the hallway, listening to every sound rustle before turning any corners. Taking a semi step at the corner, the strike of a blade swooped to the right, alarming Aoh to move back. She removed the bow from over her head and wrapped it over his. The guard swung his arms, trying to grab her, choking violently. Running backwards, he slammed her against the wall. Falling, Aoh grabbed one of several arrows that fell from her quiver, shoving it into the guard's foot and then into his throat.

Grabbing her bow and the fallen arrows, Aoh panted heavily, progressing down the hallway and, following the path that led to the open space near one of several guards. Aoh's heart pounded in her chest in fear, quickly running back to hide at the corner behind a column, trying to catch her breath. Swallowing hard, Aoh breathed in and out as slow and deeply as she could, unable to stop the fear from crawling around her arms and legs.

From her left, she heard the loud sounds of armor. At least a dozen soldiers rushed towards her from across the way.

Moving to the other side of the column, she heard one of them shout, "You are ordered to reveal yourself, betrayer of Egypt."

Removing her bow and preparing the arrows, she calmly took a heavy breath. She paused, following the clinking of their movement and shadows on the wall before her. She watched them run, revealing their swords, passing between columns and large leafy plants. Feeling the fear slowly fading from her, she released several arrows, killing them as they turned the corner, charging at her like horses. She aimed between their armor, striking their necks and heads.

Running out of room, Aoh backed up two steps, killing at least five of them. Bringing the bow over her shoulder, she ran past the guards down the hallway to the nearest set of steps. Feeling a hand pulling her quiver and the other just barely grasping her hair, Aoh let out a painful scream.

Turning, she swiped him in the throat with the arrow clutched in her hand and kicked him into the first of many rushing after her. Running up the stairs, she removed her bow, preparing three arrows, containing her heavy breaths. The moment a guard or soldier emerged from the stairs she followed them, looking down the line of arrows and fired.

She ducked when arrows were fired in her direction. The narrow stairs contained the whistle of the arrows, soaring quickly upon released. Preparing three more, she fired again, killing three more as they collapsed onto the stairs, colliding into each other.

The horses screeched, coming to an abrupt halt as the chariots covered in sand and dust roared one last time. Stepping out of the chariot, the pharaoh looked in the distance, seeing the small glow of flames and dark figures sitting and standing scattered among their horses. The pharaoh wrapped his robe tightly over his body, quickly looking to the sky, unable to see the moon hidden behind layers of clouds. He rolled his lips, keeping a hand at his waist, as the rest of the chariots slowed to a solid stop, forming at least three straight lines.

Laggus walked to his side, staring ahead at the dark shadows and slow movement in the distance. He panted, turning around to watch the soldiers beginning to remove furniture from the chariots, gathering their weapons and supplies, feeding the horses and checking the chariot wheels. They wrapped dark sashes over their mouths, keeping lit torches to a small kindle, ensuring they stayed low to the ground.

"Is this where you saw them?" the pharaoh asked.

"Yes," Laggus replied, wiping a hand over his scruffy mouth.

Hearing the sounds of the men setting up a small camp, the pharaoh watched them.

"I want them to remain back. We'll wait here, observe and see what happens, but by no means are we to engage first."

"Yes, my king," Laggus replied.

"If anything should happen to me, Laggus, for Egypt and for my family, do not let them take my body. Carry me back."

The bottom of his long cape dragged across the floor as he stormed towards two closed doors – as the constant sounds clashing of the struggle echoed off the walls. Sefkh rushed into the room, nearly bursting the door open. He saw Senmet standing out on the balcony overlooking the kingdom, gazing in the direction the pharaoh traveled in silence.

Senmet looked to the sky, waiting for the moon to reveal itself, listening to distant sounds of jackals barking and fighting. He heard Sefkh's armor and cape brush against the large doorframe, sweeping across the floor, and turned around. Sefkh rested his right hand over his sword handle, lowering his gaze for a moment before speaking.

"Daimina and her servant were not in her chambers," he stated roughly, pushing the left side of his cape off of his shoulder behind him.

"Which means they are hiding somewhere in the palace," Senmet replied calmly.

Sefkh's gaze lowered again before adding, "One of them has been leaving dead guards and soldiers in their wake. We've found several killed with arrows."

Senmet's relaxed demeanor turned from mild surprise to beastly anger.

"There was a trail of blood," the general informed the vizier. "We followed it back to Daimina's chambers."

The wrinkles upon Senmet's face tightened, and a sense of deep heaviness suddenly fell upon the room. His slow steps slapped across the floor, violently releasing an aurora of intensity. He stopped inches from Sefkh's face, staring at him with growing anger and deep dissatisfaction.

"You call yourself a general. You…call yourself a general," Senmet spat. His teeth ground against each other, like nails dragged across the floor. He shook his head. "You are a strategist, a warrior, a killer. I do not care how you do it, but find them …AND KILL THEM!"

Sefkh's eyes clasped shut, his ears ringing.

Senmet gripped Sefkh's face between his hands, staring into the general with wide eyes of insanity, "KILL THEM BOTH! Neither Daimina nor Aoh lives!"

Senmet's outburst startled Sefkh, biting into his lips, struggling to refrain himself from responding.

Running to the top of the stairs, Aoh ducked at the sight of a guard's blade near her face, hiding behind a potted tree. She knocked him down with a swing of her bow and quickly drew another arrow, killing him. Straining her arms, she shoved his body down the stairs, colliding into oncoming soldiers.

Taking one of the torches from the dead guards on the floor, Aoh ran down the hallway to dip it into the nearest fire pit, seeing more guards rushing towards her like a wave of death. Lighting the torch, she knocked the fire pit down, casting a wave of flames and ashes forward across the floor. Her shadow raced across the walls, rushing up the nearest stairs and ducking below a guard swinging forward.

Kicking him down the stairs, Aoh fled upward, feeling another soldier grab the back of her leg, tearing the bottom of her dress, and pulling her down. Aoh's body jolted against the stone steps, feeling her breath nearly knocked out of her chest. The torch flung from her grip, laying too far out of reach. She watched the vibrant flames eat away at the wood, slowly decreasing in strength.

Taking an arrow from her quiver, she slashed at the guard's hands, kicking and struggling to escape. Shoving her other foot against his neck, she leaned forward and then back, stretching her arm, and slashed him in the face. Aoh listened to him scream with each roll of his armor against the stone until he slammed into the wall at the bottom of the stairs, crushing his skull.

Coughing profusely, she spat trails of blood onto the stone, dragging herself up, trying to get onto her feet. Forcing herself back up the steps, she felt a rush of cold air from the open door. Grabbing the torch, she smiled with relief, wrapping her arm around the bottom of the column at the top of the stairs and stumbling forward.

Keeping her firm grip on the four arrows in her hand, now painted with light drops of blood, she sprinted into the night. The cold air struck her body, nearly extinguishing her inner flames of pain and adrenaline. She barely took a moment to breathe, rushing to the side, looking down at the beautiful garden of tall palm trees.

Dropping the bow and arrows, Aoh pulled her arm back and threw the torch at the nearest trees below her with a loud grunt. The leaves caught fire within seconds as a giant rush of smoke rose to the sky. The heat from the flames surrounded the gardens, burning every leaf, branch, and flower petal. The glow of the red and yellow flames rose with thick, black smoke above the palace.

The loud outburst of screaming alarmed Sefkh and Senmet. They followed the tumult to the hallway, finding all of the greenery swallowed whole by malicious flames. The intense heat spread across the hallway, creating a blinding light. Soldiers and guards screamed, covering their heads and faces from the falling burning branches and trees. Pieces of the trees snapped and spewed onto the palace floor, spreading the fire across carpets and curtains.

Senmet raised his wrinkled eyes upward to the tops of the trees, spotting Aoh on a balcony, preparing her bow. A solid moment of silence filled him as every memory he had of her flashed before his eyes like lightning strikes. His suppressed rage bottled to the top and exploded.

"KILL HER! Kill her now!" he screamed, pointing at Aoh.

Sefkh nodded, and turned to the two soldiers next to him.

"Kill her," he ordered.

The soldiers hesitated, looking to each other, confused by his drastic order.

"I ordered you to kill her. Do it, now!" Sefkh screamed.

"General Sefkh, we-"

The blade slashed both throats, with one strike, spewing blood down their bodies like poured a rich wine. They gurgled and sputtered, falling to their knees, trying to breathe before collapsing dead onto the floor. Sefkh's eyes widened in horror, looking at Senmet, whom carefully whipped the fresh blood from the blade with the inside of his linen robe, undisturbed by his actions.

Senmet panted, staring at the blood spewed across the reflective surface of the blade. He stared at his reflection in the blade, imagining himself younger, full of life. See the smooth skin that once attracted women.

His eyes, once so pure, could trick any that dared question him.

Turning to face Sefkh, he curved the blade. Sefkh, unable to speak, stared at the dead bodies of two men he trained. He knew the moment they arrived that they had to become soldiers to provide better lives for themselves and their families. They looked to him, they trusted him. A rush of despair flooded through him, leaking from his eyes.

"Any soldier or guard who hesitates upon an order cannot be trusted, Sefkh," Senmet justified, calmly clenching his teeth together. "If they will not do as they are told, they are traitors to us."

Sefkh's eyes lowered to the dead soldiers at his feet, carefully taking several steps away from the flow of blood that spread across both bodies, slipping into the small cuts grooves of the floor.

"Keep the queen and the pharaoh's mother locked until this task is complete," the vizier demanded. "I do not need unnecessary palace cats to interfere tonight."

Sefkh sniffled, continually clearing his throat.

Tucking the blade back on to the inside of his open sleeve, Senmet ordered, "Find a way to put out that fire, and wait at the palace entrance."

"Wait for what?" Sefkh asked, rubbing his nose and mouth, his eyes glossy wet.

"That fire can now be seen for miles. The pharaoh will send Laggus ahead of him, so he will arrive first. Didn't I promise you could kill him?"

Sefkh's glossy eyes ran dry. The deep sorrow for the dead soldiers disappeared. Dropping his hand from his face to rest upon his sword, he nodded as a small, disturbing smirk formed from the left corner of his mouth.

46

"I don't understand it. They can see us, clear as day, and yet they do nothing," Laggus stated, looking ahead of him with the pharaoh by his side amongst the small group of soldiers.

"So it seems," the pharaoh commented. Boldly, he asked the questions no one else could utter. "You think it's a distraction to keep us focused here and not somewhere else?"

"Unlikely. They seem to just…" Laggus paused, lowering his head, understanding the pharaoh's point.

"Send a small group of scouts west of here, just to make sure they aren't sending men into our borders."

"Yes, sir." Laggus walked back into the tent where several soldiers argued over their position on the map, which was visible in the firelight. Their tall shadows casted against the inner walls of the tent, dancing from the flames. Entering the tent, he watched them bicker like animals sharing a meal.

"The pharaoh has ordered that several are to head west," Laggus ordered. "Make sure none of the Hyksos get by our eyes. This could be a distraction. Do not engage."

Two of the soldiers folded their mighty arms across their chest in response, unmoved by the order. Laggus stood his ground, staring at them silently. The last of several soldiers leaving single file out of the tent nudged the tallest of the two, shifting his eyes side to side. Glaring at Laggus, the remaining soldiers left the tent as one entered.

"Laggus," the newly-arrived soldier called, walking towards him.

Laggus glanced at the soldier whom he had been training with, and then returned his attention to the map on the table. Using figurines to represent the Hyksos, Laggus observed their placement.

"Perhaps, we should speak to them ourselves? It's obvious they know what we are doing."

"We can't risk putting the pharaoh in danger," Laggus argued.

"Come now, Laggus, even you know he's not in any danger. You were unsure about this from the beginning. They don't hesitate."

"No, I was not unsure. We cannot take chances," Laggus repeated.

The soldier titled his head, unconvinced.

"Before someone makes a mistake, we should at least be the ones to come to them peacefully. Explain ourselves truthfully. They did not leave with spite in their hearts. They agreed to the alliance," the soldier explained firmly. "The way they are grouped…they are just families, traders." Taking a step closer to Laggus, he continued, "These men are antsy. They are not used to sitting around and waiting."

Laggus silently walked around to the other side of the table, to view the map from a different angle.

"What troubles your mind?"

"It is not the Hyksos that troubles me, but a greater threat that I fear is drawing near to Egypt once again," Laggus answered, looking closer at the drawn desert on the map. He couldn't ignore the graffiti he saw on several walls. Those three words did anything but settle his worried mind. Taking a deep breath, he continued, "I concur with your statement. We should…"

Laggus' voice trailed off when he noticed a brightened color in between the small gap of the back of the tent. Pulling the drape back, the red, yellow, and orange color burned rose, sending with it clouds of grey and black smoke into the night sky.

"My king! My king!" Laggus called in a panic, running out of the tent. "Look! There!"

The pharaoh turned around and saw the flames, loud and wild, burning in the distance.

"It's coming from the palace. I must go!" he screamed.

"No, pharaoh. I will go. It could be a trap," Laggus insisted.

"I cannot risk your life, Laggus, you are not like the other men who serve me. You're the only one I trust!"

"Then let me serve you, my king. Let me go and protect your queen, Daimina, and your people."

Biting his lips together, frowning deeply, the pharaoh bellowed in the darkness.

"Go!" he yelled, pointing in the direction of the palace. The pharaoh turned his attention to the soldiers nearest him, and shouted, "All of you, follow him! Go, now!"

Taking to his horse, Laggus rode out into the desert with fifteen men following behind him.

Aoh's eyes followed two guards as they ran up another set of stairs from the tip of her aligned arrow. Her arm was drawn back as her fingers curled tightly around the taut string. She waited patiently, following their movements, ignoring her surroundings.

"We are given very few things to control. This is one of them. This arrow…is controlled by you."

With one release, the arrow flew from the bow, striking the second guard in the forehead. Drawing quickly, Aoh followed the first guard and struck him down without hesitation. After watching him fall dead, she exhaled, grabbing another arrow and preparing to fire, anticipating another guard. Instead, she heard them calling out from the right side.

Turning, she released the arrow, striking the next guard running as he ran in between columns. Backing up quickly, she drew another, then another, and another, killing three more; like the rhythm of plucked harp strings rushing from the doorway.

"It is with discipline and concentration that decides whether the arrow kills or spares. Do you understand me?"

She could feel the weight of the quiver on her back becoming lighter each time she drew arrows. She heard yelling below her and ducked as several arrows flew by her, narrowly missing her face.

Aoh panted heavily, feeling her heart racing in her chest, struck with a moment of pure terror knowing she just missed death. She waited, listening as another round of arrows were fired, whistling into the air above her before disappearing into the sky.

As terrified as she was, the moment the sound of the bow releasing the arrows disappeared, she rose to her knees and fired back. The arrows killed the first two archers on the ground as the others immediately hid behind columns, preparing their bows.

With one side turn, they fired as Aoh dodged them, quickly moving to the offensive, firing arrows, and killing them one by one just as guards rushed the stairs again. Turning around, she fired her arrows, striking them down, noticing the pile of bodies beginning to build.

Taking a deep breath, she pulled another arrow from the quiver, feeling it becoming lighter than before. She waited on her knee, her eyes focused on the arrow and what laid before it. Seconds later, she released upon seeing the face of another guard.

I knew that, at any moment, I was going to have to pick up a sword and physically fight them. Knowing I had no choice terrified me. Was this my destiny? To be a killer of men like the soldiers? Like Laggus?

Watching from the balcony, growing intensely angrier by the sight of Aoh stopping every guard and soldier that rushed her, Senmet turned and faced another general and several men behind him.

"Send as many soldiers as you can at once, up every stairway. She will not be able to kill them all. Not with the amount of arrows she has left."

"Yes, sir," the general replied.

"Do not take her alive. Make sure she is dead and bring her body to me. I want to see it for myself, understood?" he growled.

"Yes, sir," he replied firmly with a loud cry in his voice.

Impressed by the triumphant roar, Senmet spoke again, "You sound quite eager to kill her."

"She was pretending to be the mistress' servant. She won't be missed," the soldier validated with a firm tone.

"Well, if that be the case, if you find Daimina, bring me her dead body as well," the vizier ordered.

The soldier glanced at Senmet with a hint of hesitation in his eyes.

"You heard me. She must be killed before she ruins Egypt to the point of no return."

"As you command," the soldier answered.

Swiftly tossing his cape over his shoulders, he left, slamming the doors closed behind him. Alone, Senmet listened to the struggle of the palace under siege from within. Every time he heard the dying voice of a failing soldier or guard, his eyes heavily closed. His impatience was building…

Walking over to his chair positioned across from where the pharaoh would sit when playing games, he exhaled heavily. His wrinkled left hand squeezed the animal skin draped over the chair tightly, turning his knuckles white.

He imagined the pharaoh's bright smile as each move they made across the board brought him excitement and thrill. The chase of one trying to capture the other in a game of chance and fate would carry on for hours until a winner emerged.

Drowning out his surroundings, Senmet smiled faintly, remembering the first time he held the pharaoh in his arms. What a small child he was. So tender and sweet, not yet aware of the world he was born into and the glories that would fall upon his lap one day. He looked like a king. The glow from his eyes proved as much.

The sounds of jackals barking in terror and fear distracted his thoughts. He rushed to the balcony, following the source of the chaos. In the faint distance, he could see fast movement. Dark shadows moved towards the palace with great speed grabbed him. The left door to the room opened gently as steps moved behind him with the sound of rubbing linen.

"Here lies the snake," Kha'y spat, draping his thin arms over his chest.

Senmet turned around and replied, "Indeed."

"You said that Aoh would be mine," he growled with a heavy frown.

"Aoh is a threat, as you can blatantly see," Senmet replied, holding out his arm to guide Kha'y towards her direction.

Kha'y turned and saw Aoh killing the guards and soldiers from the top, nearly invisible between the large flames that slowly burned, disintegrating every plant it consumed. His eyes widened in wonder, amazed by her skill as he watched speechlessly. He raised his arms, watching her kill them with such precision, and concentration, and beauty. She looked nothing like the servant he had seen in the palace.

Her hair was untamed, makeup removed, linen dress covered in blood. The intensity in her eyes burned brighter than the fires, lighting his heart as the heat burned him from within. She became a goddess in those short moments. She emanated passion. Senmet's slow steps moved towards Kha'y, keeping both of his arms behind his back.

"The gods brought her to this palace for me," he whispered. He gasped aloud, feeling his heart beginning to ache intensely. Clutching his chest, he nearly fell onto the floor. "The gods brought her here for me, Senmet. They promised her to me."

"The gods brought her here because of Daimina; because our king's heart is so big he had to love two women," Senmet bluntly stated.

"You dare disobey the gods?!" Kha'y screamed, standing up.

"No, Kha'y, I dare to disobey you."

"I warned you-"

"And now I will warn you," Senmet interrupted, taking another step forward.

"You warning me?"

"If she dies, there will be no witnesses of tonight…" the vizier explained.

Kha'y shook his head, raising his hands dramatically.

"She is not the only woman in Egypt."

"I want…no other woman of Egypt… You will pay for what you have done! You will not go quietly!"

Senmet took another step forward, unyielding to Kha'y howls.

"The gods will-" the high priest attempted to cry, interrupted again by Senmet.

"The gods can be replaced," the vizier hissed. Taking one last step forward, Senmet deepened his voice, "Everyone can be replaced, Kha'y. That is the only truth in a world of lies."

With one movement, Senmet revealed the blade he concealed, stabbing Kha'y in the chest below the golden pendant. Removing the blade, he stabbed him twice more as Kha'y collapsed onto his knees, spitting up blood. Unable to respond, he placed his hands on the floor, attempting to hold his body. His long arms shook.

Senmet watched him collapse. His eyes following the blood spreading across the floor and onto the animal skin carpet. He looked down, seeing the blood across his garb when he heard mumbling. Turning his gaze, Kha'y spat horrid curses aloud in between blood. His eyes remained wide, glaring at Senmet as he released one last heavy breath, falling limp.

Senmet raised both hands, as the long sleeves rolled down to his elbows. Waving his hands, speckled with Kha'y's blood, he spread the droplets onto the floor around the high priest's body.

Looking at him and shaking his head slightly, he noticed something residing in the left sleeve, slowly soaking in the flowing blood. Bending down, Senmet grabbed the small fragile scroll. Upon opening the scroll, he read the content quickly. Intended for the pharoah, it detailed every facet of Senmet's plot. Reading it tempted him to spit onto Kha'y's dead body. Stepping over him, slipping past the puddle of blood, he dropped the scroll into the burning fire pit, watching it burn into nothing but ashes.

"You people," he whispered, shaking his head.

47

Pulling back heavily on the reigns of his horse, Laggus stopped at the large doors to the realm of the pharaoh. His eyes lifted to the top, watching for archers as the fifteen men stopped behind him. The vicious flames hovered over the palace, creating monstrous shadows that towered over Laggus.

Citizens fled their homes quickly, fading into the darkness. Their startled screams muted the dying flames, just barely seen over the top of the palace. Getting off his horse, the fifteen men repeated the action, drawing their swords and standing behind him.

"All of you, find and protect the queen, pharaoh's mother, Daimina, and her servant," Laggus ordered, firmly. "Do not let them out of your sight. Go, from the sides of the palace. If anyone tries to stop you, kill them."

They nodded, following to the large threshold. Laggus pushed himself into the door, opening it slowly. Through the small gap, the fifteen men entered single file, splitting into two groups and keeping their eyes at a constant rotation. Rushing towards both the left and right sides of the palace, they disappeared into the darkness.

Hunched over, drawing swords and bows, they remained in the shadows. Laggus lifted his right hand over the sword handle. His eyes followed every slight sound as he walked deeper into the darkness.

Laggus remained at the bottom of the white steps, listening to every movement. Panting, he watched both stone lions before running up the stairs, noticing that the palace doors were partially opened. He paused and drew his blade, looking through the small open space. His sandals scuffed the stone as he raised his hand towards the left door. Carefully moving towards the door, he quieted his breath, reaching to touch the door with the tips of his fingers. Barely moving his head, he listened…

Without warning, he slammed himself into the door, smacking into Sefkh who was hiding behind it. Sefkh screamed, cursing repeatedly, clasping both hands over his face as Laggus ran. Growling, Sefkh threw his spear across the room, hitting the wall several inches from Laggus, stopping him. Laggus stared at the spear, slowly turning around.

Sefkh spat onto the floor, followed by wiping his mouth with the knuckle of his right hand. He grinned from the corner of his lips, breathing heavily.

"I've waited a long time to kill you," Sefkh declared, walking towards him with his sword drawn.

The general swiped his hand over the blood on his face and in his hair. He leapt at Laggus, striking outward with his sword. Swinging forward, Laggus blocked the strike with ease, moving slightly to the left.

"What makes you superior compared to men born of this land?" Sefkh howled. "What is so great about you? Everyone knows you'd be nothing if it weren't for the pharaoh."

Swinging several more times, Laggus blocked, panting heavily, drenched in his sweat.

"I have no desire to kill you, regardless of how much you want to kill me," Laggus defended as he circled behind a column.

Hearing silence, Laggus waited, keeping his sword steady.

Sefkh swung, missing Laggus and striking the column, cutting into the stone images of peasants and farmers across their necks and chests. Laggus remained still against the column, staring into the eyes of a man he had fought twice for a chance to become a soldier and lost… A respected, beloved general. His eyes were infused with a combination of hatred and joy.

Sefkh exhaled heavily, rubbing his hand over the drying blood and cleaning the skin around eyes.

Above them, they heard feminine grunting and the sounds of arrows whistling through the air. Men shouted repeatedly, as the struggle above them continued to unfold. Sefkh's grin widened, opening his mouth with an expression of ecstasy across his face.

"Sounds like someone is running out of time?" the general goaded.

Laggus didn't answer, keeping his eyes focused on Sefkh.

"This is the last time, Laggus. Run away while you still can."

"I'm not running," Laggus replied firmly.

Surprising Sefkh, Laggus moved towards him, grabbing his arm still holding the sword and throwing him onto the floor. Failing to grab Sefkh's sword stuck in the column, Laggus used his sword to block Sefkh's attacks with a short blade he drew from his belt.

Remaining on the defensive, Laggus blocked each strike. Upon every object he collided into, Sefkh's left his mark; slicing, cutting, jabbing the short blade through marble, granite, and limestone. Taking his chance, Sefkh rushed Laggus, dipping underneath him as Laggus' raised his arms and head-butted him.

Stunned, Laggus stumbled momentarily, temporarily losing sight. Wrapping his arms around Laggus' neck, Sefkh squeezed, attempting to choke him. Desperate, Laggus dropped to his knees and flipped Sefkh over him. Gasping for air, Laggus looked for his sword, finding it having slid across the floor…almost completely underneath a tall statue of Horus made of blue granite. Running for the handle, he heard something move and dropped as the short blade missed him, striking the column behind the statue.

Grabbing the sword handle, Laggus turned and threw it, striking Sefkh in the chest. Laggus watched Sefkh's disgusted face, morph from anger to severe pain to nothing… Falling over silently, Laggus released a heavy breath, coughing violently. Blinking intensely, he regained his breath, feeling a burning sensation around his neck.

Getting up, he looked at the Horus statue, panting, swiping the spit and sweat from his face. He nodded, respecting the protection. Freeing Sefkh's sword from the column, he rushed for the stairs. Looking up, he heard the sounds of guards storming up the solid steps and then the echo of Aoh screaming, striking them with arrows. He heard their final breaths, collapsing onto the floor, fiercely cursing her name.

"Aoh!" Laggus called, when suddenly a rush of metal fire struck his lower left leg.

Grinding his teeth, Laggus released a painful roar. Looking down, he saw Sefkh had plunged his sword into the back of Laggus's leg, trailing light streams of his blood across the floor.

"If I die, you will die, too," Sefkh bellowed, vomiting blood from his mouth, dripping down his neck and onto the marble floor.

Laggus raised his arm and, with one last swoop, slashed Sefkh across his neck and chest, as an excessive amount of blood spewed onto the floor and steps. Frowning deeply, feeling immobile from the pain, Laggus ripped the sword from his leg, letting out another cry of wild pain.

Taking his sword back from the fallen general, he slumped against the wall, hearing guards above him like stampeding animals. He wailed loudly, unable to move his leg an inch without wanting to collapse. He bit into the pain, dragging himself up the steps in between breaths.

From the stairs leading to the doorway, Laggus killed each guard, cutting them down without a second thought, gritting through the pain, and spraying their blood onto his face. His voice roared like a mighty lion, his strength uncanny, barely moving his wounded left leg.

Aoh reached for another arrow, only to realize she had none left. As another guard came rushing for her, she quickly swung her bow, smacking him in the face, and then swung it a second time, knocking him off his feet. Removing an arrow from the nearest victim, she slammed the sharpened tip into his neck before getting knocked over by another guard. She rolled across the floor, feeling her body ache with each turn, several feet away from her bow. Getting onto her knees, she ducked as the guard swung his blade and, in turn, rolled over her back and fell off the balcony and onto the ground below.

Aoh screamed, feeling her hair grabbed from behind and seeing the blade about to be slashed across her upper body. Bending her arms inward, the sword cut into the leather made bracelets that covered the length of her lower arm. Her scream was cut short when she felt the monstrous force of the guard's other hand clasp itself around her neck, applying pressure on her arms.

Lowering her head, she thrust it back and into his face, feeling him release his grasp momentarily as she lowered her arms. He dropped the sword, but reached for her hair and clasped closed both hands over her neck. Aoh dropped to the ground, reaching for a sword before feeling her body being dragged away. Struggling against the guard, he grappled her.

Rolling across the floor, he applied excessive force, trapping her body beneath him. Aoh gasped, feeling her throat being crushed, barely able to keep her eyes open… She released one last scream before hearing her voice disappear. Her hands couldn't clasp the barbaric arms – they were as …solid as stone. His distorted face haunted her eyes, as the sounds of her own struggle echoed in her ears. Her legs couldn't budge under the weight. …

The guard's body suddenly jolted as Laggus thrusted the sword into his back fiercely. Stunned, eyes wide and mouth agape, the guard released Aoh, collapsing on top of her.

"No traitors shall live," Laggus growled, dragging the dead guard off of her.

Aoh coughed uncontrollably, feeling as though little to no air was filling her lungs each time she struggled to breathe. She craned her neck, feeling her chest tighten with every small breath. Panic took hold. Laggus fell to his knees, alarmed, seeing Aoh struggle to breathe.

"Aoh. Aoh, look at me. Look at me," he ordered.

Aoh looked at him, wheezing. Her face red, and eyes stricken with fear, she was unable to stare at anything else but him. Holding her upward, he grabbed her left arm, pressing her hand against his chest.

"Breathe. Breathe," he ordered quickly, keeping her hand over his heart.

Her hand graced the rough leather armor, as her fingers curled over the edge, touching the linen over his chest. Feeling his heart, Aoh tried to mimic the breathing. Each beat she tried to follow, she coughed loudly and wheezed. With a loud gasp, the air returned to her slowly. As her hand tightly gripped his chest, she took deep breaths, feeling the world around her again. Hearing Aoh's breathing returning, Laggus let go of her hand, relieved.

Coughing light droplets of blood that, trickling down her chin, Aoh strained her voice.

"L-Laggus…"

The pharaoh slammed the doors open violently and saw the back of a tall soldier as he suddenly turned to the side and fell, spewing blood from his mouth, revealing his terrified vizier holding the bloody knife in his shaking hand.

His eyes were filled with terror, dropping the blade, uncontrollably shaking. His eyes rose from the soldier he killed to the pharaoh standing in the doorway, stunned to see him covered in layers of blood.

"My king…thank the gods you are alright!" Senmet shouted,

shaking and sputtering.

"What happened?!" the pharaoh screamed.

"I don't-don't know. I—all of a sudden guards and soldiers were kicking doors in. They were killing servants. It was Kha'y and the priests, my king. They...were behind all of it."

The pharaoh looked around him seeing dead servants lying on the floor, motionless in their blood. Soldiers, as well as Kha'y, lie lifeless, filling the room with a heavy scent of death. The pharaoh heard the last of the guards' yelling fade away. The burning trees were nothing but a smoldering fire and black ash.

"It was mass panic, my king. They were killing everyone. He was rambling about the gods, decreeing him to be the true king, not you," the vizier added, shaking his head. "He was willing to do anything to take the throne himself. He craved it."

The pharaoh stared at the dead body of the high priest. Rolling his lips, he couldn't look away from the puddles of blood. The sight of furniture knocked over, pieces spewed across ruined carpets, captured his attention. It was everywhere, as though it had fallen from the ceiling.

"Where is my mother, my queen, and Daimina?" the pharaoh asked vehemently, narrowing his eyes.

"I-I don't know. I don't know where they are," Senmet answered, stumbling forward.

"My King!" a loud voice called.

Swinging the doors open so roughly they slammed into the walls and, cracking them.

"My King!" the voice called again.

Senmet remained still, witnessing the pharaoh backing up.

Moving to the side, Aoh and Laggus approached slowly, limping forward, covered in blood and sweat, holding onto each other. Laggus slumped forward slightly, nearly pulling her down as she tried to keep him upward, struggling to keep him steady as every movement created pain that radiated up and down their bodies.

He dragged his left leg, releasing a low pitched growl with each step. Trying to speak, Aoh cleared her throat, wincing intensely each time she tried to breathe. She forced herself onto her knees, struggling to keep her balance as she felt Laggus support her. She kissed the floor at the pharoah's presence. Senmet watched, growing increasingly angrier.

"I-" she squeaked, raising her face, keeping herself low to the floor.

She swallowed hard as Laggus tried to stand properly so Aoh could touch her throat.

"I…know where Dai…mina…is."

The pharaoh shoved himself into the statue, using all of his strength to push it, revealing the small door. Running his hands erratically over the outline, he pulled the stone, removing it with aggression. In the dim darkness, he heard a soft voice call out to him. Bending down, he found Daimina curled in the small space with her legs drawn to her chest.

Seeing him with half open eyes, she held out her arms and revealed a small smile. Nearly crying, the pharaoh bent downward to pick her up and into his arms. Aoh and Laggus watched as he carried her, rubbing his forehead against hers, nearly weeping at the sight of her.

He repeated her name, listening to her soft whispers; he was relieved to see her alive. He cradled her body tightly against his in a loving embrace. He whispered into her ears softly with narrowed eyes.

Laggus looked at me the same way on the rooftop, saving me from death. There was no way I could ever repay him. As I watched the pharaoh cradle Daimina, I heard light tapping of a liquid touching the floor. Looking down, I saw small beads of blood drip from the bottom of the Senmet's dress . A wave of red splashed over the white, still running around his fingers… I looked at him, and his eyes told me everything I needed to know as he watched the pharaoh and Daimina in heavy silence.

Noticing Aoh looking in the direction of Senmet, Laggus turned to look at him as they panted heavily.

"Thank the gods. Thank them-" the vizier muttered.

The pharaoh's eyes rested upon my weakened state and a stream of tears slipped from his eyes of gratitude.

"Thank you," he spoke.

I felt Senmet's eyes on me...and the comforting grip of Laggus' hand on my shoulder.

48

The chirping of insects played continually with the light sounds of fish swimming to the top of the Nile River, startling croaking frogs and sleeping ibises. Soothing scents filled the hallways as the sounds of fresh wine were poured into large basins and vessels. The sounds of papyrus being collected and rolled drowned out the crackling of fires burning incense. The palace cats rolled over near each other, curling their long tails and preparing to sleep in the comfort of the open windows.

Slipping past the same wall scenes since the day she arrived, Aoh entered the room at the end of the hall, isolated from the rest of the chambers. She quietly closed the door behind her so gently that the sound was nearly silent. Removing her lightly bruised hands from the door, she turned around slowly. Her minor cuts were covered in smooth wraps smelling like freshly planted herbs. For the first time, she was beginning to see the progress of healing, unlike Laggus' wounded leg.

He laid on the soft sheets of the long couch, surrounded by fresh air. He rested, craning his neck to look out the large open windows, listening to the insects and the whistle of the breeze dancing with the silk drapes. The wood hissed in the fire pits placed at the furthest corner of the large white and dark blue room.

Aoh hesitated from approaching him, watching from behind the nearest column, lifting one of three large potted palm tree leaves. Laggus stirred gently, shifting to the left. Seeing Aoh from the corner of his eyes, he turned. Aoh stepped forward slowly and bowed before him.

"Why did you bow when you entered? You are not a servant anymore," Laggus questioned.

"Old habits," Aoh replied weakly. She sat at the end of the couch where Laggus laid, even though she was afraid to.

Laggus looked at Aoh from behind his thin bangs, watching her eyes shift from his face to the nearest window.

"Thank you for protecting Daimina. You risked your life," he stated, looking at her.

"I only did what I was supposed to. That is why the pharaoh brought me here."

"I brought you here," Laggus corrected.

Aoh's eyes froze, feeling her heart beginning to race uncontrollably.

"I'm relieved you're talking again," he admitted, blinking heavily.

Aoh touched her throat gently, still tender to the slight touch, covered in a thick bruise she hid with a necklace she received from the pharaoh. She faked a smile, lowering her gaze to Laggus' wound wrapped in new medicated cloths. He groaned slightly, trying to shift to the side, as a sharp pain grasped the entire lower half of his leg.

"How is it?" she asked, looking at his leg.

"Acts up now and again, but I'll be fine," he replied lowly, trying to bear with the pain.

Aoh nodded, returning her gaze to the window, unable to control herself from running her hands through her hair, struggling to control the butterflies in her stomach.

"I tried to visit you sooner," she confessed.

Her eyes shifted to him repeatedly, while his remained upon her.

Not even the sounds of desert jackal's barking in the distance disrupted his concentration.

"Aoh, you're avoiding telling me something?" he asked.

Aoh's lips curled momentarily before lying flat on her face. Concerned, he questioned her.

"I can see it on your face. What is it?" he asked.

"I have a suspicion that…Senmet was behind everything," Aoh admitted, pulling her hair over her left shoulder.

"So do I."

"This…isn't over, is it?"

Laggus shook his head and replied, "No."

Aoh nodded again, and released a heavy sigh knowing he was right.

"Now, are you going to tell me what it is you are avoiding telling me?"

Aoh paused, unable to separate her eyes from his gaze. The deeper she stared at him, the more intense the warmth she was feeling grew.

"I couldn't sleep," she admitted.

"Neither can I," Laggus replied.

"You never could, could you?"

"No."

Aoh rubbed her left shoulder, slowly curling her fingers over the linen fabric. The covered wounds tormented Laggus as he stared at them. A wave of unexpected guilt washed over his small eyes.

"I didn't want to be alone," Aoh admitted.

Stretching his long arms, Laggus released a hearty groan and yawn, shifting his body again and, tucking his head deeper into the pillow.

Blinking heavily, he declared, "Then I will stay up, until you fall asleep."

As the fire crackles deepened in sound, turning the wood into ash and the hours of the night slowly moving to the gentle breezes, Aoh remained relaxed in the chair next to Laggus. They sat in silence, listening to the sounds they sometimes forgot to listen to.

Aoh slipped into the comfort of her chair able to, for the first time in a while, empty her mind. Her eyelids grew heavy, her arms and legs near weightless. Hearing the sound of peaceful breathing, she turned, finding Laggus fast asleep. She smiled, watching him sleep when she heard the distant sounds of music coming from outside. She could just hear the soft music dimly playing, recognizing it almost instantly from the window at the back of the room.

Getting up, she approached the closed window and opened it. Immediately, the shine from the half-moon glowed in the sky, spreading the white light around her. A gentle breeze twirled her hair over her shoulders, brushing the sides of her linen dress and tickling her nose. The music continued coming from the town beyond the sleeping city. It was the same music she heard as a child. The same music she hadn't heard in six years…

The soft, yet powerful, sounds of the wooden flute danced through the air, following the wind, encircling the town and city, reaching the highest peaks of the palace and catching Aoh as she absorbed the moonlight. Laggus stirred awake, blinking heavily. Leaning forward, he saw Aoh standing in the faint glow of the half-moon. She smiled, feeling overjoyed to hear such music again. Such music she missed…and long thought was dead.

She caught a glimpse of an winged shadow flying past in the faint moonlight. Though she could barely see it, she knew it was her friend the kite, with her as he always had been. His presence brought a sense of relief and reassurance that he will always be there.

Laggus asked the pharaoh to relieve me of my duties. However, I chose to remain at the palace. He was afraid that I would be targeted, not as Daimina's servant but, now as her protector.

There were days when I caught myself wanting to brush her hair, wanting to follow her through every hall. I had to remind myself the days of being her servant were over. The pharaoh allowed Laggus to return to guarding the city streets, but he refused. He never told me why, but I knew he wanted to stay because of me. I don't know if he knows how much I love him, how I would do anything for him. I don't know if I will be able to tell him.

For now, I live day by day, in a new light of the palace. I never need an excuse to speak with Laggus or to be with him. He never used an excuse to speak to me or to be with me. I never found out what happened to my family. I don't know if I ever will find them. But even as I stand here, looking out at the desert, listening to the flute being played in the distance, I know I am home.

The End

Jennifer Renson-Chiappetta's passion for writing began in childhood. Her writing career spanned from articles in Lost Treasure Magazine to her self published poetry books; *Delightfully Dark: A Collection of Poems and Tales*, *Eo: Go, walk, ride, sail, pass, travel* and *Uncharted*. She is the author of the modern-day fairy tale novel *Carousel*. Presently she is a mother and wife; she enjoys spending her time with her family and friends, writing, crafting, specifically cross-stitching and reveling in Victorian Era ambiances while living in New Jersey.

Made in United States
North Haven, CT
17 April 2024

51464916R00221